COLD-MOULDED
AND STRIP-PLANKED
WOOD BOATBUILDING

Other books by Ian Nicolson

*Ian Nicolson Omnibus (Sea Saint,
    Log of the Maken, Building the St Mary)
 Dinghy Cruising
 Outboard Boats and Engines
*Small Steel Craft
*Surveying Small Craft
 Designer's Notebook
 Marinize Your Boat
*Yacht Designer's Sketchbook
*Boat Data Book
 Build Your Own Boat
 Improve Your Own Boat
*Race Winner
*Build a Simple Dinghy

*Also published by Sheridan House

COLD-MOULDED AND STRIP-PLANKED WOOD BOATBUILDING

Ian Nicolson FRINA, C. ENG.

SHERIDAN HOUSE

First published 1991 by
Sheridan House Inc.
145 Palisade Street
Dobbs Ferry, NY 10522
Reprinted 1996

Printed in Great Britain

ISBN 0–924486–14–7

ACKNOWLEDGEMENT

The Author and Editor would like to acknowledge with thanks
the following, who have been helpful in providing information
or photographs used in this book: McGruer & Co., Rosneath,
Dunbartonshire; Fernando Sena and Structural Polymer
Systems, Cowes, Isle of Wight; Tony Castro; Rob Humphries;
Anthony de Kerdrel and Whisstock's Boatyard, Woodbridge,
Suffolk; Peter Wilson, Aldeburgh Boatyard, Aldeburgh,
Suffolk; Gustaaf Versluys; Richard and Michael Riggs;
Thomas Sprecher; R. Franklyn Pierce of Franklin-Eldridge
Wooden Boats, Windermere, Cumbria.

To Dom Benedict Sankey and Fr. George Carrick

CONTENTS

PART 1

APPROACHING THE PROJECT

Why Wood?

Wood has advantages such as a valuable strength-to-weight ratio, resistance to fatigue and shock loads, ability to stand up to different types of damage, repairability, adaptability, and ease of handling and working. Cold-moulding retains these virtues, and is particularly good in terms of strength/weight and resilience. It is consequently an attractive option for racing craft of all kinds – sailing dinghies, powerboats or large offshore racers – as well as small tenders, fast launches and rescue boats. Strip-planking is also light in weight and easy to build, but less good in terms of strength and resistance to damage, ease of repair and longevity. For commercial craft, however, the conditions of use tend to favour steel in most cases.

As economic pressures increase there is a tendency to build boats for the widest possible market. Design has gone towards short bow and stern overhangs, ample beam and high topsides because these proportions suit land storage and marinas, where charges are based on length, and allow maximum accommodation space. When a yacht is wanted that is not short and fat the choice in fibreglass becomes very small, and this is where cold-moulding becomes especially attractive as it suits such hull shapes and is viable for small production runs. Long, narrow, fast and light launches of the type used on lakes and rivers, where they combine high speed with minimal wave-making wash, are another example, and like rowing shells they have been made in this way for decades.

Both methods particularly suit one-off or 'custom' building, as for racing yachts and dinghies, or short production runs. A set of moulds may be reused for sister ships, are easy to store in between, and compared to a fibreglass mould are much quicker to make and perhaps a quarter the cost. The shape of the moulds can also be altered quite a lot without total rebuilding. This is a unique and valuable asset because racing boats tend to change gradually. When a designer has a successful shape one year, next year's boats are likely to be similar and the old moulds can be modified in a few days.

Wood itself is not a particularly expensive material. Just how its cost should be realistically compared to other boatbuilding materials is much debated. Comparison by weight alone ignores building costs, storage, the density of the material, the cost of buying, handling and working, and so on. Cutting away the forest of prejudices, most experienced people would agree that steel is the cheapest material, with wood and ferrocement about equal second, then fibreglass, and aluminium the most costly. However these relationships change according to the size of craft involved and the amount of series production. One advantage of cold-moulding is that the cheaper pieces of suitable timber can be used, since long lengths and expensive wide boards are seldom needed. Good quality timber is still necessary, though, and always costs more than rubbish.

Another aspect which makes both cold-moulding and strip-planking attractive to amateurs is that they can be done by people who are short of woodworking skills, and by a small team such as a club or even one person working virtually alone. By careful planning most of the jobs can be handled by semi-skilled labour, and this is also an attraction for professional builders who want to stay in business. Second year apprentices can do much if not all the work, and material stocks do not have to be large.

Anyone worried about his competence should start with a dinghy. Unless the boat is clearly a disaster it will be useful or can be sold, and it will give experience as well as confidence. If building is started but cannot be completed, the materials are not difficult to sell and the experiment will have been cheap.

One disadvantage of all wooden hulls is that they are not impervious to marine borers unless sheathed under water. However the sheathing need not be expensive copper. Cascover, which is a tough nylon cloth embedded in epoxy resin, keeps out worm and is stronger and lighter as well as cheaper. So for the tropics cold-moulding and strip-planking are still attractive, especially as the wooden hull, deck and cabin top make good insulation.

Because wood is an insulator, and above all because it is so attractive, cold-moulded hulls do not need lining provided the interior is well finished, and glue spillages have been minimized and wiped away before they harden. Furniture is quickly and easily joined to the hull, and given plenty of manpower for laminating the shell a cold-moulded boat can be afloat in a very short time after the design is complete. A fibreglass boat from an *existing* mould is built quicker, but if the pattern and mould have to be built then the wooden one will be afloat much sooner. So where speed of building matters, cold-moulding is sometimes the best choice.

Finally, a well built cold-moulded boat should last as long as a carvel-planked one, say fifty years; however, strip-planking is not likely to have the same longevity.

Cold-moulded Hulls

The term 'cold-moulding' covers a number of related building techniques, but essentially consists of gluing layers of thin wood skins or planks together like a multi-layer sandwich. The result can be considered a composite material, and is very different from traditional wood boatbuilding in which separate pieces are fixed together with metal fastenings (sometimes assisted by glue) so that in use each part can move very slightly in relation to its neighbours. A cold-moulded hull is rather like the shell of a nut; the waterproof outer shell is also the strong structure which makes the nut so tough. If a nut's shell has a weakness it is at the join of the two halves, and in the same way cold-moulded boats (like fibreglass) unless properly designed and built tend to have less strength at the deck/hull join. The analogy does not hold true, however, in the advanced form of construction seen on some racing boats, where the hull shell is largely to keep out the water and contributes much less to the rigidity and strength of the whole. An internal space-frame takes over much of the structural role as well as linking the stresses from the rig, keel, etc that would in the conventional version be taken partly by floors, framing, stringers and so on as well as the hull shell. However, a hull built in conjunction with a space-frame structure is still laminated, though more lightly.

Cold-moulding is the best way of using wood because it accentuates its good properties and gets round most of the problems. Many woods are subject to faults such as cracks as a result of uneven drying-out or thunder shakes; a sound tree has curly grain near knots and other variations.

But by using thin narrow planks one can be virtually certain of eliminating all faulty wood; if there is a hidden defect it must be small since each piece is small in section. The tendency to warp or shrink, which varies according to the species of wood and how it is cut and dried, has always been a nuisance. Laminating veneers or thicker layers together contributes to dimensional stability, and modern glues used with well dried timber result in a long-lived and stable shape. Naturally paint and varnish have to be kept up, but cold-moulding does not suffer from the drying-out cracking and open seams sometimes found on carvel hulls, solid timber and laid decks after exposure to hot sun.

The strength of wood is of a special kind. Tough stringy fibres are bound together by a gluey substance so in a collision it deals with the distorting forces in two ways. Part of the energy of the blow is absorbed by crushing, as the wood is progressively compressed; this is an excellent way to react to damage because the force is decelerated. At the same time the fibres bend, steadily building up resistance which further helps to absorb the force. This springiness, which remains in cold-moulding and strip-planking, is remarkably effective in minimizing damage. It also absorbs vibration, so slamming against steep seas, or the vibration of a mast in a gale, are neutralized by a wooden hull.

Chafe damage, such as a boat suffers when grinding against a quay or pontoon, affects a cold-moulded hull more severely than carvel or clinker, much more than steel, but less than fibreglass. Such damage to wood is easily repaired if it is slight, and is not really difficult (though it is time-

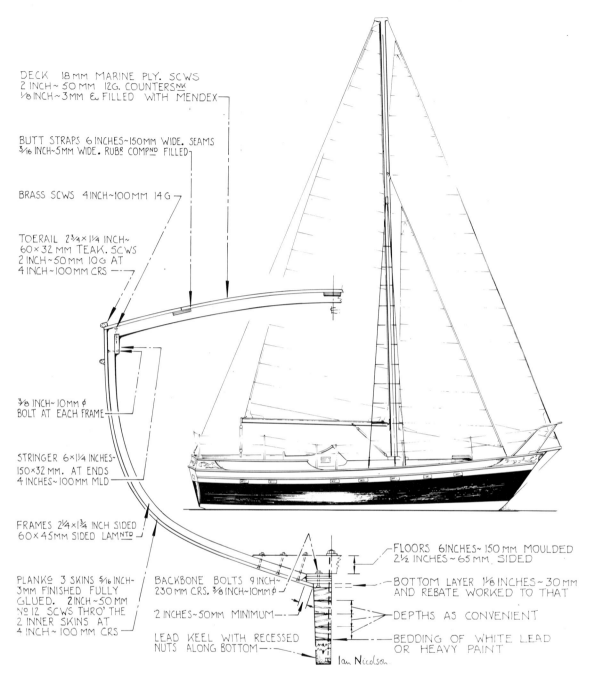

DECK 18MM MARINE PLY. SCWS
2 INCH~50MM 12G. COUNTERS^NK
1/8 INCH~3MM & FILLED WITH MENDEX

BUTT STRAPS 6 INCHES~150MM WIDE. SEAMS
3/16 INCH~5MM WIDE. RUBR COMPND FILLED

BRASS SCWS 4INCH~100MM 14G

TOERAIL 2¾ × 1¼ INCH~
60×32 MM TEAK. SCWS
2 INCH~50MM 10G AT
4 INCH~100MM CRS

3/8 INCH~10MM ⌀
BOLT AT EACH FRAME

STRINGER 6×1¼ INCHES~
150×32 MM. AT ENDS
4 INCHES~100MM MLD

FRAMES 2¼×1¾ INCH SIDED
60×45 MM SIDED LAMNTD

PLANKS 3 SKINS 5/16 INCH~
3MM FINISHED FULLY
GLUED. 2 INCH~50MM
NO 12 SCWS THRO' THE
2 INNER SKINS AT
4 INCH~100 MM CRS

BACKBONE BOLTS 9 INCH~
230MM CRS. 3/8 INCH~10MM ⌀

2 INCHES~50MM MINIMUM

LEAD KEEL WITH RECESSED
NUTS ALONG BOTTOM

FLOORS 6INCHES~ 150 MM MOULDED
2½ INCHES~65 MM SIDED

BOTTOM LAYER 1⅛ INCHES~30 MM
AND REBATE WORKED TO THAT

DEPTHS AS CONVENIENT

BEDDING OF WHITE LEAD
OR HEAVY PAINT

Ian Nicolson.

consuming) if it is deep. Fibreglass is very vulnerable to quite mild abrasion and even if this is repaired just by filling and painting, so many coats are needed and the paint is not the cheapest, that repairs are relatively expensive. Steel of course is the ideal medium where conditions are rugged; it stands up to a lot of abuse without any harm except to the surface coating. However it is heavy, massively so when compared with a carefully designed cold-moulded hull. Aluminium is com-

A heavy duty cruiser designed by A. Mylne & Co. of Rosneath for owners who wanted a yacht capable of taking the ground at low tide on the rocky shores of the Scottish east coast. As a result she is unusually strong, with no cabin top to break the continuity of the deck. Her overall length is 38ft and she was originally designed with a ketch rig. The two men who built her had no previous experience in boatbuilding, so the construction was worked out to avoid difficulties like reverse turns near the garboard.

parable in weight and toughness, but less so in cost until the larger sizes are reached.

There is nothing so dangerous as a claim that one particular boatbuilding method is lighter than another. Each material and technique has the backing of designers, suppliers and owners who constantly promote their favourite. Big companies have invested millions in fibreglass, so they have no intention of letting the material fall behind in popularity for want of advertising, research, press trials, development and so on.

Sticking my neck out with the certain knowledge that howls of protest will arise from many quarters of the boatbuilding world, I quote from the Henry and Miller paper before the 1978 meeting of the U.S. Society of Naval Architects and Marine Engineers, with an updated comment* for cold-moulded (see page 14).

Since the advent of epoxy resins the techniques of cold-moulding and strip-planking have gained

considerably, not only in respect to the improvement in bond strength. The further development of epoxies for wood composites has altered the way in which these resins can be used, and considerably extended them beyond the gluing role. To take advantage of these new qualities greater control of the working atmosphere and moisture content of the timber are necessary, but the benefits are great. There is limited soakage from inside or out. The resin fills and seals the surface and small gaps left accidentally. As it penetrates the dry wood and excludes water, the strength is maintained because water absorption of itself tends to weaken wood, quite apart from the rot and staining it brings in its train. Maintenance is reduced and frost damage becomes less of a threat. Rot, of course, is a condition of wood where there is no strength left, apart from its other detrimental effects, so its defeat by this technique is perhaps the biggest recent advance in wood boatbuilding.

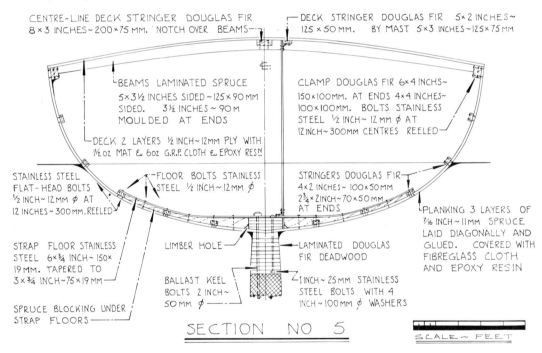

SECTION NO 5

Section 5 is near the mid-length of a yacht, in this case a light but strongly built 65ft (20m) WL ketch from Alan Gurney. The ample use of Douglas fir confirms that she was built in North America where this wood is used much more than in Europe.

Epoxy resin and glassfibre cloth cover the hull to give extra strength and protection against marine borers. In the event of a collision there is a chance that the skin will

remain intact and keep out water even if the wood is fractured.

It is worth noting the way the floors terminate at a stringer to avoid hard spots at their tips; the floor depth is tapered out at each end. There are plenty of fastenings because the strength and value of a component is limited by the effectiveness of its fastenings.

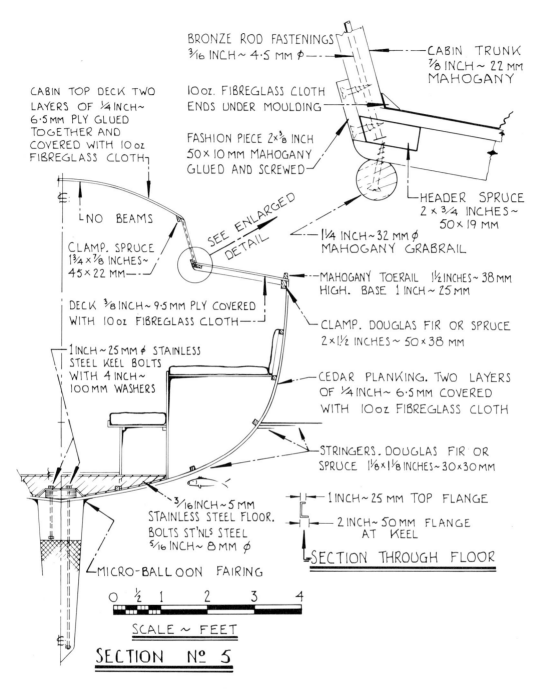

BRONZE ROD FASTENINGS
³⁄₁₆ INCH ~ 4.5 MM ⌀

CABIN TRUNK
⁷⁄₈ INCH ~ 22 MM
MAHOGANY

CABIN TOP DECK TWO
LAYERS OF ¼ INCH ~
6.5 MM PLY GLUED
TOGETHER AND
COVERED WITH 10 oz
FIBREGLASS CLOTH

10 oz. FIBREGLASS CLOTH
ENDS UNDER MOULDING

FASHION PIECE 2 × ³⁄₈ INCH
50 × 10 MM MAHOGANY
GLUED AND SCREWED

SEE ENLARGED
DETAIL

HEADER SPRUCE
2 × ³⁄₄ INCHES ~
50 × 19 MM

NO BEAMS

CLAMP. SPRUCE
1¾ × ⁷⁄₈ INCHES ~
45 × 22 MM

1¼ INCH ~ 32 MM ⌀
MAHOGANY GRABRAIL

MAHOGANY TOERAIL 1½ INCHES ~ 38 MM
HIGH. BASE 1 INCH ~ 25 MM

DECK ³⁄₈ INCH ~ 9.5 MM PLY COVERED
WITH 10 oz FIBREGLASS CLOTH

CLAMP. DOUGLAS FIR OR SPRUCE
2 × 1½ INCHES ~ 50 × 38 MM

1 INCH ~ 25 MM ⌀ STAINLESS
STEEL KEEL BOLTS
WITH 4 INCH ~
100 MM WASHERS

CEDAR PLANKING. TWO LAYERS
OF ¼ INCH ~ 6.5 MM COVERED
WITH 10 oz FIBREGLASS CLOTH

STRINGERS. DOUGLAS FIR OR
SPRUCE 1⅛ × 1⅛ INCHES ~ 30 × 30 MM

³⁄₁₆ INCH ~ 5 MM
STAINLESS STEEL FLOOR.
BOLTS ST'NLS STEEL
⁵⁄₁₆ INCH ~ 8 MM ⌀

1 INCH ~ 25 MM TOP FLANGE

2 INCH ~ 50 MM FLANGE
AT KEEL

SECTION THROUGH FLOOR

MICRO-BALLOON FAIRING

0   ½   1   2   3   4

SCALE ~ FEET

SECTION N⁰ 5

Mid-section and inner edge of side-deck, details of a 25ft 10in (7.87m) WL racing yacht by Alan Gurney. They show a light strong boat designed round multiple stringers, with only two laminates of planking but a covering of glassfibre which might almost be considered an extra thin laminate. Fitting glass cloth to a hull should be done when the boat is still inverted and still in the warm and dry building shed.

As always with Gurney designs the details are worth studying. There are no beams under the cabin top decking nor is there a conventional side-deck carline, the floors end at the berth front to avoid a succession of hard spots, the cabin coamings are secured and made extra strong by vertical bronze bolts which are unusually thin, and so on.

13

Type of construction	Comment	Weight of hull per ft (30.5cm)
Traditional carvel wood	Now dying out due to high cost and shortage of craftsmen	182lbs (83kg)
Wood construction to Herreshoff's Rules	Requires a very high standard of boatbuilding	159lbs (72kg)
Fibreglass (GRP)	New techniques which call for more expensive building will reduce this weight	144lbs (65kg)
Welded aluminium	Development work has not been widespread, but this figure could come down soon	132lbs (60kg)
Cold-moulded wood	*Figure correct for 1978 but weights continue to come down	126lbs (57kg)

Selecting an Appropriate Design

Before deciding on a particular set of plans, it is worth considering the choice of designer. Long gone are the days when the yacht designer would one week produce a new class of racing dinghy, the next a 50ft cruiser, and a month later settle down

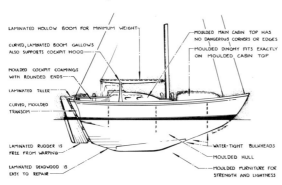

LAMINATED HOLLOW BOOM FOR MINIMUM WEIGHT

CURVED, LAMINATED BOOM GALLOWS ALSO SUPPORTS COCKPIT HOOD

MOULDED COCKPIT COAMINGS WITH ROUNDED ENDS

LAMINATED TILLER

CURVED, MOULDED TRANSOM

LAMINATED RUDDER IS FREE FROM WARPING

LAMINATED DEADWOOD IS EASY TO REPAIR

MOULDED MAIN CABIN TOP HAS NO DANGEROUS CORNERS OR EDGES

MOULDED DINGHY FITS EXACTLY ON MOULDED CABIN TOP

WATER-TIGHT BULKHEADS

MOULDED HULL

MOULDED FURNITURE FOR STRENGTH AND LIGHTNESS

Some of the special advantages of cold-moulding show up on this sketch of a long-range cruiser. The forward and main cabin tops may be made from the same basic mould, modified to suit the different sizes of the two structures. The same mould can then be used to make a strong light dinghy which will fit exactly on the forward cabin top, where it will take up no foredeck space and lie safely without needing special chocks.

The boom gallows corners makes a useful handhold, may support the hood over the front of the cockpit, and could even form the base of the mainsheet horse.

to draw a vast power yacht intended for elegant progression round the more fashionable shores of the Mediterranean. Designers specialize: some concentrate on boat types, a few on construction methods. Obviously a man who has made a name producing cold-moulded or strip-planked boats is the person to approach, and you may be able to look at built examples of his work.

It is worth writing out your basic requirements before going to a designer, not least because the act of putting pen to paper concentrates the mind on exactly what is wanted. Almost always they should be broadly stated, because the designer's experience is wanted and he should not be fenced in by too-precise details. After the early discussions the exact owner specification can be written out, but this will often be done by the designer from his notes.

The owner will probably have told the designer that he wants a cold-moulded or strip-plank hull, but he should, if he can, elaborate on the reasons why. If a principal aim is to get inexpensive construction the hull form should be simple, with no reverse turns or hollows anywhere. If there *have* to be hollows or reverse turns, they may be formed after the hull has been completed, by fairing with micro-balloons or other fillers, or less commonly by adding solid wood chocks or shaping the

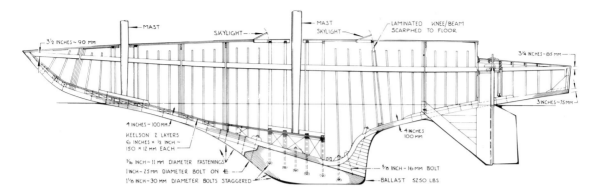

Galway Blazer II was more than once rolled right over when being sailed singlehanded in high latitudes on a circumnavigation. The hull suffered no trouble, which speaks very well for this specialized Angus Primrose design. (42ft × 30ft × 10ft 5in max. beam × 8ft 2 in WL beam × 6ft draft. Displacement 4.5 tons.)

backbone. (Adding extra veneer layers is less simple than it sounds.)

It is also easier to build a hull that is small enough to be made upside-down and then turned over with the available equipment, but there is no reason apart from convenience why a hull should not be built right way up.

Hollows or reverse turns are important because they make the work slower and sometimes more difficult. The layers tend to spring up and flatten,

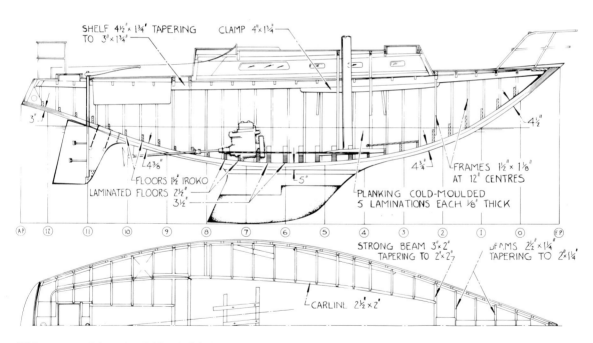

With an overall length of 33ft (10.2m) this auxiliary sloop is a good example of a light yet strong boat. The scantlings are not so delicate that she could not stand up to severe weather, nor so heavy that she will be handicapped by carrying around excess poundage. She is an example of a partially laminated boat, with a cold-moulded hull, continuous laminated backbone, lam-inated main floors and knees, but solid beams, frames, carlines and beam shelf. The deck follows what is the very usual practice of being of ply, $\frac{5}{8}$in thick, covered with Cascover. The coachroof deck only has beams by the mast and is cold-moulded from three layers of $\frac{3}{16}$in marine ply covered with Cascover.

so they need careful fitting and much more stapling, and probably narrower timber. Provided the laminates will easily follow the hollow the job is possible, so an obvious approach is to set up a rough jig and see how easily the wood to be used will bend into the required curve. With strip-planking the problem is that the planks need coaxing to fit in, and if the hollow is curved in two directions this may be very difficult. With strip-plank a hollow flare is not too difficult provided the curved section is not much more than say 1 in 16, but those oval hollows seen on some IOR racers near the rudder and skeg are fiendishly difficult to work because the individual planks have to bend inwards, then reverse out again, in a short length. This is usually hard, sometimes impossible. If on top of this each successive piece is set in from its neighbour the job would be almost impossible in strip-plank even for the most skilled team.

In cold-moulding localized hollows are not so difficult, and I have seen 'dents' of 1 in 8, with curvature in both directions, achieved with narrow veneers and lots of long staples. Certainly a hollowed *flare* of 1 in 8 presents little difficulty because the curvature is only concave in section view but convex in plan view. Sharp turns at garboards and bilges can be designed so that the curvature is nearly all in one plane.

Another problem arises where a ballast keel is narrow at the top, relative to its depth and surface area. The size and shape of such a keel give rise to high stresses, which because of the small top area become very localized onto the keel bolts. Even on steel hulls this is a problem, especially when the maximum width at the top is less than about one-fifteenth of the keel's vertical length.

On power boats the effect of a hollowed flare to the bows can be achieved by fitting rubbing strakes which stand well out from the deck edge, at or slightly below it. They may be horizontal on the top surface or slightly angled down towards the outboard edge, with the lower edge steeply sloped up and out. This looks smart, sheds water and dirt, gives a professional finish and throws clear a lot of spray and even solid water.

Ease of building must not totally dominate the design, otherwise the boat will look odd. This fault is seen in merchant ships, which have become progressively uglier as commercial pressures have forced designers into every sort of contrivance from square-section funnels to corrugated deck-houses. Because small craft can be encompassed easily by a single glance, because their essential characteristic is that they *are* small, it is vital that they are not designed solely with a view to easy building.

To make a boat simple to plank it is a help if all hull curves are gradual and minimal. An extreme example of this would result in a saucer-shaped section with a wide transom and no great beam for its length. Tumble-home makes the builder's job more difficult, but it is not so awkward that a design should be rejected just because it has tumble-home. A 'lifeboat' or Colin Archer stern, or indeed most forms of double-ender, are awkward and probably best avoided unless the builder is experienced and skilled in the technique to be used; however it may be easier in cold-moulding than in carvel.

A special design is costly and may be as much as a tenth of the cost of the boat, if she is small and complex. Often the designer saves the builder more than the design fees and expenses, but even more often the builder will not believe this before he starts work. Consequently, many builders try to buy stock plans. These are not all they seem. Sometimes, quite often I suspect, they are old sets of drawings which a designer is using to generate extra income, though he knows the plans are out of date. The builder will find that materials and equipment specified are no longer available, or have been superceded by something better or cheaper or easier to use.

Stock plans may be a help if the builder can inspect a boat recently built to the drawings. If he can talk to the team which built her he may find out about any problems. In fact the supply of stock plans for cold-moulding and strip-planking is not great, and many of them were done before epoxy glues and the new widespread practice of glassing-in bulkheads and similar components. If the main reason for buying a set of stock plans is to save money, the true saving has to be carefully calculated. Time (which is money) is saved if the list of scantlings tallies with locally available timber. Not only must the timber types be available, but the available standard sizes should be worked into the plans. The same applies to fastenings, deck covering material, even ballast keels.

A neat way to speed up construction and save money is to use a standard fin keel designed for another boat, when building a sailing cruiser. The

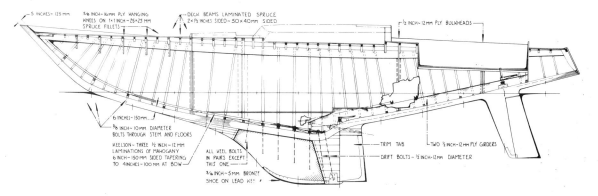

The angled frames were something of a trademark of Angus Primrose, who designed this offshore racer *Hypercon* (44ft 9in × 33ft × 13ft 5in × 7ft). The quick double bend in the keel by the aft end of the ballast shows one of the advantages of laminated construction. As with many Primrose designs, the only things not laminated are the toothbrush handles and as a result the total weight is exceptionally low.

designer will make the decision about the weight, size and shape required, and then see what is available from stock patterns. It may be necessary to get permission from another designer to use the pattern and pay a small royalty, but there may still be a useful saving.

Good plans will show the stations for the offsets exactly at the locations of the building moulds. For a boat 60ft on the waterline there will be displacement stations 6ft apart, and this will normally be too far apart for the building moulds. But the chances are that when drawing the lines the designer will find it necessary to put in half-sections at bow and stern. These half-sections can be drawn in throughout the length of the hull and used as mould stations.

There is an interesting division of opinion between amateur and professional cold-moulders. Amateurs like to build around bulkheads, also using them as building moulds on which the longitudinal ribbands are set up. They like lots of partial bulkheads located at the half-length of berths, at the fore end of the foc's'le, under the cockpit, just ahead or astern of the rudder stock, and so on. Their view is that there is a valuable time and materials saving if these full and partial bulkheads combine the jobs of strength members and building moulds. Professionals have in the past disliked this approach, though it is not easy to get them to say why. Sometimes they may hope to use the moulds for subsequent boats to the same design. Another reason may be that it is hard to avoid scratching or even doing serious damage to bulkheads which are installed very early. More than once I have heard professional builders say that using the bulkheads as moulds does not save time, and not much material. (The cost saving in wood is easy enough to work out, since it is the volume needed to make the building moulds.)

Some of the best designs are based on station spacings of about 6ft 6in or 2m. This is ample length for a full-size berth; toilet compartments may be conveniently made half the length, and also the chart table and a small galley; a good-sized galley might be the full length. A very useful hanging locker is made one-quarter of the basic unit, and a cockpit for a small or even medium-sized boat may be this length. For a boat under about 35ft (10m) the berth length might be reduced to about 6ft 4in (1.93m), which is then used as the station spacing.

There are various tricks associated with this technique. If a little extra space is needed the bulkheads bounding a standard spacing can be packed away from the frames they are secured onto by wood spacers which can be up to about 1½in (40mm) thick without inconvenience. As the spacers can be either side of the station, the standard interval can be enlarged or contracted by 5 × 1½in, since the spacers can be on either side of the station line.

It is the mark of a good design that there are plenty of standardizations. There may have to be extra strong beams at each end of the cabin top and in way of the mast, but a plan which requires more than three different beam sizes is a nuisance. Where weight saving has to be rigorous, there will be far less standardization because the only way to reduce the total tonnage is to cut out unnecessary weight in every individual part.

Cold-moulded hulls are light for their size, and to a lesser extent so are strip-planked ones. This is a main reason why designs for building in other materials should not be adapted. There are possible exceptions, such as for deep-sea cruising under power or sail. It is hard to make extended voyages in a light displacement yacht because so much gear, food and water has to be carried. Also, ocean cruising tends to be hard on a boat, so she needs reserves of strength and scantling thickness to cope with bashing in harbour, very heavy weather at sea, and periods when maintenance is limited.

The best plans for adapting to cold-moulded tend to be those which are for conventional carvel wood construction. Sometimes little change will be needed in the deck and cabin top, accommodation, engine installation, perhaps in the wheelhouse and cockpit. Much of the steering, ballasting, appearance and the detail work can be the same. But adapting is only justified when the case for it is strong: the size and lines plan must be particularly suitable, the accommodation must need little alteration, and existing boats to the plans must be entirely proved and satisfactory. Since a new construction plan still has to be drawn, and this takes as long as all the other plans put together, adapting is only worthwhile when the case for it is overwhelming.

A further characteristic of cold-moulding and strip-planking is the relative cheapness of the resulting craft. Thus these techniques are likely to be used when money is short. It follows that the plans should reflect this. For a given amount of enclosed space it is cheaper to have a high-freeboard hull and the minimum of superstructure: it is almost always even cheaper to increase the hull length or beam or both, in order to cut down the number and size of deckhouses, coach roofs and other erections above the deck. This basic rule applies to power and sail, to pleasure and commercial craft, and to just about every type except where there are special circumstances. Since the weight per square foot of topsides is small, raising the sheerline or extending the overall length is acceptable from the point of view of total displacement. It is a convenient bonus that the trend in small craft design for the last sixty years

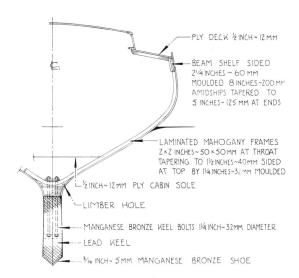

Midship section of 44ft *Hypercon*, a Class I offshore racing yacht by the late Angus Primrose. The frames are sophisticated since they taper in both planes, but in many respects this is a modernized version of traditional boatbuilding at its best.

has been towards ever higher topsides, so it will also look fashionable and acceptable to have ample freeboard.

The basic rules for amateur building are, briefly:
1. Build small. It is true that size is a measure of speed, comfort, seakindliness and often of seaworthiness. But boats tend to cost more than the amateur expects, take longer to build than anticipated, and cost more than expected to maintain, moor and insure. Most yacht owners have a boat which is too big for the money available for upkeep. The cost of large fittings and equipment rises disproportionately.
2. Keep it simple. Better one mast than two, one engine than two, portable plastic water tanks and hand pumps rather than an electric plumbing system, the minimum gadgets, and above all the fewest possible devices using electricity.
3. Try to build with sufficient help to complete the boat in less than 24 months. More than this and interest will sag till momentum is lost and the boat will never be completed. Timber and any stored materials may start to absorb moisture and deteriorate in other ways. You may even have to begin maintenance on the shed or the work already completed, further cutting into the time and funds available to finish the boat.

PART 2

PREPARATION AND MATERIALS

Building Spaces and Timber Storage

Because the most important part of cold-moulded and strip-plank construction is the gluing, it is essential to build under cover. If no suitable shed is available a temporary one must be put up. One might think that where the sun shines reliably and rain is infrequent and possibly predictable, build-ing in the open would be possible. But even then a shed is advisable, to keep off the heat of the sun and drying wind.

It is sensible to take a lot of care even when making a temporary building because one leak causes more trouble than all the labour preventing it. In some localities (and in the U.K. at present) a temporary shed attracts no rates (taxes) and does

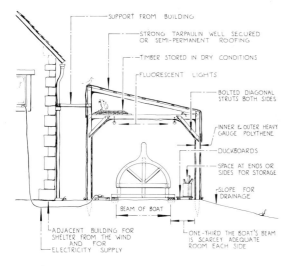

SUPPORT FROM BUILDING
STRONG TARPAULIN WELL SECURED OR SEMI-PERMANENT ROOFING
TIMBER STORED IN DRY CONDITIONS
FLUORESCENT LIGHTS
BOLTED DIAGONAL STRUTS BOTH SIDES
INNER & OUTER HEAVY GAUGE POLYTHENE
DUCKBOARDS
SPACE AT ENDS OR SIDES FOR STORAGE
SLOPE FOR DRAINAGE
BEAM OF BOAT
ADJACENT BUILDING FOR SHELTER FROM THE WIND AND FOR ELECTRICITY SUPPLY
ONE-THIRD THE BOAT'S BEAM IS SCARCEY ADEQUATE ROOM EACH SIDE

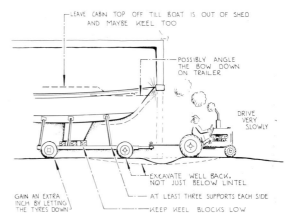

LEAVE CABIN TOP OFF TILL BOAT IS OUT OF SHED AND MAYBE KEEL TOO
POSSIBLY ANGLE THE BOW DOWN ON TRAILER
DRIVE VERY SLOWLY
GAIN AN EXTRA INCH BY LETTING THE TYRES DOWN
EXCAVATE WELL BACK, NOT JUST BELOW LINTEL
AT LEAST THREE SUPPORTS EACH SIDE
KEEP KEEL BLOCKS LOW

All sorts of places can be used for boatbuilding, ranging from the shelter given by bridges over unused railway tracks, to disused church halls. But for amateurs especially, the best is very close to home.

This sketch shows some of the things desirable for a boat shed. The framework may be made from second-hand timber covered with a tarpaulin, or roofing boards which can also be bought used. Of course the whole shed can be second-hand, and some trade papers advertise them. The structure should be so rigid that it does not creak or move in the strongest gale. It may be best to sling the roof beams between two existing buildings, though this calls for cooperative neighbours. If there is a permanent building each side the top of the shed and the ends should be made translucent where possible. Boatbuilding needs plenty of daylight and artificial light. Before the shed is set up the local regulations and planning permission rules should be studied.

Before beginning to build a boat, the shed door should be measured to ensure that it's larger than the finished hull. An allowance has to be made for the trailer, though in the old days it was common to fit a cradle round the boat and slide her out. This, with care, used up less height than a trailer.

Sketched here are a few ideas for getting a big boat out of a medium-sized doorway. It is often hard, sometimes expensive and always tedious raising the top of the doorway. Lowering the floor by the exit may be quicker and easier, but it needs thought. The drop should not be just under the doorway, especially if the bow extends forward, and each side of the excavation should slope gently so that there is no sudden lurch to tip the boat off the trailer. This is why there should be at least three supports each side of the hull, notwithstanding the dangerous habit of risking life and limb with just two. If one goes the boat may swivel sideways, then crash over. Which is frustrating, especially if the builder is underneath at the time.

not need planning permission, so that even for a professional builder it has advantages. There is one type of temporary structure which is particularly suitable, because it is easy to control the environment inside. This is the inflatable building, which is like an air-tight half sphere or ovoid. A fabric skin keeps the air inside and a simple blower inflates the whole building. The blower is run off the normal electrical supply, and a standby diesel generator with its own fan can be provided. The disadvantage of an inflatable building is the limited access, as the doors have to be air-locks. Once the boat is finished the building has to be deflated and removed from around it, but this involves no great labour. Suppliers of this type of building normally rent out as well as sell, and there is a wide range of shapes to suit any size of project. It is surprising how vandal-proof this type of inflatable is, because the material is so thick, tough and rip-proof.

Working in wood is not suited to rough or damp conditions. For steel boatbuilding the shed can be rough and dirty; but it is hard to get grubby oil marks off wood, indeed it is sometimes impossible because the oils soak in and stain it deeply. Even planing off $\frac{1}{8}$in (3mm) may still leave a stain. Wet ground should be avoided, and if a garage is being used the first job is to dispose of all the oil and greasy muck. The floor, workbenches, materials store and roadway must be blitzed clean, otherwise the boat will get grubbier as the work proceeds. Even if everyone concerned changes their shoes before starting work the oil will still get onto the boat.

Whatever site is being used, there must be plenty of space all round, unlike finishing off a GRP hull where a cramped shed which fits tightly around it may sometimes be used. It might be possible to build a boat with a space of about a third of the maximum beam clear on each side, but most people would consider that the boat's width to port and starboard was cutting things fine. So the building shed needs to be at least twice as wide as the maximum beam, and there must be the same clearance at each end.

A short shed can sometimes be extended temporarily by jamming open the end doors and roofing them over, then putting in a new end closure. This lengthens the shed by the doors' width, but it tends to reduce its resistance against vandals. A professional builder who has previously been working with fibreglass boats may

well need a longer (or wider) shed as GRP boats tend to be short and nearly plumb-ended. The high cost of GRP means that bow and stern overhangs are kept to a minimum. With cold-moulding there is less reason to go for a short-ended hull, so more room may be needed.

The building berth should be near a source of electricity. If a portable generator has to be used it is worth arranging a good distance between the noisy engine and the boat, though it must not be so great that there is a voltage loss in the cable. Cables are expensive, also vulnerable to wheeled traffic and even in some cases to rodents! So the wire should be protected, and it may be best to have the generator not too distant but with some soundproofing round it. It is helpful to have a water supply, but not essential. A gas supply is useful as a quick and often cheap way of raising the temperature of a building. In cold or even in temperate climates warmth is needed for glue curing, and moisture control may be necessary also. For epoxy saturation techniques, and for composites, it is essential.

Because cold-moulded and strip-plank techniques are specially suitable for amateurs, and for one-off construction, some details of temporary sheds are worth considering here.

An economical way to convert an open space is to rig up a series of wooden frames shaped like goalposts but with one side higher than the other so that when tarpaulins are laid on top the roof has a slope of at least 1 in 4 to shed rain. Alternatively the framework can be in the form of a conventional building with centreline ridgepole. With either configuration there should be plenty of battens and diagonals from framework to framework so that they are well braced and the tarpaulins do not sag: a gap of 10in (25cm) is about right. Wire ropes from the top corners of the framing down to stakes driven in the ground help to keep the whole building rigidly supported. The stakes are like outsize tent pegs and should extend at least 18in (50cm) below the surface.

Green canvas tarpaulins are best. A modern form is made of a synthetic man-made fibre which is dyed the same green as the old-fashioned heavy flax tarpaulin so that the latest type is easy to confuse with the less hard-wearing old-fashioned canvas. The trade name for one of these new materials is Durathene. Tarpaulin makers will provide covers to a given set of dimensions so that one can get them to fit exactly.

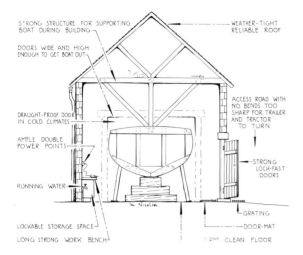

Labels for left diagram:
STRONG STRUCTURE FOR SUPPORTING BOAT DURING BUILDING — WEATHER-TIGHT RELIABLE ROOF
DOORS WIDE AND HIGH ENOUGH TO GET BOAT OUT
ACCESS ROAD WITH NO BENDS TOO SHARP FOR TRAILER AND TRACTOR TO TURN
DRAUGHT-PROOF DOOR IN COLD CLIMATES
AMPLE DOUBLE POWER POINTS
STRONG LOCK-FAST DOORS
RUNNING WATER
GRATING
LOCKABLE STORAGE SPACE
DOOR-MAT
LONG STRONG WORK BENCH
CLEAN FLOOR

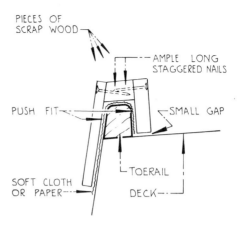

Labels for right diagram:
PIECES OF SCRAP WOOD
AMPLE LONG STAGGERED NAILS
PUSH FIT
SMALL GAP
SOFT CLOTH OR PAPER
TOERAIL
DECK

It is not enough to be sure that a boat can be worked out of its shed when complete: the road leading away from the premises must be suitable for the vehicle. At least one boatyard is prevented from building boats as big as it would like because of sharp bends, steep hills and narrow streets just beyond the building shed.

These days the shed must be proof against vandals and thieves. Windows and doors must be protected and stout. Ideally there should be occupied dwellings nearby. The roof should not only keep out rain but be secure against future gales, because these often bring rain. And everyone knows that gales occur on Friday nights so the resultant leak from lifted roofing is not discovered till Monday morning, by which time a lot of damage has occurred. Sheds housing amateur built boats naturally loose their tiles on a Sunday night, so that the owner does not discover it until he comes back on Saturday morning.

Facilities should include running water, toilet and plenty of electric power points. These should be double or quadruple sockets, to take all the necessary tools, heaters and lights. A cat to keep away mice and birds is also an asset.

Conventional tarpaulins let in only limited light and so the sides of the shed, and perhaps short lengths of the roof, should be covered with translucent material. Ordinary polythene sheet, even the heavy type (sometimes designated 1500 mil) will not stand up to strong gusty winds for long. However, there are various types of reinforced polythene and one of the best uses nylon netting: small-gauge netting with about $\frac{1}{2}$in (12mm) squares or even smaller is needed for long life. Even so, expect it to begin to deteriorate after about a year, certainly within two years. The heavy reinforced plastic used in the construction industry may last longer.

Everyone working onboard should wear clean soft-soled shoes, but even so protection is needed on all surfaces that can be marked during the final stages of construction. Cockpit coamings, breakwaters, anything which stands up and may be trodden on should have a guard such as this one. It is no good putting on a protector with sharp edges and forgetting the layer of soft cloth or paper. Some coats of paint or varnish will be applied before the guard is fitted.

The doorway width and height are critical. One of the advantages of cold-moulding is that the coachroof or superstructure can often be added after the finished hull has been hauled out of its building shed, so the height may not need to be more than the hull's depth. Ballast keels and in a few cases the skeg and lower part of the keel of a power craft can be added outside. However, outside work is never quite as satisfactory as inside work, especially in wet climates. High winds also hamper work outside, and of course many places are plagued with vandalism. So a high, wide but strong door is essential.

If a doorway has to be changed it is not always necessary to make the lintel higher: at times it is better to sink the threshold downwards. However this needs some planning, possibly a scale drawing. Just digging a local trench across between the doorposts is not enough. The ends of the boat are normally higher than amidships due to the sheer so the wheels of the trailer must start going down well before the bow or stern reaches the lintel. The depression in the ground must continue well beyond the doorway too, so quite a bit of excavating may be needed and raising the lintel may after all be the least work. Sinking the door sill is likely to introduce drainage problems too.

A cold-moulded hull shell before it has beams fitted would be squeezable if the moulds were taken out; a light hull might well be pinched in by more than 5 per cent of its total beam. There may be a temptation to use this squashability to get a wide hull through a too-narrow doorway. The idea has been tried and it is thoroughly bad. Not only is the hull likely to be damaged, it may be very hard to get the precise shape back.

Because these hulls are also light they can sometimes be laid over on their sides to go through a high narrow doorway. A well-built and well supported hull will withstand 'this provided it is done gently.

Apart from the space needed for the hull, there must be room for a workbench and power tools, for preparing the timber, gluing up frames and beams, space for the heater unit and above all space to keep the timber.

Timber should be stored well away from heaters to prevent over-drying and then cracking. Over-dry wood is brittle, so the veneers crack when handled. Ideally a hygrometer should be obtained, to ensure a relative humidity of not less than 45 per cent can be maintained. If there is a risk of the humidity dropping below this a few buckets of water should be put near the wood, if necessary with cloth wicks to extend the surface area. Increased ventilation and decreased temperature

help to raise the humidity, but once gluing starts the area round the hull or parts being laminated has to be kept free from drafts and in the temperature and humidity range decreed by the glue manufacturer. This may well mean that the timber has to be stored in a separate building. It is not unusual to see professionals working on a hull which has a tent of polythene sheet over it, because this is such an effective way of eliminating drafts and keeping the temperature up without using a lot of fuel.

All timber ought to be kept completely protected from rain, roof leaks and damp from the ground. None of the wood should be on the ground or floor, nor even on small chocks, which will soak up water from a wet floor. A row of battens spaced say a foot apart with polythene sheet over them, make a good support for the building timber. Another row of battens on top of the polythene, each upper batten resting on one below the protective sheet, will allow air to circulate round the pile. From all this it is obvious that the wood used for building should be delivered from the mill just before the building is to begin. It should be protected from the weather during transport and be unloaded under cover, or on a day when the weather is fine.

Building Bases

To build any boat a firm base is needed. It is a good idea to think of this as a gigantic workbench, firm and free from movement regardless of how hard it is punished. Vibrating tools, heavy-footed helpers, dropped baulks of timber should all leave the building base unmoved. Totally. A building base which sags when a ballast keel is added to the hull, or flutters when a massive drill bears down, is inadequate.

All building bases must extend at both ends beyond the hull by about 18in (50cm) for every 20ft (6m) of boat length. This overhang is for securing stems, transoms, end moulds and so on. However, bases that stand up above the floor should not reach right to the end wall of the shed; there must be at least a gap large enough to walk through. This may mean setting it diagonally across the shed to get the maximum length under the roof.

A wood floor over the whole building area may seem the ideal basis on which to start. It is,

provided that it can stand up to the high local loads. A heavy engine or keel needs massive joists if there is to be no sagging or splintering crash as the floor is asked to support a big weight. Standard floor joists are available for known loads, so the size required is easily determined once the largest weight the floor must support is known.

In practice reinforced concrete floors are used in modern boat-building premises. Here again the largest probable load is decided, then the floor is designed to take this, with a suitable factor of safety to allow for future expansion in the number and weight of craft. Concrete floor design is detailed in text-books on reinforced concrete building.

Once laid, concrete has a number of disadvantages. Nothing can be conveniently joined to it, it will not take nails, it is usually laid flat and smooth without recesses for props or hooks, so it is altogether a bit inconvenient for the practical boatbuilder. Many of his difficulties disappear if wood baulks are recessed into the concrete. They must be of the hardest, most stable wood locally available and secured down with lag bolts. If no fastenings are put into the concrete they may pull out when heavily loaded; for instance a baulk may dry out and become slightly slack in its recess, then it may be made to tilt or take a strain upwards and the result can be that it lifts out.

Baulks recessed every 1 or $1\frac{1}{2}$ yards (1–1.5m) apart suit most builders. They should be wider than the beamiest boat under construction, and ideally extend across the shed. The wood should not be less than 6in (15cm) deep, but here it will be sensible to buy the size in stock. The width of each baulk will also be determined by what is available without further sawing. Bearing in mind that wedges have to be nailed on, sometimes moulds secured down, prop ends possibly recessed slightly, the baulks should be at least 8in (20cm) wide and 12in (30cm) is much better.

All this wood is expensive because it is no good using anything but a rot-resisting, non-splitting dense hardwood. So instead of having so many baulks, a saving can be made by having slotted steel plates recessed flush with the concrete floor. These plates will be 12×12in (30×30cm) or more and quite $\frac{1}{2}$in (12mm) thick, with T-shaped slots to take hooks and bolt heads so that all manner of components can be fastened down. The T-slots must be large enough to take stout bolts about $\frac{3}{4}$in (20mm) thick, and the lag bolts holding the plates into the concrete must be commensurate. Wood baulks can be bolted to these plates to hold moulds, eyes used to take tackles for turning the boat over or haul the keel in place, chocks secured to hold props, and so on.

Instead of a series of steel plates, continuous angle-bar may be recessed across or along the concrete floor for the same purposes. Alternatively eye-bolts with rings may be set flush with the top of the floor. Whatever is used there should be no upstanding part to make it difficult to move the finished boat out of the shed, and nothing to trip on after a hard day's grind.

If the shed floor is of earth, duck boards round the hull help to keep everything clean. They must be deep enough to remain clear above the ground even after they have been well trodden in. Boards less than 3ft (1m) wide are a nuisance. If they are well secured down with stakes they can be used for *minor* jobs such as holding secondary mould supports or low staging.

The purpose of the building base is to give perfect support to the moulds and in time the whole hull. Whether a wood, concrete or earth floor is used, on top of it there is usually a fore-and-aft structure, well fixed in place, onto which the moulds are bolted or screwed. This spine is often made of two planks set on edge. They must be exactly level, and parallel in both plan and section view. Any type of wood can be used provided it has seasoned well; second-hand planks may be best, being well matured. Hard or soft wood, knotty or clear-grained, anything sound will do.

These two planks take the whole weight of the boat until it is turned over, and maybe after that. So they must be strong enough for the loads and must not sag. Close-spaced supports will ensure that light planks do the job, but it is a mistake to use planks much less than 8in (20cm) deep per 20ft (6m) of hull length, and about $1\frac{1}{4}$in (32mm) thick for every 20ft of length.

If these two supports are set very far apart they give good athwartships stability to the moulds, but the hull will curve inside them well before the stem and the stern. If they are close together they remain inside the topsides for most of the length, but the moulds may have a slight tendency to 'shoogle' sideways. A compromise which usually suits strength and convenience involves setting the supports about one-quarter of the maximum beam off the centreline. Each plank needs supporting athwartships and underneath. If the floor is earth, stakes are hammered in alongside planks and nails driven across. Diagonal supports from the bottom of one plank to the top of the other, in pairs of crosses as used on joists, are secured at about ten intervals along the length of the base. To take the load of these planks with the boat growing above them, there must be some well-spread structure underneath if the ground is not firm. A row of railway sleepers (ties) makes a practical foundation.

Using second-hand material makes sense for the whole building base. Steel joists welded or bolted together may be used for both the fore-and-aft members and the athwartships ties. A grid of rolled steel sections is wonderfully strong, and only suffers from the risk that during welding distortion may occur. (Avoided by using a proper welding sequence and minimizing heat output.)

For small boats a base of heavy grade Dexion angle-bar has many handy features. It is easy to add on pieces, easy to secure the moulds to the holes already there, easy to bolt on diagonal bracing. Dexion is not cheap, but it can be found second-hand and then resold, and for a more permanent building base it has attractions.

Overhead beams are a tremendous asset. The beams and side pillars of the shed can help secure the moulds, or take the ends of struts to the stem and transom, or shores with wedged ends for jamming the backbone down into position, and so on. If necessary a little doubling and reinforcing of the building's structure may be put in, just to make sure that in a burst of energy, forcing some part with wedges driven under props, or tackles hauled too heartily, the building does not shift or come crashing down.

Hand Tools

Good tools speed a job through, stay sharp longer, last well, save time and add to the pleasure of doing a job. Perhaps most important, they impart pride of ownership which is a great morale booster, especially when a job is hard and tiring. The finest tools are not necessarily the most expensive, but they will not be cheap. Most people built up a kit over the years, shopping around to get the best quality. My own experience is that tools made in Britain, Germany and America are reliable, especially if bought from an established trade supplier. Products from other countries are often cheaper but too often shoddy.

There is no agreement among boatbuilders as to the ideal tool list. Professionals make some of their own, amateurs tend to be short of money for buying tools, and everyone has their own idiosyncrasies. Some people can work with few tools; I built myself a 30-footer which carried me across the Atlantic and through several subsequent gales using a set of tools which fitted into a box 3ft × 10in × 8in. The whole collection cost little more than an average week's wages.

Most people like a lot of tools, partly because they are a pleasure to own, partly because they speed up certain jobs and partly because they make a few almost impossible jobs easy. Professionals tend to use more and more machinery, which reduces the need for hand tools. They also buy in completed boat components, which further cuts down their requirements. Amateurs are following the same paths, but are so often short of money that they have to compromise. The best way to save money is to buy the best, but only when the need for a particular tool arises. There is no need to rush into buying the whole of the following list right away. Take heart from my young sons, who solve many problems with a Mini-Mole Grip and a multi-blade Swiss Army knife!

Bench vice with soft jaws. I like to have both a wood and a metal vice, set on the same workbench and lined up so that a long or heavy piece of metal or wood can be held by both vices. The metal-faced vice needs clip-on soft jaws. The height of the vice matters, but as it is not easy to adjust a bench height a set of duckboards to stand on may be used to give the correct distance.

Claw hammer. 12in (30cm) long, weighing about $1\frac{1}{2}$lbs. The type with its handle made from compressed leather washers has a good grip and can be used all day without discomfort.

Pin hammer. About 12in (30cm) long and 6oz weight.

A selection of screwdrivers. Pump screwdrivers earn their keep repeatedly when boatbuilding. They are called 'Yankee' screwdrivers in Europe, but not in North America. One about 14in long (36cm) suits a variety of jobs provided it has a selection of blades including Philips blades. Additional screwdrivers are handy and sometimes essential. For cramped places a stubby one is needed. I like all my screwdrivers to have a square shank which goes right through the handle so that a hammer can be used on the end; the square section makes it easy to clamp on a Mole Grip for extra turning leverage. For boats up to about 35ft (10.5m) a heavy screwdriver 13in (35cm) overall with a $\frac{3}{8}$in (10mm) blade width copes with most problems. A medium screwdriver may not be needed if there is a pump one, but a small one typically 9in (23cm) long with a blade $\frac{3}{16}$in wide (5mm) or less is important. Those small screwdrivers made principally for electricians are not needed much except when putting in electrical components, but the type with a test lamp in the handle for detecting electrical current is wonderfully useful. For really heavy work there is nothing to beat a screwdriver bit in a ratchet brace. The best types are reversible, with different size blades at each end.

Pliers, assorted. Electricians' pliers about 7in (18cm) long and a Mole Grip cover most situations. Wire cutters come in various forms, and for clenching work, which admittedly is rare except on bent timbers, the 'end nipper' type is best.

Hand-drill. The best type has an enclosed wheel which holds grease well, whereas the open type loses its lubrication and occasionally catches clothing. The chuck should take up to $\frac{5}{16}$in (7mm) bits. Some people like the short handle type because it fits into tight spots; I do not share this enthusiasm, preferring to use a right-angle drive on an electric drill for inaccessible corners. The electric drill fanatic may do without a hand drill entirely.

Breast drill. Not always needed, especially if an angle brace is available, or a heavy duty electric drill. The two-speed breast drill is recommended, with a chuck size up to at least $\frac{1}{2}$in (12mm).

Angle brace. The ratchet kind is needed for working in confined spaces.

Set of wood bits. For most work a range from about $\frac{3}{8}$–1in (10–25mm) is adequate. A variable diameter bit is useful but should not be asked to do prolonged work in hard woods. A countersink bit is likely to be needed, but some people use a metal countersink drill for wood or metal, though it tends to clog at times.

Two boxes of small drills, $\frac{1}{16}$–$\frac{3}{8}$in (1.5–10mm). Two sets are needed because these small drills break and get blunt often. For moderately soft woods I sometimes make by own drills out of hard wire: the end of the wire is flattened by hammering, then ground to a spear point with sharp cutting edges. Most boatbuilders make up a few of their own tools to save money and because the needed item is not available, not easily found, or not quite right when factory produced. I make up small batches of these low-cost drills.

Countersink drills. The type with a short cylindrical section backing up the conical nose is best. They are great time-savers as they make the two sizes of hole and countersink all in one pass.

Long drills, to suit the sizes of long bolts being used. Few ordinary hardware shops stock them but specialist tool suppliers have them. Alternatively, ordinary drills can be lengthened by having hard steel rods welded on top. The rods should be the same diameter as the drill, fully welded all round, the weld being ground smooth after it has cooled. It may be cheaper to have a batch of drills lengthened this way than to buy new long drills.

Hole cutters. Not essential for many boats but useful when working on plywood. Cutting out widows, locker door holes or vent holes are typical jobs speeded up with a set of these.

Planes. There is much disagreement here, partly because the size of plane which can be conveniently worked depends in part on the strength of the hands holding it. To complicate matters it is now hard to get planes with wooden bodies, which are lighter than the typical steel-bodied plane though the latter are easier to set and adjust, and fairly cheap. It is sometimes possible to get second-hand wooden planes; if the plane body has warped it can be trued by passing it carefully over the bed of a planing machine. The sole may need a new base, which is made by gluing on a doubler piece. Old planes tend to have superior blades which have an almost soft, slightly greasy touch, I've been assured. 'Something like old English silver' were the words used – neatly confirming my view that anyone involved in the use of tools gets lyrical about them. While a professional will probably favour a 10in (25cm) long steel plane with a $2\frac{5}{8}$in (7cm) wide blade, amateurs may be happier with an 8in (20cm) plane having a blade width of $2\frac{1}{4}$in (6cm).

A trying plane is needed, for straightening long edges though plenty of boats have been built with wood largely trued in the mill and finished with a standard plane. Trying planes about 18in (50cm) long are good all-rounders but heavy work for many amateurs; this is where a wood plane helps. A long plane might be thought good for finishing off topsides, but a short plane is essential for this job because lightness is important especially when not working down-hand.

A little *hand plane* is valuable for furniture work, bevelling and so on. A good size is about 6in (15cm) overall by perhaps $1\frac{1}{2}$in (4cm). It is very light and so can be worked all day without fatigue, besides being more quickly sharpened than its larger cousins.

Wax candle end. This is not just to use when the lights all fuse because someone has overloaded the mechanical planer by asking it to cut a hardwood too deeply! Its principal purpose is to lubricate the plane bases, especially when the wood is not perfectly dry.

Chisels and gouges. These are used less every year in boatbuilding due to the increase in machinery.

Mechanical woodworking tools are now so versatile and cheap that they are ousting the chisel, which tends to be slow. If a professional finds himself doing a lot of chisel work he is probably losing money and should reassess the job. An amateur should follow this lead, because he will want to save time also.

Boxwood handled chisels tend to have good blades, but are not widely sold. Plastic handled chisels are easy to get and suit most jobs, but the cheap wood-handled chisels should be viewed with suspicion. It's surprising how many boats have been built using no more than two chisels, perhaps a $\frac{1}{2}$ and 1in (12 and 25mm). Chisels are needed for rebating, but even here so much rebating is either eliminated or machine cut that chisels are less used.

Mallet. The rectangular-headed mallet is universally used, apart from in my workshop where we had a series of minor accidents. Because my sons were too small to use a full size mallet I bought a carver's mallet which has a head like an egg with both ends chopped off. It was well made, but when being quite carefully used the handle sheared off just below the head. Looking for something to do one day, my elder boy drilled out the end of the broken handle in the head and pushed in a 10in (25cm) length of $\frac{3}{4}$in (25mm) diameter steel tube to make a new handle. The result is one of my favourite tools, not least because it has the right balance and can be used for hours without fatigue.

Sharpening stones. A medium stone is needed for taking off the first stage of bluntness, after any grinding wheel work has been completed. A fine stone finishes off the edge. Amateurs save money, they think, by getting a reversible stone, medium on one side, fine on the other. Professionals reckon this is a waste of time, and dislike the way the oil runs off when the stone is inverted. Setting the stones in wooden cases, with wooden chocks at each end so that the blade can be run beyond the very ends, results in even wear, and the stones last a long time even though used a lot; professionals sharpen tools twice or three times as often as beginners.

Sharpening gauge, for holding chisels or plane blades at just the right angle when sharpening. A help for everyone, but especially a beginner.

Oil can, for holding oil for the sharpening stones and for lubricating every tool with moving parts, or parts likely to rust.

Surforms. A selection of these is worth having because they are versatile and easy to use. Blades should be bought in packs, and when blunt should be kept for finishing work. The difference between a new and an old Surform blade is akin to the difference between a rip-saw and a tenon saw: one is for quick chopping and the other for fine finishing.

A selection of files. Files are less used now, partly because Surforms fill the bill, partly because power grindstones do some filing jobs quicker and with less effort. The best files still seem to come from Sweden, regardless of how hard other countries try.

Shears or heavy-duty scissors, such as sailmakers' scissors. If wood laminations about $\frac{1}{8}$in (3mm) thick are being used it is possible to trim the edges with shears or scissors, though the cut must not be right against the marked line and final planing along the edge will be necessary.

Knives. Instead of using shears some builders like to trim laminations with a knife. A Stanley knife or gutting or sailmaker's knife suits the job.

Saws. Even if various power saws are available, hand saws are almost certainly going to be needed. There is a strong trend towards disposable saws which are thrown away when the teeth are blunt – fine provided the saw does not snag a hidden nail the first day it is used. Some professionals always keep one or two old saws for risky situations and only use their favourites when the wood is above suspicion. New saws have Teflon coatings to ease the passage of the blade through the wood, especially when there is moisture about, but as in planing rubbing over with a candle end is probably best, not least because it can be frequently renewed.

A cross-cut saw with about ten teeth to the inch (25mm) deals with a variety of work. Rip-sawing may be done by an amateur with a circular saw on a drill. But if this involves assembling and dismantling, the time wasted will be unpopular, so a rip-saw with perhaps six teeth to the inch will be worth having.

For sharpening a saw a set of small files is needed, and a suitable long clamp which holds the full length of the blade. A saw setter is not used every time the teeth are sharpened, so it is not needed if the saws are sent to a saw doctor every so often for the full treatment.

A tenon saw about 8in (20cm) long with about fourteen teeth to the inch suits a variety of fine work, but is rather small for jobs like trimming off bent timber ends, where a 12in (30cm) size is more popular and gives a quicker cut.

Hacksaw. A pistol grip handle is better than one in line with the blade for almost every job. An adjustable saw is best because it will take whatever size of blades are available, but if it is a fixed length tool it should be for 12in (30.5cm) blades. Selections of blades, always bought in packets since many break or wear out, are needed. A mini-hacksaw is a valuable tool, used by some professionals for cutting wood mouldings and similar small jobs. One version has an adjustable handle which makes it possible to fit it into awkward corners.

Cramps or *clamps.* For jobs like laminating a long backbone many cramps are used. For general boatbuilding three G-cramps about 8in long (20cm) and three more about 3in (75cm) cope with a lot of situations. Two sets of sash cramps are needed for making up furniture, doors and so on; they need to be at least as wide as a big door, which will be about 2ft 6in (76cm) across. For larger assemblies two sash cramps can be bolted together after the end bolts have been removed.

Carpenter's square. A 14in (26cm) size is good for boatbuilding, but for loft work a larger one is an asset over and above a really big one, perhaps 5ft (15 cm) along each edge. For truing up edges of wood a tiny engineer's steel square just 2in (5cm) long is used by careful woodworkers. This tool, like so many, is very personal; one person will claim it is impossible to work without it, while fifty others will be just as sure it's far from essential.

A triangular set-square as used by draftsmen can save time, especially for furniture work. The plastic type about 12in (30cm) along one edge covers many situations.

A steel or fibreglass tape measure at least as long as the boat. Anything shorter is inconvenient. The old cloth type stretches and is not reliable.

A folding rule. I've noticed amateurs use 2-footers and professionals use 3-footers. It may now be best to have a rule with metric units on one side and feet and inches on the other. Steel engineer's rules 6 or 12in (150 or 300mm) long are fairly popular but not easy to read in bad light, and more appropriate to precision indoor work than building hulls.

Straight edge. This usually takes the form of a strip of stable, well seasoned wood with one edge carefully trued up and about 6ft (2m) long, but the longer the better. My own preference is for one the length of a berth (6ft 3in or 1.9m) and a second long one up to 15ft (4.5m) long.

Plumb bobs and lines. Two are needed even for a small boat, and four for over 25ft (7.5m). Can be homemade.

Chalk-line and reel. For loft work, and in the building for making long straight lines. Where a subtle but even curve is needed the trick is to pluck the string sideways as well as away from the wood, so that when released it gives a gently curving mark. This takes little practice and is a handy way of drawing slight curves without resorting to battens.

Wooden battens made up as needed. They will be required for loft work first, and some should taper at one end, if not both, for variable curves. A typical range will be $\frac{1}{2} \times \frac{1}{2}$in (12 × 12mm), $\frac{3}{4} \times \frac{3}{4}$in (18 × 18mm), and 1 × 1in (25 × 25mm), each 60 per cent of the overall length, perhaps with a second set half this length.

Spirit level. While everyone agrees that this should be the biggest that available money will buy, most people go for one around 3ft (1m) long. The little ones, about a third this length, are not much good for boatbuilding, and larger sizes are awkward when doing joinery work inside the boat. It must have levels for horizontal and vertical use.

A long length of transparent plastic tube is a great help for levelling up hulls. Water finds it own level, so the two ends of the tube are set up athwartships and fore and aft, then the waterline on the hull is made to coincide. Colouring in the water makes the level in the tube easier to see.

Sanding block. A wood block made to fit the hand is a pleasure to use. It should have $\frac{3}{8}$in (10m) of cork glued on the base. Commercial sanding blocks are all cork or all rubber; the latter are best for wet-and-dry rubbing down.

A bevel gauge. As with so many marking tools, a big one is wanted on the mould loft floor, a small one in the confined spaces inside a hull. The type with one leg of about 10in (25cm) is popular, and I've seen lots of miniature versions made up by shipwrights.

HB (medium hard) pencils. There is a pencil with a flattened oval section, called a carpenter's pencil; it has a thick lead and won't easily roll, nor does it need resharpening in the middle of marking in a very long line. But these assets hardly justify the extra cost.

Spanners (wrenches) to fit all the nut sizes used.

A large adjustable wrench or Footprint. Since this tool is (on small boats) not often used, it may be borrowed or hired. I prefer the type made by the Rigid Tool Co. which is available in a range of sizes with renewable jaws and light alloy handles. Mine is 20in (50cm) long and adequate for all the jobs on craft up to 40ft (12m).

Mole Grip. These can be used as small cramps and one version has a clamp attached to the handle so it can be used as a bench vice. Working single-handed, perhaps the most important use is tightening a bolt when the nut is not accessible from the same side as the bolt head. The Mole Grip is clamped onto the nut and secured so that it cannot rotate while the bolt is tightened.

And so on. There are omissions in this list because some tools are going out of fashion and are hard to find, or because the increasing use of power tools and the need to get jobs done quickly is making them obsolete. I used to use a drawknife and spokeshave often, but neither are easy to buy now, and they tend to be found mostly in the kits of dedicated craftsmen. The adze and the boatbuilder's axe are now seldom used in industrialized countries and virtually never by amateurs.

Power Tools

Nothing cuts down the hard labour of boatbuilding like the availability of power tools, except the help of more skilled hands. Even the most penniless amateur putting together a simple un-decked 20-footer will have an electric drill. It is the basic power tool, with attachments for all sorts of other jobs: circular saws, jigsaws, disc and drum sanders, grinding stones and routers, not to mention orbital sanders and pillars.

The smallest size of drill, with a chuck to take bits up to $\frac{1}{4}$in (6.5mm) diameter, is not a good choice. The next size up, $\frac{5}{16}$in (8mm) is much more versatile, tends to last longer and work harder, and generally gives better service. For amateur or professional, this is the size for so many jobs. The bigger $\frac{3}{8}$in (9.5mm) is beginning to get a bit heavy to handle all day, especially for amateurs. It is sometimes made more bulky too, so that it will not fit into small spaces. Both the $\frac{5}{16}$ and $\frac{3}{8}$in sizes are made with high and low speed settings and this is a worthwhile extra.

Any professional building boats bigger than about 25ft (7.5m) will find a $\frac{1}{2}$in (12mm) size drill an asset, especially for bolt holes in the backbone, pilot drilling for the rudder tube, and so on. An amateur might consider buying a drill this size second-hand (with a guarantee) or hiring it while assembling a backbone structure.

Electric hand tools are made in two grades, for amateurs and for professionals. The former are cheaper but less rugged, they are surprisingly long lasting, but they do not like being overloaded and repairs sometimes cost half the price of a new tool. For serious boatbuilding and especially when taking a ten year view, it is best to buy tools designed for full time professional use. Some yards use air-driven hand tools because they are safer, more reliable, hard to damage, and unlikely to be stolen as they are no use in the typical household or workshop which lacks a supply of compressed air.

Having bought an electric drill or two, the boatbuilder is faced with a dilemma. Does one go on to buy a separate jigsaw next, or a vibrator sander, or maybe a hand-held power planer? A professional will buy the lot, because for him time is money and these tools pay for themselves in the first year. An amateur chooses according to the kind of boat he is building, and what he can borrow or hire.

For cutting out ply bulkhead, furniture, windows and so on, a jig-saw or sabre saw is a great asset. Blades are available to slice through fibreglass, plastics and thin aluminium as well as wood. One of the few limitations of this tool is swinging room. The body of the saw extends behind the blade so when cutting round a curve there must be room to work the whole saw round outside the cut. When cutting the doorway through a ply bulkhead, the top and bottom of the opening must not be too near the deckhead and sole, if the bulkhead has already been installed, otherwise the saw cannot be used in the space available. In practice this means: (a) cutting out all possible access holes, doorways and so on before the component is put into the boat; (b) making sure that all cuts made inside the boat are well clear of limitations such as adjacent parts that are at right angles to the piece being cut. This is not such a hardship because in any case it is bad engineering to cut near the edge of a bulkhead and leave just a narrow weak border round a hole.

An orbital sander, sometimes called a vibrating or oscillating sander, is a useful tool for finishing work. It should not leave marks on the wood, the way disc sanders so often do, but it has strict limitations. It cannot work right into a corner, it is slow, it is nothing like so good for fine finishing as a well handled plane, and it sometimes leaves undulations.

Belt sanders have similar limitations but they work faster. They tend to be heavy to use, but they are a great asset to the unskilled amateur and the professional in a hurry. Disc sander attachments for electric drills are a dubious asset, but the drum type have all sorts of uses, some professionals even using them to bevel off sharp edges of components which have been built in. For all sanding machines paper with aluminium oxide grit is far better than the traditional type of sandpaper. Its cost is more than offset by longer, harder service.

A hand-held router is a useful machine for a job like cutting the recess for a window, but it is a dangerous tool. The spindle rotates at about 2,000 rpm so if it breaks pieces of sharp-edged metal may zip about, slicing whatever may come in the way. I have heard of one which broke and a chunk of metal ricocheted from wall to wall before finally coming to rest. To cut down the danger when routing it is best to have a guide against which the machine is pressed as it is taken round the shape. Guides should always be bolted rather than clamped in position. They are useful for all manner of jobs, such as planing bevels with a bench planer, using a batten of wood secured along one side of the plane base, so that the wood is tilted up one side.

Hand-held power planers are not much used, very seldom by amateurs. They tend to be heavy and need skill, but the type which can cut a rebate is at times useful for backbones, if a router cannot do the job. There is always a temptation with this sort of tool to work too fast. I once used an electric planer when making a mast; getting impatient after a long hard slog, I reset the blade too deeply and the next minute I had sheared away too much wood. As a result, for five years I sailed in the shadow of a mast just slightly too thin and whippy.

A hand-held circular saw is useful for cross-cutting, for speeding up the cutting of a backbone rebate, maybe for tapering a hog or slicing off the surplus where a deck extends out beyond the topsides. A selection of blades are needed, with fine, medium and coarse teeth.

One attachment for an electric drill which is worth having is a pillar, to convert the portable tool into a bench-mounted one. The type of stand which has a vice on the base is best. To further enhance this tool, it is possible to buy a hand-held brake which slows the drill so that materials like brass can be drilled properly.

So far all the tools mentioned have been portable. They can be moved about, taken into the hull, or used in awkward corners as the need arises. Being portable, there are limitations on size and weight, which in turn this means that the power which can be packed into the machine is modest. For really hard work a static power tool is needed, on its own steel bench which is secured strongly to the ground. Ahead and beyond, whether it is a saw or planer, there must be plenty of space to handle long pieces of timber. If the room is small the walls are pierced with doors or windows which can be opened to allow long baulks to be brought up to the machine, through it and away at the far end. The height of the window sill must be the same or slightly lower than the bench so that wood can be worked through the machine while protruding through the window. It's no good having a busy main road outside the window; the machines must be located in such a way that they can handle the longest component without undue drama. I've more than once been mixed up in situations which involved holding up the traffic. Drivers join in the fun the first time, the second time they are prepared to be tolerant: after that they get irritable. If necessary angle saws and planers diagonally across the shop.

A bandsaw is probably the most useful major tool for amateurs and professionals. For general boatbuilding a saw with a reach of about 2ft 8in (80cm) is good, with a second one for minor jobs about 18in (50cm). This smaller size on its own suits amateurs turning out a boat about 33ft (10m) overall. The reach, or 'swallow' is the distance from the blade to the vertical pillar which supports the top wheel. For some operations this distance is critical, since it limits the width of wood which can be passed through the saw. Suppose a piece of wood is being cut down the middle: if its total width is more than twice the swallow the saw cannot cope with the job. If the wood has to be cut say 17$\frac{3}{4}$in from one edge but 4ft from the other, then a saw with an 18in reach can just manage provided the cut is straight and parallel with the near edge. A curved cut may be out of the question, though, and this is why the swallow is so critical.

Bandsaw blades come in two styles, for re-sharpening or disposable. Modern blades tend to be thrown away when they are blunt or broken. They stay sharp longer than the older type, but it is impossible to sharpen them. They suit anyone who lives far from a saw doctor, but they are a nuisance for those who break blades often, or have to use wood which is permeated with sand (teak being the most usual example) or second-hand timber which may have hidden nails. Anyone building boats seriously must keep at least one spare blade of every type, but if using disposable blades it will be sensible to have several spares.

Blades are made with different types of teeth for fine work, for fast cuts, for aluminium and so on. When buying the blade make sure that the maker's label says that it suits the saw, and gives the speed of 'feed per minute'. This is the rate at which the blade can cut through the workpiece. When the feed rate drops either the electric motor needs attention or the blade is becoming blunt. Accidents occur when wood is forced against a failing blade. A regular clicking sound is an indication that the blade has a fault, which is usually a warning that a breakage is imminent. Accidents can be minimized by keeping the adjustable vertical guard as low as possible, just above the wood being fed through. For curved cuts a thin blade is used, for long cuts and thick timber a broad blade. The fading note of the motor is a sure sign that it is being overloaded, and this applies to planers as well as all types of saw.

Boatbuilders are different from other wood workers in that they seldom use straight lines or right angles. They need band and circular saws with tiltable beds for cutting at a bevel. Circular saws which tilt have lift-out sections of the table by the blade, otherwise as the table is angled it binds the blade.

Professionals will select a saw with a blade diameter of about 18in (50cm) and a second for small parts about 12in or even down to 8in (30 or 20cm). Amateurs will probably go for the 12in size. A variety of blades is needed, including coarse for bold cutting, planer blades to give a finish which needs little if any further planing, and perhaps a special one for cutting Perspex or polycarbonate plastic.

A circular saw also needs a gate, which is a steel fiddle parallel to the blade and adjustable so that wood can be cut to a predetermined width. The gate allows a series of pieces to be cut all to exactly the same width, like a jig. The modern type of adjustment has a hand screw with a vernier and this is much to be preferred to the older type, which has no scale and no handy means for slight adjustments.

Where there is a shortage of space or money, a 'universal wood-working tool' is sometimes the answer. It is an electric motor driving a spindle, mounted on a variable base so that the spindle can be turned to any angle in a horizontal or vertical plane; the base travels on a rail or pair of rails. On the spindle, circular saw blades, routers, or various other tools can be mounted. The machine is akin to an electric drill with attachments, only it is much larger, in some ways more versatile, and because it is on a bed with travelling guides it can be used for accurate cuts, precise channelling and so on. It is not a safe tool but it is extremely handy and will do so many jobs provided that the wood can be brought to it and fixed down for the cut to be made. A serious danger is that the blade is unguarded for the most part.

For finishing timber a professional will probably prefer a planer with a width of about 18in (50cm) and a second one half this size. Amateurs will probably put a power planer well down the list of priorities, but it may pay for itself quickly since sawmills now charge a lot to finish wood. Once a cutting list has been worked out a timber yard can be asked to quote for the wood 'off saw' and 'finished all round', meaning planed on all four long sides; or 'd 2 s' which is short for 'dressed two sides', i.e. planed top and bottom but not along the edges. The price difference between the rough and planed timber will show whether it's worth buying a power planner. Of course even if the price difference is not enough to pay for the tool there is the tremendous convenience of being able to clean off wood on site.

Small tools do not always have dust extractors, but for major machinery a built-in vacuum cleaner is a real asset. On a planer especially it saves a lot of sweeping up and a shed full of flying sawdust.

Building Sequence

Boatbuilding is both an art and a science, and the order of working varies. Factors such as the time available for building and the exactness of the people who cut the wood will dictate some aspects of the job. Or, for instance, it may not be possible to have the use of a good building shed for long. This should not delay starting work. In one quite small room construction can start on components such as frames, coachroof coamings, rudder, hatches and berth fronts, which can be finished almost to the penultimate coat of paint or varnish. There are other good reasons for starting on minor parts before the main hull. If the builders are amateurs they gain skill, confidence and know-

how on less important items. In a new or expanding yacht yard a skilled team does not spring instantly into being. As men join the firm it is sensible to put them onto minor jobs while they find their feet, while the management learns their capabilities and while the leaks in the roof are being fixed.

A normal building procedure, in brief, is as follows.

The hull is laid off full size on a mould loft floor. It is usual to complete all the loft work at once, but some builders prefer to make the moulds as soon as the hull has been lofted, leaving the cabin and cockpit coamings, rudder and other parts to be

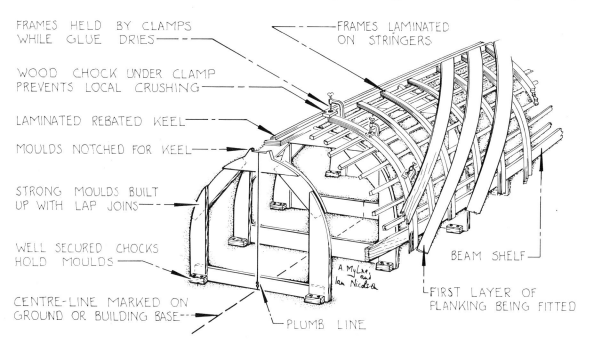

FRAMES HELD BY CLAMPS WHILE GLUE DRIES

FRAMES LAMINATED ON STRINGERS

WOOD CHOCK UNDER CLAMP PREVENTS LOCAL CRUSHING

LAMINATED REBATED KEEL

MOULDS NOTCHED FOR KEEL

STRONG MOULDS BUILT UP WITH LAP JOINS

WELL SECURED CHOCKS HOLD MOULDS

BEAM SHELF

FIRST LAYER OF PLANKING BEING FITTED

CENTRE-LINE MARKED ON GROUND OR BUILDING BASE

PLUMB LINE

A Mylne and Ian Nicolson

Stages in building. At the left a building mould is shown being set exactly on the centreline and precisely vertical with a plumb bob. Each side is well fastened to the floor or a building base with wood chocks. Moving to the right, a mould is seen with the backbone fastened into the recess by one or two screws driven upwards so that it can be removed when planking is complete. This mould has the stringers fitted and frames are being laminated over them.

While the glue in the frames dries, clamps hold the laminates together. Each clamp has a pad of wood under each jaw because crushing would weaken and

disfigure the timber.

The first planking laminate is just going on. Each plank is laid parallel with the first, with a gap for another. All the planks which have been laid need no extra shaping; they are just as they come from the mill, with parallel sides. The intermediate planks are laid on the gaps and marked with a pencil from below, then trimmed and dropped in place. If the plank timber is 4in wide the gaps for these must be about 3½in or less, to insure that the intermediate planks are wide enough to fill the gaps in spite of the curvature around the hull.

lofted later. Very occasionally lofting is not needed, in the case of a very small boat or where a full set of moulds is already available.

The building base is set up, made exactly level and thoroughly fixed down to the ground.

The backbone structure, which is like the spine of a vertebrae, is now made, possibly working from templates or direct on a moulding jig. Occasionally it may be made on the loft floor although there must be protection to prevent the loft line being rubbed out or otherwise obscured. And of course the loft floor must be protected from glue and so on. In some cases the backbone structure is laminated up on the erected moulds. All this is described fully in a later chapter.

The building moulds are made, with allowances for the difference between the full-size lines and the size of the moulds, which must be less than the hull planking; a futher reduction is needed for the ribbands put on over the mould.

At this stage the beams and frames may be made, particularly if there has to be a wait while the glue of the backbone structure is hardening. In practice some frames are glued direct onto the finished hull shell, and bent (steamed) timbers are made at the same time as they are fitted.

The moulds and transom are set up; as described here, for the hull to be built upside-down. They should be very well supported vertically and horizontally, fore and aft and athwartships. It should be possible for two heavy men to stand on the building base at any corner of any mould without its deflecting.

Battens or stringers that will support the hull shell from inside are laid over the moulds and checked for fairness.

The backbone is now put over the moulds and built up by laminating *in situ*.

The veneers for the hull skin, machined to the correct size, are now taken from the mill and stored close by the building base. Alternatively, if the builder is doing his own machining the kiln-dried timber is taken in, machined and stored close by the building base.

The hull is laminated up layer by layer to form the outer shell, and excess glue cleaned off inside and out.

The outside surface should be finished up to the third last and possibly the penultimate coat of paint or varnish.

The keel of a sailing boat (not including the ballast) may be fitted at this stage, before the hull is turned over. It may also be decided to fit twin fins, or the bilge keels of a power boat, the skeg of a sailing or power boat, etc before turning over.

The rudder tube and stern tube holes may be drilled before or after turning the hull over. It is more usual to do it after getting the hull the right way up but occasionally it is more convenient earlier.

The hull is turned the right way up, very firmly supported, and trued up so that it is again exactly level fore and aft and athwartships. (The DWL and station marks will have been transferred from the moulds to each layer, for reference.) At this stage it should be possible for three heavy men to stand on the gunwale at any point without the hull deflecting out of true in any way: the moulds and ribbands are still in place, otherwise the hull would be floppy and distort.

The true sheer is now marked in, the top and bottom of the boot-top, cove lines and so on.

The moulds are removed progressively and the battens follow, as the beams and carlines, bulkheads, frames, floors and stringers (as required, since the last three may not be fitted) are built in.

Some internal painting or varnishing should be carried out at this stage. A lot of structure and equipment should be put in before the decking goes on to gain the advantage of ample light and easy access to the inside of the hull. Engine bearers and engines, sole and sole bearers, knees, where feasible furniture, wiring and piping, tanks, steering system and rudder, skeg, keel, ballast and so on may all be fitted before the decking, always provided the hull is rigid in every plane and the extra weights can be carried safely without distortion.

The decking is fitted onto the beams followed by coachroof coamings and cabin top beams and decking.

At this stage finishing will proceed according to the availability of equipment. Toerail or bulwark, hatches and skylights, deck fittings, tiller, wheel steering etc are all put in place.

At each stage protection should be put on to prevent the wood being damaged (see sketches). For instance, there should be special battening over cockpit coamings and over the toerails, at least in way of the ladder over the side, and cabin steps should covered. In spite of all this everyone who comes aboard must wear clean shoes with soft soles.

It is no bad thing to have a detailed list of the

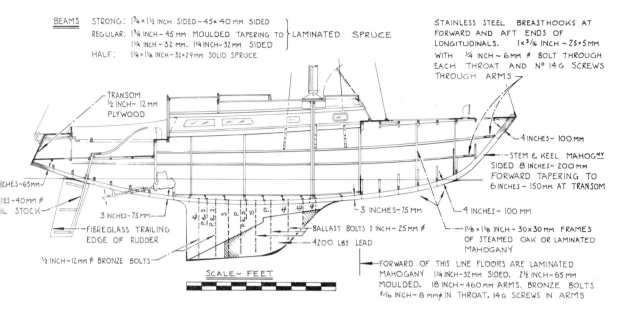

BEAMS STRONG: 1¾ × 1½ INCH SIDED ~ 45 × 40 MM SIDED
REGULAR: 1¾ INCH ~ 45 MM MOULDED TAPERING TO } LAMINATED SPRUCE
1¼ INCH ~ 32 MM. 1¼ INCH ~ 32 MM SIDED
HALF: 1¼ × 1⅛ INCH ~ 32 × 29 MM SOLID SPRUCE

STAINLESS STEEL BREASTHOOKS AT FORWARD AND AFT ENDS OF LONGITUDINALS. 1 × 3/16 INCH ~ 25 × 5 MM WITH ¼ INCH ~ 6 MM ⌀ BOLT THROUGH EACH THROAT AND N° 14 G SCREWS THROUGH ARMS

TRANSOM ½ INCH ~ 12 MM PLYWOOD

4 INCHES ~ 100 MM

STEM & KEEL MAHOGNY SIDED 8 INCHES ~ 200 MM FORWARD TAPERING TO 6 INCHES ~ 150 MM AT TRANSOM

CHES ~ 65 MM

ES ~ 40 MM ⌀ L STOCK

3 INCHES ~ 75 MM

3 INCHES ~ 75 MM

4 INCHES ~ 100 MM

FIBREGLASS TRAILING EDGE OF RUDDER

BALLAST BOLTS 1 INCH ~ 25 MM ⌀

4200 LBS LEAD

1⅛ × 1⅛ INCH ~ 30 × 30 MM FRAMES OF STEAMED OAK OR LAMINATED MAHOGANY

½ INCH ~ 12 MM ⌀ BRONZE BOLTS

SCALE ~ FEET

FORWARD OF THIS LINE FLOORS ARE LAMINATED MAHOGANY 1¼ INCH ~ 32 MM SIDED. 2½ INCH ~ 65 MM MOULDED. 18 INCH ~ 460 MM ARMS. BRONZE BOLTS 5/16 INCH ~ 8 MM ⌀ IN THROAT. 14 G SCREWS IN ARMS

Hotfoot was designed by Alan Gurney in New York and has proved exceptionally successful, having had a long racing career with no structural problems. She is 25ft 10in (7.87m) LWL and intended to be fast without being extreme.

To save weight the beams (detailed top left) are kept as light as possible and beefed up where extra strength is needed. The keel bolts are in pairs or staggered each side of the centreline so that they have better leverage for holding the keel tight.

Close study of this drawing shows up interesting details, such as the sensible size of cowl vents, the location of the deadlights clear of the immediate area of the mast, Z-section metal floors which double as sole bearers, an adjustable backstay arrangement which leaves the aft deck clear, and a backbone which is parallel in moulding for much of its length. (See also the section drawings of this yacht.)

work to be done laid out in a column. In adjacent columns will be lists of the materials required, the fastenings needed and the correct finishing. This list is a help for both amateurs and professionals since it will allow work to proceed to other jobs if one is held up.

A list of work in the correct sequence is useful if material or equipment is not available in the specified quantity or style. For instance, the cockpit coamings may be extensions of the cabin coamings. If timber in sufficient lengths is not available the cabin coamings will be made and fitted first and the cockpit coamings will probably be made much later and fastened on the outside of the cabin coamings to give a neat join. (Butting

cockpit coaming ends against cabin coaming ends seldom looks right, and is very often not particularly strong even with proper corner posts.)

Items like tanks should be small enough to go through the cabin door even though they are fitted before the decking goes on and perhaps even before all the beams are in. Tanks eventually have to be renewed and it is seldom convenient cutting them up inside the hull: if they are fairly thick metal and have contained fuel then cutting them up may be altogether too exciting.

Engines have to be taken out sooner or later, so if the hatch is too small for the engine there must be a removable section of deck.

How Thick, Wide and Close?

By far the most common way of deciding the correct plank or veneer thickness, frame size and spacing, number and spread of stringers, and indeed all scantlings is on past experience. Very rarely is a boat so unique that there are no comparable craft of the same general size which can be used as a reference. Ample sea-going experience is available to show what will or won't stand up to racing, stresses of weather, accidents, careless handling, commercial pressures and lack of maintenance. These are the factors which set construction standards, and often they indicate the materials. The majority of construction drawings are based on the designer's own experience

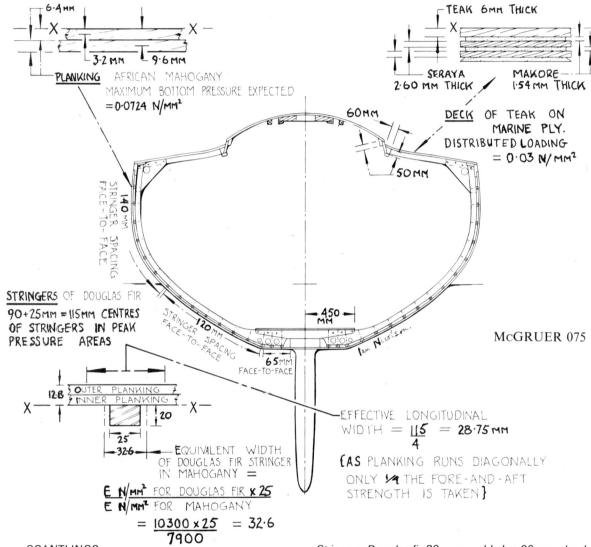

PLANKING AFRICAN MAHOGANY
MAXIMUM BOTTOM PRESSURE EXPECTED
$= 0.0724 \text{ N/mm}^2$

6.4 mm
3.2 mm   9.6 mm

TEAK 6mm THICK

SERAYA 2.60 mm THICK / MAKORE 1.54 mm THICK

DECK OF TEAK ON MARINE PLY.
DISTRIBUTED LOADING
$= 0.03 \text{ N/mm}^2$

60 mm
50 mm

140 mm STRINGER SPACING FACE-TO-FACE

STRINGERS OF DOUGLAS FIR
$90+25 \text{mm} = 115 \text{mm}$ CENTRES OF STRINGERS IN PEAK PRESSURE AREAS

STRINGER SPACING FACE-TO-FACE 120 mm
65 mm FACE-TO-FACE

450 mm

McGRUER 075

OUTER PLANKING
INNER PLANKING
12.8
20
25
32.6

EQUIVALENT WIDTH OF DOUGLAS FIR STRINGER IN MAHOGANY $=$

$$\frac{E \text{ N/mm}^2 \text{ FOR DOUGLAS FIR} \times 25}{E \text{ N/mm}^2 \text{ FOR MAHOGANY}}$$

$$= \frac{10300 \times 25}{7900} = 32.6$$

EFFECTIVE LONGITUDINAL WIDTH $= \dfrac{115}{4} = 28.75 \text{ mm}$

{AS PLANKING RUNS DIAGONALLY ONLY ¼ THE FORE-AND-AFT STRENGTH IS TAKEN}

Ian Nicolson.

SCANTLINGS
Backbone: laminated iroko 79mm moulded throughout main piece
Frames: laminated iroko in one piece except frames 1, 2 and 3

Stringers: Douglas fir 20mm moulded × 30mm, glued and nailed to planking, through-fastened to frames
Planking: two layers 6.4mm African mahogany skins glued together and stapled where necessary. Sheer strake 33mm thick with check for diagonal planking

Rudder skeg: 75mm iroko tenoned through backbone
False keel: solid African mahogany bolted to lead keel
Deck beams: laminated African mahogany
Beam brackets: 9mm Makore ply BS1088
Main deck and coachroof: two thicknesses of 5mm ply to BS1088 covered with 5mm teak
Deck-edge stringer: 70 × 20mm African mahogany, laminated, screwed and glued to top strake and nailed to beams.
Coachroof deck carling: 60 × 50mm African mahogany
Coachroof carling: 50 × 25mm African mahogany
Transom quarter knees: laminated iroko 50mm thick

FASTENINGS
Keelbolts: 35mm stainless steel
Frames to backbone: 9.5mm diameter aluminium bronze bolts
Plank to stringer: Glue and 1in × 10g Gripfast barbed nails
Plank to stringer to frame: 2.5in × 8g Gripfast nails
Beam brackets to frame and beam: 1in × 8g screws
Quarter knees and breasthook: 8mm bolts except 9.5mm throat bolt in breasthook

HULL STRENGTH CALCULATION
Typical example based on the McGruer 075, a Three-quarter Tonner. The drawing shows the midship construction section, with enlarged details of the main strength members. The working out of the scantlings is shown below. E is Modulus of Elasticity.
E for African mahogany, parallel to the grain = 7900 N/mm² (Newtons/mm²)
E for African mahogany, at right angles to the grain = 250 N/mm²
E for teak = 11,000 N/mm²
E for makore, parallel to the grain = 9310 N/mm²
E for makore, at right angles to the grain = 340 N/mm²
E for seraya, parallel to the grain = 6900 N/mm²
E for seraya, at right angles to the grain = 140 N/mm²
E for Douglas fir = 10300 N/mm²

For comparison of this design with conventional cold-moulded shell or transverse frames:
Conventional cold-moulded shell on transverse frames:
weight/ft ÷ frame spacing
22mm mahogany planking	12.98kg
50 × 44mm iroko frames	3.98kg
Total	16.96kg

McGruer 075
13mm Planking	7.67kg
25 × 20mm Douglas fir stringers	2.57kg
50 × 45mm iroko frames	4.10kg
Total	14.34kg

This represents a weight saving of 16 per cent.

Maximum bottom pressure expected = 0.724 N/mm² (From the Norske Veritas power boat chart)

Stringer spacing up forward between frames = 90mm. Using 45° double diagonal skins this represents a 127mm span along the grain

Planking African mahogany, see detail top left of drawing.
D_{na} (i.e. distance of neutral axis from assumed axis X–X)
$$= \frac{\Sigma (E \cdot t \cdot d)}{\Sigma (E \cdot t)}$$
$$= \frac{(7900 \times 6.4 \times 3.2) + (250 \times 6.4 \times 9.6)}{(7900 \times 6.4) + (250 \times 6.4)}$$
$$= 3.40mm \text{ below X–X}$$

Taking 1 metre width:

Item	A(×10³)	Y	AY²(×10³)	Total 2nd lg(×10³)	Mt.(×10³)
1	6.4	0.2	0.2560	21.8453	22.1013
2	6.4	−6.2	246.0160	21.8453	267.8613

adding last column
$$I'/metre = 289.9626 \times 10^3 \text{ mm}^4$$
$$E_p = \frac{\Sigma (EI)}{I'}$$
$$= \frac{(7900 \times 22.1013) + (250 \times 267.8613)}{289.9626}$$
$$= 833.0922 \text{ N/mm}^2$$

Considering as clamped along all edges
$$\therefore \delta \text{ (deflection)} = \frac{0.018 \times P \times W^4}{E_{pw} \times t^3}$$
$$= \frac{0.018 \times 0.0724 \times 127^4}{833.0922 \times 12.8^3}$$
$$= 0.1940mm$$

But allowable deflection = Span ÷ 300 = 0.30mm

Maximum Bending Moment produced by loading
$$= 0.05 \times P \times W^3$$
$$= 0.05 \times 0.0724 \times 127^3$$
$$= 7420 \text{ N/mm}^2$$

Maximum permissible B.M.
$$= \frac{fE_p I}{EY} \quad \text{and } f = 9.3 \text{ N/mm}^2$$
$$= \frac{9.3 \times 833.0922 \times 289.9626 \times 10^3 \times 0.127}{7900 \times 3.4}$$
$$= 10622 \text{ Nmm}$$

Deck teak over Thames marine ply (see detail, top right)
Distributed loading is taken as full crew spread typically over the deck (equivalent to approx 10ft or 3m head of water). Loading = 0.03 N/mm²
$$D_{na} = \frac{\Sigma (E \cdot t \cdot d)}{\Sigma (E \cdot t)}$$

where D_{na} is the distance of the neutral axis from the assumed neutral axis X—X
$= [(11,000 \times 6 \times 3) + (9310 \times 1.54) (6.77 + 10.91 + 15.05) + 140 \times 2.6 (8.84 \times 12.98)] \div [(11,000 \times 6) + (9310 \times 4.62) + (140 \times 5.2)]$
$= 6.16$mm below X–X

Consider 1 metre width:

Item	A($\times 10^3$)	Y	AY²($\times 10^3$) Ig($\times 10^3$)	Total 2nd Mt($\times 10^3$)
1	6.00	3.16	59.90	18.000	77.900
2	1.54	−0.61	0.60	0.305	0.905
3	2.60	−2.68	18.70	1.467	20.167
4	1.54	−4.75	34.75	0.305	35.055
5	2.60	−6.82	121.00	1.467	122.467
6	1.54	−8.89	121.80	0.305	122.105

I'/metre = 378.599×10^3
total

$E_{pa} = \dfrac{\Sigma \, (EI)}{I'}$

$= [11,000 \times 77.9 + 9310 (0.905 + 35.055 + 122.105) + 140 (20.167 + 122.467)] \div 378.599$
$= 6240$ N/mm²

Consider as supported by beams only but continuous fore and aft where the maximum deck beam forward of the turtle deck is 3.28m.
δ (deflection)

$= \dfrac{0.0055 \times \text{panel width(mm)} \times \text{distrib. load} \times \text{span}^4}{E_p \times I'}$

$= \dfrac{0.0055 \times 3280 \times 0.03 \times 350^4}{6240 \times 378.6 \times 10^3 \times 3.28}$
$= 1.048$mm

Maximum allowable δ $= \dfrac{\text{Span}}{300} = 1.17$mm

Maximum B. M. by loading $= \dfrac{W \times P \times L^2}{12}$

$= \dfrac{3280 \times 0.03 \times 350^2}{12}$
$= 1,004,500$ Nmm

Maximum permissible B. M. $= \dfrac{f.E_p.I}{E \cdot Y}$

for teak f = 16.5 N/mm²
$M = \dfrac{16.5 \times 6240 \times 378.6 \times 10^3 \times 3.28}{11000 \times 6.16}$
$= 1,886,903$ Nmm
for makore f = 16.5 N/mm²
$M = \dfrac{16.5 \times 6240 \times 378.6 \times 10^3 \times 3.28}{9310 \times 9.66}$
$= 1,421.661$ Nmm

Stringers see detail bottom left of drawing
E for African mahogany = 7900 N/mm²
E for Douglas fir = 10300 N/mm²

Item	A	Y	AY	AY²	Ig
1	368	6.4	2355	15080	5030
2	652	−10.0	−6520	65200	21733
Totals	1020		−4165	80280	26763
				26763	

Adding 80280 + 26763 = 107043

$\overline{Y} = \dfrac{4165}{1020} = 4.08$mm below X–X
$-A\overline{Y}^2 = -17,000 \; \therefore I_{na} = 107043 - 17,000 = 90043$mm⁴
$I/Y \text{ plank} = \dfrac{90043}{16.88} = 5340$mm³
$I/Y \text{ stringer} = \dfrac{90043}{15.92} = 5660$mm³

Frame spacing = 370mm centres in peak loading area
= 370 − 45 = 325mm unsupported span.
Assuming virtually fixed end connections due to continuous stringers.
Maximum BM $= \dfrac{0.0724 \times 115 \times 325^2}{12}$
$= 73,100$ Nmm
Reduce Factor of Safety and use Basic Stress instead of Grade Stress because of local nature of slamming loads.
Permissible BM$_{\text{planking}}$ = 5340 × 13.1 = 70,000 Nmm

Permissible BM$_{\text{stringer}}$ $= \dfrac{5660 \times 16.5 \times 7900}{10300}$
$= 70,000$ Nmm
∴ the stringer spacing in the slamming area is to be no greater than 115mm centres.

and his knowledge of other successful boats. Throughout this book there are illustrated numerous examples of scantlings that have proved successful. (Drawings appearing in apparently unrelated sections of the text may also show useful details of scantlings.) Those who wish to work out from basic principles just what the scantlings should be will get guidance from the following paragraphs.

The pressure of water on the hull increases with depth at the rate of 0.445lbs/sq in per foot immersed. The lowest point of the hull structure which has to be stressed is the planking by the keel, but it is no good taking the static draft of the boat and working out the pressure at this depth. At sea the draft varies as the boat plunges into a head sea: at times she will immerse her deck so that solid green water lands on board. The exact depth

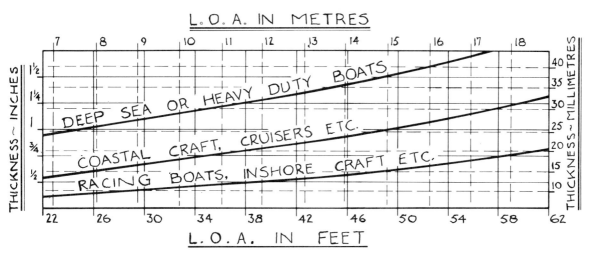

L.O.A. IN METRES

L.O.A. IN FEET

To obtain a preliminary idea of the correct finished plank thickness, first decide the category of the craft. Three curves are given here, for light, average and extra strong boats. When in doubt the higher curve should be selected, or at least a mean between two. In any case thickness should not be decided solely on the basis of these figures. If there are numerous frames or stringers or both the planking can be thinner. A reduction of perhaps 10 per cent, sometimes more, might be acceptable for a hull sheathed with Cascover or Dynel.

The plank thicknesses given are for finished work, so some allowance should be made for cleaning off. Even on the heaviest hull it is unlikely that much more than $\frac{1}{16}$ in (1.6mm) will be taken off, but this amount may also be taken off a very light hull. Generally speaking the more experienced the boatbuilder the less he will need to take off for final smoothing. If in doubt, add $\frac{1}{8}$ in (3mm) for this and as an additional safety factor, unless weight is absolutely critical.

The lower scale should only be selected for boats intended for light duties and with a full crew. Hulls planked this thinly are likely to have a limited life unless exceptionally well built and maintained. 'Racing' use may mean hard driving or occasional fair weather use: adjust dimensions accordingly.

below the surface in the worst conditions has to some extent to be guessed, basing the estimation on the observed behaviour of boats at sea in severe gales. Boats remain buoyant as long as their hull and deck are intact, and it is rare for craft under 60ft (18.3m) to have a depth of water on deck in excess of one-twelfth of the overall length. Using this rule of thumb we see that the greatest pressure on the planking and frames is given by adding together:

the static draft, in feet

the maximum freeboard, in feet

and one-twelfth of the overall length, in feet

Multiply this sum by 0.445 and this gives the loading (in pounds) down by the keel per square inch of bottom, as a result of the hydrostatic pressures alone.

In addition, movement through the water imposes further pressure loadings over the forward two-thirds of the hull. (It sometimes adds extra stresses to the aft third, but these are normally dealt with by the reinforcing supplied by the engine bearers, A-bracket doublers, the safety factors in the static pressure calculations, and so on.)

There is an empirical formula, loosely based on kinetic energy theory, which states:

$$\text{Pressure due to velocity} = \frac{1.34 \times \text{Velocity}^2}{1000}$$

(Pressure is in lbs/sq ft, velocity in knots.)

To find the total pressure on the hull shell, the hydrostatic pressure is added to the pressure due to velocity. There is implicit in this addition a factor of safety, because it would be extraordinary if the loadings due to the boat's speed peaked in the same area as the hydrostatic pressure. The latter must be at its greatest down along the keel, when the hull is plunging down, whereas the velocity pressure is more likely to be at a maximum in way of a wave near the surface.

Once the forces which have to be contained have been determined it is necessary to work out the correct thickness of planking and frames to stand up to this loading. Some authorities assume that a plank-and-frame hull securely fastened by clenches, bolts or nails can be taken as one homogenous unit. Others say that glued-only components are sufficiently well bound together to be considered as a single entity. Bearing in mind that in boats the planks are pressed by water pressure onto the frames, it seems reasonable to assume they are all of one piece, when calculating their strength.

Simple beam theory is applied, using a single frame and the planking extending halfway to the adjacent frame each side. This gives a T-section beam with a greatly extended bar across the top of the T. Some designers will only take half the plank length from frame to frame, on the basis that the planks will bow in when very heavily stressed. Where the planking is supported longitudinally by stringers, instead of frames, the theory is similar.

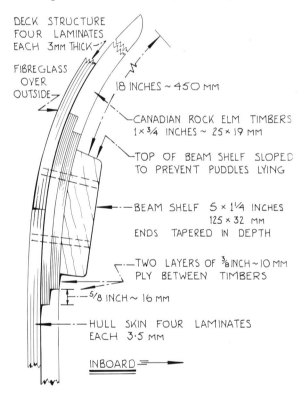

DECK STRUCTURE
FOUR LAMINATES
EACH 3MM THICK

FIBREGLASS
OVER
OUTSIDE

18 INCHES ~ 450 MM

CANADIAN ROCK ELM TIMBERS
1 × ¾ INCHES ~ 25 × 19 MM

TOP OF BEAM SHELF SLOPED
TO PREVENT PUDDLES LYING

BEAM SHELF 5 × 1¼ INCHES
125 × 32 MM
ENDS TAPERED IN DEPTH

TWO LAYERS OF ⅜ INCH ~ 10 MM
PLY BETWEEN TIMBERS

⅝ INCH ~ 16 MM

HULL SKIN FOUR LAMINATES
EACH 3·5 MM

INBOARD

The hull of *Galway Blazer II* blends into the deck at a curved edge. This makes a tremendously strong structure, ideal for the ocean cruising in severe weather for which she was designed. This drawing should be studied in conjunction with the main hull plan, earlier in this book.

One advantage of stringers is that they tend to come together towards the bow, which suits the higher loading likely to be found forward. Also stringers are easily arranged so that they are close together where the stresses are most likely to be great.

The whole of the scantling calculation up to this point has been based on the sum of the static and velocity pressures. An alternative source of information about probable pressures is the Norske Veritas power boat chart. This is used in the worked example of the McGruer 075, illustrated in this chapter.

Power boats driven into a head sea have exceptionally large stresses on the bottom. The impact is most severe between about 20 and 50 per cent of the length from the bow. Loading figures are detailed in various technical publications (see Bibliography).

When designing sailing craft the information available for power craft will be used with modifications, including the following considerations.

1. Under some conditions modern sail-driven vessels exceed their displacement 'hull speed' and plane or 'surf' so that speeds of 20 knots have been sustained.

2. A vessel going to windward will be heeled. The angle of heel must be taken as the most unfavourable when calculating the angle of impact between sea and hull.

3. When taking into consideration the weights, allowance should be made for crew weight forward, since there are times when half the crew may be wrestling with a headsail on the foredeck. An allowance should also be made for bilgewater, a load of sodden sails and so on.

4. Under extreme conditions the hull may broach and be knocked down with the mast horizontal. In this condition the ballast keel and rudder will probably be out of the water and may be subject to shock loadings.

5. A boat plunging at her mooring or anchor in heavy seas will place large and alternating tension and compression stresses on her foredeck, perhaps for a long period.

A set of experimental data which will at times be useful to designers and builders is given below. *Note*: a factor of safety has to be introduced into the calculation. In addition, each load must be multiplied by a second factor which depends on the type of wood to be used; for pitch pine 0.95, white pine 0.50, oak 0.78, western red cedar 0.64. The term 'moulded' means the dimension perpendicular to the outboard surface of the member: in a beam this is more or less vertical, and the 'width' is the fore-and-aft dimension; in a frame the width is again fore and aft and the moulded depth perpendicular to it, being fairly horizontal near the deck edge and becoming more vertical towards the keel.

LOAD THAT CAN BE SUPPORTED BY A BEAM 1IN (25MM) WIDE, LOAD EVENLY DISTRIBUTED

Beam 6in moulded × 1in (150 × 25mm)

Beam length		Load	
6ft	1.83m	5160lbs	2340kg
8ft	2.44m	3870lbs	1760kg
10ft	3.05m	3100lbs	1410kg
12ft	3.66m	2580lbs	1170kg

Beam 8in moulded × 1in (200 × 25mm)

Beam length		Load	
6ft	1.83m	9180lbs	4170kg
8ft	2.44m	6880lbs	3120kg
10ft	3.05m	5500lbs	2500kg
12ft	3.66m	4580lbs	2080kg

Beam 10in moulded × 1in (250 × 25mm)

Beam length		Load	
8ft	2.44m	10,750lbs	4880kg
10ft	3.05m	8600lbs	3900kg
12ft	3.66m	7070lbs	3210kg
14ft	4.27m	6150lbs	2790kg

Beam 12in moulded × 1in (300 × 25 mm)

Beam length		Load	
8ft	2.44m	15,500lbs	7040kg
10ft	3.05m	12,500lbs	5670kg
12ft	3.66m	10,330lbs	4690kg
14ft	4.27m	8850lbs	4020kg

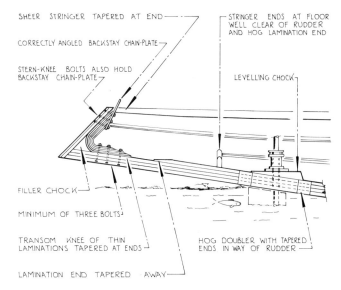

SHEER STRINGER TAPERED AT END

CORRECTLY ANGLED BACKSTAY CHAIN-PLATE

STERN-KNEE BOLTS ALSO HOLD BACKSTAY CHAIN-PLATE

FILLER CHOCK

MINIMUM OF THREE BOLTS

TRANSOM KNEE OF THIN LAMINATIONS TAPERED AT ENDS

LAMINATION END TAPERED AWAY

STRINGER ENDS AT FLOOR WELL CLEAR OF RUDDER AND HOG LAMINATION END

LEVELLING CHOCK

HOG DOUBLER WITH TAPERED ENDS IN WAY OF RUDDER

Longitudinals can be tapered out towards the stern because the bending moment reduces. However, the rudder imposes severe strains in heavy weather so the hog may need doubling in way of the rudder tube.

It is particularly important to save weight near the ends of a boat, to help her lift easily to passing seas and reduce pitching. The same bolts that are used to secure the transom to its knee hold the backstay chainplate. Not all stringers extend the full length of the hull. One set is shown ending on a floor deliberately positioned away from the tapered-out lamination of the hog and the high-stress area in line with the rudder. There will also be a floor in way of the rudder.

As a final warning to anyone who favours the straight calculation approach to boat structure design, it is worth quoting the Timber Research and Development Association of High Wycombe, Bucks, England. When invited to suggest methods of calculating suitable scantlings of cold-moulded craft, they replied: 'None of the research papers that we produce, or know of, can be used sensibly to work out the stresses of a cold-moulded hull even accepted that certain approximations could be made. Previous parallel excercises which we have carried out, making assumptions of the type necessary in this sort of calculation, end up predicting member thicknesses often two or three times those which prove adequate in practice.'

All of which proves that wood is wonderful, and at its best when allied to a lot of hard experience. Which is why there are so many examples in these pages of successful designs.

Building Moulds or Shadow Sections

To build a boat a temporary pattern and former is needed; this might be considered a male mould. Before starting construction a rigid, reliable and accurate temporary shape is assembled and the skin is built over it. It is made as cheaply as possible and designed so that it can be taken apart and removed when the hull or hulls are finished: therefore when making the moulds and setting them up no fastenings must be put in which cannot be removed from *inside* the hull after it has been turned right way up. Once the moulds have been erected battens or ribbands are extended fore and aft over them. The resulting framework looks like a gigantic simple canvas canoe before the canvas is put on.

The hull shape is defined by moulds evenly spaced from bow to stern. Each mould is like a bulkhead except that it is not continuous right across but a stout, broad wooden ring with cross-bracing at half-height and down the centreline.

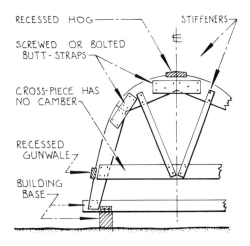

RECESSED HOG

STIFFENERS

SCREWED OR BOLTED BUTT-STRAPS

CROSS-PIECE HAS NO CAMBER

RECESSED GUNWALE

BUILDING BASE

Moulds must be rigid, so strong good wood is used. The different parts are joined with bolts or screws, and diagonal braces prevent distortion. Each section is set up exactly vertical, precisely on the centreline with the sheer at the correct height above the levelled building base.

The hog and gunwale protrude from the mould by an amount equal to the thickness of the ribbands. Where possible neither hog nor gunwales should be fastened to the moulds, because in time the latter are removed. However there must be some temporary fastenings, perhaps in alternate moulds, and these should be designed so that the planking does not cover them.

Moulds are made of cheap, non-splitting, dimensionally stable wood such as a local pine, of whatever sizes are to hand without further cutting. A typical thickness would be about $\frac{5}{8}$in (16mm) for every 20ft (6m) of hull length, and the plank width will be about 4in (10cm) for every 20ft of length. There is a temptation to use any old wood because the moulds have a short life, so unplaned rough lumber found lying about is sometimes made up into moulds. Yet professionals who seldom waste any money tend to make their moulds rather well. They use wood which is planed all over, and seasoned timber since warping and capping can be a great nuisance. They use screws or bolts rather than nails. This is not just pride of workmanship: the moulds need the centreline and waterline marked on them and it is often helpful, if not essential, to have other lines. Marking these on unplaned timber is difficult, less precise and asking for trouble.

Furthermore, once the first boat or batch of boats has been built the mould may still have value. If the design is a good one someone may be prepared to buy the complete set of patterns, and even if slight modifications are needed they may

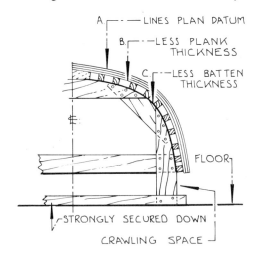

A ---- LINES PLAN DATUM

B ---- LESS PLANK THICKNESS

C ---- LESS BATTEN THICKNESS

FLOOR

STRONGLY SECURED DOWN

CRAWLING SPACE

The mould profiles are not made up to the same shapes as the body sections, because thickness allowance has to be made for the planking and battens over them.

If additional plank thicknesses are to be put in, say over the lower part of the hull in way of the ballast keel, or in the area of the mast stresses, they will be put in once the hull has been removed from the moulds.

still be reusable or saleable. The selling price will depend at least partly on the moulds' strength and appearance, so quality matters.

Each mould is normally made up of a top athwartships piece like a beam, four side pieces (two each side), and one piece extending down to the keel on each side. If the shape is suitable fewer pieces may be needed; right forward, apart from the beam piece only one side piece may be required since the shape will be triangular. When all the pieces are assembled the outside edge is exactly the shape of the hull at that particular section, so the more curved the hull form the more parts will be needed to achieve the final shape. (It is slightly inaccurate to say that the mould shape is *exactly* the same as the hull shape since the mould is made smaller by the plank and ribband thicknesses.)

The pieces of the moulds can be butt-strapped or lapped. Lapping calls for some care and it may mean that the edges have to be bevelled at the ends of the top cross-piece and wherever the lap extends forward of the station line. So usually a mould is made up of long lengths of wood joined by small butt straps of cheap ply and stiffened with vertical and horizontal cross-bars. The verticals may be set with one edge exactly upright on the centreline, the horizontals with their top edges exactly along the load waterline. These two datum lines on each mould are then easy to line up along the length of the hull.

As a very rough guide, a mould is put up at each station along the hull's length. Since by convention a hull is divided into ten ordinates between each end of the waterline, this gives a spacing of about one-tenth of the waterline length. Experienced builders occasionally spread the moulds farther apart and save themselves some work. However, hulls with very sharp curves, particularly with a strong complicated flare forward and tightly rounded bow as seen on a typical motor cruiser, will need moulds at half the usual spacing, or even one-third, in way of the quick changes of shape.

The centreline is marked on the building base by a taut wire overhead or along the building base, or both. Sometimes the lower line is a pencil line, made first with a chalk-line string.

Each mould is secured to the building base exactly athwartships and with its centreline exactly aligned vis-a-vis the base. The sheerline taken from the mould loft floor is marked on each mould as it is made, and at this stage the vertical distance

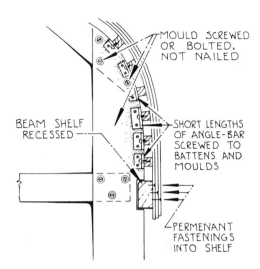

If the shelf or stringers are to be recessed into the moulds it is essential that the moulds can be taken apart to get them out of the finished hull. This is why the pieces of the mould should be screwed or bolted together, not nailed or glued. In theory the battens can be secured strongly to the moulds and lifted out in bunches, as the various parts of each mould are unscrewed and taken out. This may present some problems and it is therefore safer to secure the stringers to the mould by small angle brackets which can be unscrewed when the moulds are taken apart.

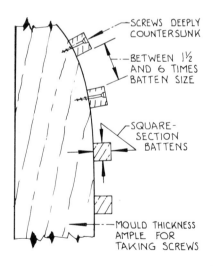

If the battens are square in section they can be fitted either way up on the moulds. They should be planed all over and their screws deeply countersunk. One reason for this is that it may be necessary later to carry out some fairing by planing away a little of the outer faces.

41

from the building base up to the sheerline is checked. When all the moulds are erected a long batten is laid on the sheer marks. Standing first near the bow at various random positions, then near the stern, the builder sights along the batten to make sure it lies in a fair and beautiful sweep. It may have been put exactly on the marks yet still need a little lifting or dropping, even though it has been set exactly as the designer's drawings indicate. What looked right on the flat paper plan may not be an elegant and seductive sheerline when seen in three dimensions, in the solid.

The spacing between moulds is also checked. They are secured to the building base by a wooden leg at each side, and a pair of diagonals extending forward and downward, or possibly aft and downwards from a point about a quarter of the beam out on the mould. This is to hold the moulds rigid until the ribbands or battens are on. Not all will need these diagonal struts; once some are properly secured temporary battens can be extended from them to hold up adjacent ones until they are all tied together by the main ribbands.

The laminated hull skin does not actually touch

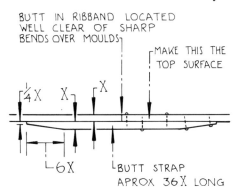

BUTT IN RIBBAND LOCATED WELL CLEAR OF SHARP BENDS OVER MOULDS

MAKE THIS THE TOP SURFACE

$\frac{1}{4}$X   X   X

6X   BUTT STRAP APROX 36X LONG

Ribbands need not be continuous from bow to stern. Some may end amidships, or indeed anywhere, provided the end does not protrude above the adjacent ones. The ribbands are only to support the laminates while they are glued up, so in theory relatively short lengths of timber can be used. But in practice it will be a help if many are long, and some the full hull length.

The sketch shows the principle of butt-strapping ribbands. The technique may also be applied to structural parts of a boat. The butt strap is made the same cross-section as the parts joined, and it tapers away at both ends. It is long enough to get five fastenings each side and to have no sudden bend. The taper is about one-third of each side of the butt and is not normally taken down to a fine point as this may splinter.

the moulds, so they do not need bevelling. So that the ribbands will preserve the correct shape, defined by the moulds' outer edges, moulds forward of the maximum beam are set with their forward faces on the station line, those aft of it with their aft faces on the station line.

A check batten that is as stiff as two people can conveniently bend in place is now laid across the moulds horizontally, then diagonally, both port and starboard. It should just touch each one. A clear-grained piece of pine about $\frac{3}{4}$in (20mm) square will suit many boats, but in way of flare, hollows or sharp tucks round the stern a lighter batten may be needed. If a gap appears between the batten and a mould, and there is no deliberate hollow in the shape which calls for a lighter batten, then the mould must be built up to meet the batten. Alternatively, the adjacent moulds may be planed away slightly. The aim is to get a fair and smooth shape free from local lumps or hollows. Provided the loft work has been well done and the moulds precisely made, very little fairing should be necessary at this stage.

The backbone may be fitted before or after the ribbands, sometimes called battens. It is often easier to get the backbone up first, while access is better. (This job is described in a later section.) Putting on the ribbands then follows, and the only problem here is how close they should be. The closer they are the more wood and work are needed, but if they are too far apart the veneer will sag in between and gaps between laminates may occur – a serious matter. Roughly, batten spacing can be about 2in (5cm) for every 20ft (6m) of hull length. (From centre to centre is 2in and the gap between is less due to the width of the ribbands. For thin veneer the gap can seldom be more than 2in.)

Ribbands extend from bow to stern, and as the girth reduces towards the ends some are stopped well back from them. To get long enough battens wood has to be scarphed or butt-strapped. To avoid hard spots and thus a tendency to bend unevenly, butt pieces should taper out over about 12 times their thickness. Ribband size will depend on the curvature of the hull and it may be necessary to do a few experiments before deciding on the finished size. The timber must be planed smooth. Battens $\frac{1}{2} \times \frac{1}{2}$in ($12 \times 12$mm) in section for every 20ft (6m) of boat length are often right.

When all the battens are in place it should be possible to put a light waterproof cover over the

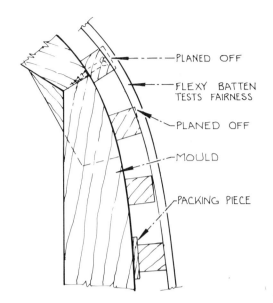

PLANED OFF

FLEXY BATTEN
TESTS FAIRNESS

PLANED OFF

MOULD

PACKING PIECE

Before applying the first layer of planking the battens must be checked for fairness, by taking a flexible batten, bending it over the screwed-on battens secured to the mould and making sure there are no high or low spots. The former are seen when the flexy check batten is lifted clear of adjacent battens and the latter when daylight can be seen clear under it. A little fairing is likely to be needed, done by planing off high spots; occasionally it may be necessary to pack out low battens with a small packing piece between the screwed battens and the mould.

resulting structure, turn it over and sail away! The cover should have no bumps, nor sag inward anywhere. This is all very fanciful, but it does give the builder a mental picture of his aim. It also reminds him that it may be necessary to run a diagonal check batten all over the hull across the ribbands, to make sure everything is still fair. This final check may show the need for a little light planing to take off the edges of some of the ribbands, especially on the more curved areas.

Not every ribband needs fixing onto every mould, but quite one-third of the intersections should be secured. When constructing the moulds and fastening the ribbands to them, remember that when the hull is turned the right way up the moulds and ribbands have to be removed. If the side pieces of the moulds are unbolted and the ribbands are sure to follow without trouble, there is no worry about putting screws through the ribbands directly into the moulds. But if the sides are heavily tumblehomed, getting the moulds-plus-ribbands out may be awkward. In that case it is better to use short lengths of metal angle to bolt or screw the ribbands to the moulds. These angles, or if preferred little chocks of hardwood, can be removed easily from inside the boat. When screws are put through the ribbands into the moulds ample countersinking is needed.

Some boats are built round stringers (permanent longitudinals that will remain part of the hull) instead of temporary ribbands, or there may be half and half. (A separate chapter covers the way stringers are handled.) In every boat there will be a substantial permanent deck stringer or beam shelf on each side, set into recesses in the moulds, and secured to them by angle brackets or wooden chocks.

To prevent glue from the shell from adhering to the ribbands plastic sheet is spread over them. This covering must be kept clear of the hog and beam shelf, where the glue very certainly must gain a hold.

Veneer, Sawn Timber and Plywood Laminates

Three forms of wood can be used for cold-moulding. Veneer is the thinnest and is available between 0.6mm ($\frac{1}{32}$in) and 3mm ($\frac{1}{8}$in) and is sold in metric measurements of thickness. It is peeled off a horizontally held revolving log by a long knife, just the way the layers for plywood are obtained.

Solid timber laminates are sawn from solid timber baulks, and for cold-moulding the minimum thickness is of the order of $\frac{3}{16}$in or 5mm. Whereas suitable solid timber is available from a great variety of timber merchants, veneer is so much a specialized product that it is not widely available. A merchant who does not specialize in it may be prepared to find a good source and handle the sale, but he will want his percentage and it will normally be better to buy direct from the makers. Names are occasionally found in the small and classified ads of yachting or wood-working magazines, and in commercial directories.

Marine plywood can be bought through many

timber merchants. It is important to use only *marine* quality ply, and every board should be inspected to ensure it is stamped with the specification type, which is BSS 1088WBP. This standard defines veneer quality, the durability of the woods, manufacturing defects and the bonding performance. Ply is sold in metric thickness, starting at 3mm. Normally it is only available in standard size sheets of 4 × 8ft (1.22 × 2.44m), though some makers produce a limited number of boards 5ft (1.525m) wide. For long lengths standard boards are scarphed end to end, or at the factory at extra cost.

Each type of wood has its advantages. *Veneer* is fairly costly per ton compared to solid timber, even allowing for the wastage when solid timber is cut down to laminating sizes. Since veneer is made into plywood by gluing, inevitably plywood is more costly than veneer. Veneer is priced per square foot in Britain, and currently is priced in an illogical way in that the cost varies directly as the thickness, whereas for other wood prices the price comes down as the thickness goes up. This is natural, since the thicker wood needs less sawing and there is a smaller percentage wasted. Admittedly, over certain widths and thicknesses the price per cube starts to climb again, because extra thick or wide pieces can be obtained only from large and valuable logs, but this applies to timber much larger than is used for laminating.

Stout scissors or shears can be used to cut veneer, which speeds up the work, and a heavy knife or Stanley knife can be used to trim the edges.

Hulls up to about 30ft (9m) are built with veneers. Much over this size, too many layers are needed to get sufficient thickness and strength. Of course a hull can be built with an extremely thin finished cold-moulded shell supported by a multiplicity of frames and stringers. Such a hull would be used when high performance is wanted and a more vulnerable shell is acceptable. People who spend a lot of time in boats tend to be suspicious of very thin cold-moulded planking, even for extreme racing craft. They point out that if a dinghy or a pontoon is accidentally bumped into the lightest, fastest, most ruthlessly designed craft, the topsides should be able to stand the impact. Anything much less than $\frac{1}{4}$in (6.5mm) final skin thickness is suspect. Veneer may also be used for the outer layers over other forms of wooden construction such as strip-planking (see separate chapters),

sawn timber or ply.

Veneer is cut from woods of the mahogany type which are fine-grained and exceptionally free from knots. Gaboon is popular, not least because it is cheap; it is also light, but not very resistant to decay, and is not recommended for the best work except perhaps for inner laminates where its lightness may be valuable.

Usually veneer is delivered in lengths of about 8ft (2.4m) and widths of around 6–12in (15–30cm); the pieces are likely to be in a guddle of different widths, and sometimes even the lengths are not consistent. It is up to the customer to sort out the wide pieces to use for the flat parts of the boat and the long pieces to use amidships, reserving the short pieces for the ends where the girth is less.

The poorest specimens are used for the hidden laminates (that is, neither the inner or outer faces) and kept away from areas of the hull where the stresses are high. By using the wide pieces where there is no double curvature the work of laminating is speeded up. Veneer 3mm thick will coggle and refuse to lie flat if it is asked to bend in two planes at once, and may have to be cut across and a wedge-shaped piece removed to make a 'tuck'.

Where one piece of laminate ends and another begins a taper butt is usual. However, when the skin is four layers thick a straight-cut butt is reasonably strong and should not raise objections. A glued scarph join is difficult because the material is so thin. When joining up lengths for the outside laminate, if varnishing is to follow the wood must be matched at the join otherwise it will be necessary to bleach and stain it.

Individual lengths of veneer are remarkably floppy and need care when handling and storing. Perhaps more important, where the grain runs across the length breaks are likely and working the piece is sometimes difficult. The finish should be 'rough planed'. When possible it pays to select the veneer and avoid curly grained pieces, but it is seldom easy or even possible to select the way that ordinary timber supplies can be graded and the unsatisfactory pieces rejected.

The large surface area and thin bulk of veneer means that its moisture content can readily alter, by drying out or absorption, which is important for gluing and especially for West System procedures.

Sawn timber is more widely available than veneer, and can be ordered in thicknesses and widths to suit the job. It can be cut with a special type of circular saw blade, called a planer saw, which leaves the wood smooth enough to use without further dressing. This saves work and sawdust (which is waste), but sawn timber cut to thin laminates still involves a fair amount of waste. How much depends on the thickness of the stock purchased, the saw thickness, the final thickness and the skill of the sawer. As the wastage factor can be less than 20 or more than 70 per cent, it is important to buy only after discussion with the timber merchant: sometimes his yard foreman will save the boatbuilder as much or more money than the yard manager. The finish wanted here is 'fully planed' or 'dressed four sides', though one might buy 'dressed two sides' and do the rest, if facilities and skill permit.

Sawn timber is used whenever a few layers are needed to build up a good shell thickness with minimum work. Its other great advantage is that being stiffer than veneer or thin plywood it can be laid over wider spaced battens.

Plywood. If a hull shell is to be built using two layers only, the inner one might be of ply. However, a ply outer layer is seldom satisfactory. When finally cleaning off with plane and sandpaper only the lightest shavings can be skimmed away before the first glue line appears, and there are few things so ugly as a blotch of glue on the topsides; beyond that the grain direction changes. Even if the hull is painted instead of varnished, it is bad practice to expose the glue under the top layer, not least because the paint will not lie well and because the inner layers of plywood are so often inferior to the outer ones.

Ply is comparatively costly but there should be little waste. It tends to be heavy for a given thickness due to the proportion of glue to wood, but against this water soakage is less, or rather it tends to take place more slowly.

When the ply arrives from the supplier it will be in standard 8 × 4ft (2.44 × 1.22m) sheets unless specified to be sawn into strips. Almost always the user will do this himself, in small quantities that let him cut the strips as wide as the hull curvature can take, and so minimize the number of planks to be laid. Where there is a lot of curvature in two directions the planks may well have to be of the order of 3in (75mm) wide even on a large boat. But along a flat middle body, or aft on a wide-transom power boat, planks may be as much as 2ft (60cm) wide, which will speed up the job marvellously.

TIMBER QUALITY

When building any boat only the best timber will do. The price difference between fairly good timber and medium quality is only a small fraction of the boat's total cost. Of course the best costs substantially more than the worst, but only a fool puts firewood into a boat. Cheap wood starts to rot soon, the rot spreads and in time the boat loses value substantially. Poor wood also splits, which wastes time and frays tempers, and may warp. Bad wood will not hold fastenings so that the boat is weak and gradually gets weaker. It is far better to leave out one or two electronic gadgets, make do with a smaller engine or have fewer sails.

A yacht built of the finest timber has a prestige and value out of all proportion to the extra cost. My firm once designed a 66ft motor cruiser which was planked in the most incredible Honduras mahogany. That wood was described variously as 'cut from the best three logs imported into Britain within thirty years', 'of the consistency of pale brown solidified cream' and 'not a flaw in any plank anywhere throughout the length of the boat'. The offcuts were prized and carried off for making all sorts of special pieces of furniture and extras on other boats in the district. Twelve years after the boat was built people are still talking about the Honduras mahogany. If the owner ever manages to steel himself to sell his yacht he starts off with a tremendous advantage. Every buyer for counties around knows the quality of that planking. Meanwhile the owner spends less on maintenance and has a better looking yacht because the basic structure is made from the best material. This is not an isolated case, and it is hard to over-emphasize the importance of good timber. During a lifetime which is spent buying things, the most expensive thing most people buy is a home. But a close second is their boat. Bearing in mind her capital value, it is common sense to make sure that her value is always kept as high as possible against the day when she has to be sold, and to keep down the running costs.

It is a mistake to use second grade timber anywhere in a boat. Just because nobody can see the furniture framework, this is no excuse for using offcuts from pallets. Wood which is hidden away is in some respects more important than that clearly visible, for the concealed part will not be noticed if it starts to rot. A sole bearer is generally considered unimportant, compared to planking or a floor. But the man who breaks his ankle when a bearer collapses can give some pungent reasons for using good timber beneath the sole.

There is a specious argument that expensive timber tends to be heavier than cheaper grades. In practice the strength of wood is roughly proportional to its density, so an expensive good quality hardwood can be used in thinner scantlings than a poor quality softwood. The end result is that less hardwood is used, and incidentally there will be less wastage so the overall costs are likely to be not much higher, using a better wood, unless it is exorbitantly expensive.

The thin veneers or planks used for cold-moulding are sensitive to temperature and moisture and may 'cup' or warp across their width. The resulting 'gutter' shape causes problems; if excessive the timber will not lie flat when stapled down and may split. Cupping can sometimes be used to advantage, however, when it can be laid to match the hull curvature, e.g. at the garboards or turn of the bilge. The cupping measurement is the height of the 'gutter'.

MAXIMUM PERMISSIBLE CUPPING

Finished thickness of laminate	Finished width 100mm/4in and less	150mm/6in	200mm/8in
mm in			
12 $\frac{1}{2}$	1.5mm $\frac{1}{16}$in	1.5mm $\frac{1}{16}$in	1.5mm $\frac{1}{16}$in
18 $\frac{3}{4}$	1 $\frac{1}{32}$	1.5 $\frac{1}{16}$	1.5 $\frac{1}{16}$
25 1	1 $\frac{1}{32}$	1 $\frac{1}{32}$	1.5 $\frac{1}{16}$
32 $1\frac{1}{4}$	None	1 $\frac{1}{32}$	1 $\frac{1}{32}$
38 $1\frac{1}{2}$	None	1 $\frac{1}{32}$	1 $\frac{1}{32}$
44 $1\frac{3}{4}$	None	None	1 $\frac{1}{32}$

Planking with Mixed Woods

When three or more layers of wood are used for planking there are good reasons for putting strong hardwoods on the outside and inside faces and softer, lighter, cheaper woods in between. A cold-moulded shell with no interior framing loses little strength if the concealed middle laminates are less strong than the outer ones; the outer fibres take the maximum stress and so need to be the strongest. When a cold-moulded hull has glued-in frames or stringers the engineering principles are not changed, but then the maximum stresses come on the outboard layers of the planking and on the inboard face of the internal stiffening members. So theory suggests that good strong hardwood should be used on the outside face and less strong cheaper timbers for the other laminates. However, the best builders tend to sacrifice the small saving in weight and use the same high-strength good quality timber for the inner surface layer to which the frames or stringers are glued.

The strength of a wood is generally proportional to its density. Cost also tends to go up as the weight per cubic foot increases, though there are many exceptions. But before deciding to save money by using cheaper timber for the inner laminates, a full investigation of costs is needed. Often it is cheaper to buy a large quantity all of one material rather than divide it between the best and a lower grade.

In racing boats weight is so important that costs are either overlooked or less crucial. Many racers have been built with outer planks of sapele which is about 40lbs/cu ft and inner laminates of gaboon which is only around 25lbs/cu ft. It is easy to work out the weight saved, but it is only right to mention that as much weight can often be saved by omitting or lightening fittings, especially anything made of metal which (except for aluminium) tends to be about ten times the weight of wood.

Mixing woods not only makes for more complex purchasing but the wastage factor is likely to be higher. Wastage varies from wood to wood and can be three times as high where the timber is full of faults compared to a clear, almost perfect species. Wastage also varies depending on how the wood is bought. The cheapest way to buy will be the standing tree, but this is rarely done. The next cheapest way, and one that professionals tend to favour, is to buy uncut logs lying in a timber yard. A wastage of over 40 per cent is usual even with a good clear-grained wood, and over 60 per cent with a knotty fault-laden one.

If timber is bought cut and planed-two-sides, as many amateurs do, there should be little wastage. So the extra cost of using two types of planking instead of one has to be worked out for the particular boat. Series builders usually have timber left over from the last boat, and expect to have some left over when the current one is complete. For them over-ordering is seldom significant, and with inflation it can be financially advantageous.

Up to now, the assumption has been that the surface laminations have been of a high grade hardwood, with a light cheaper timber for the hidden middle ones. A completely different approach might be adopted where money is really short: all the hull shell layers apart from the outside (outboard) one might be of an adequate but relatively cheap timber. This will vary regionally and from country to country with supply and demand; whatever is recommended by a good local timber merchant should be selected, bearing in mind that it should be at least moderately resistant to rot, be stable and glue well. The outside layer of high quality hardwood will be made as thin as practical, bearing in mind that it must stand up to the finishing processes and be machinable. It might be cut as veneer or sawn, and will be as thin as possible for the cutting method. If it is sawn, timber from the same log but cut to different thicknesses can be used for trim, to give the boat a homogeneous and attractive appearance.

When building up the hull shell with different woods a good theoretical case can be made for laying the adjacent veneers at 45° or even at 30° to each other, in contrast to the usual 90°. The argument is based on the known different expansion and contraction rates for different woods. The idea is to keep all the laminates roughly in line, at a smaller angle to each other and within each layer as parallel as possible, so that they all come and go roughly the same way and the same amount.

In practice the elasticity of wood is such that different woods seem to be able to live together in the marine environment, even when glued to each other with the grains at right angles. However, fractures and unexplained faults sometimes occur, and may be where the wood's natural elasticity has not been able to accommodate the conflicting forces. The argument for keeping the laminates all running roughly the same way might be summed up as so far 'not proven'.

PART 3

LAMINATING AND FASTENING

The Laminating Process

It is possible to build a cold-moulded (or indeed a strip-plank) boat with no laminated beams, frames or knees. But in practice laminated components tend to be found frequently in these boats because they are light, strong, attractive, resist rot and stay watertight; and perhaps because the builder has become oriented toward the technique.

The laminating procedure is:

1. Cut out or buy wooden strips.
2. Set up a jig, a simple wooden pattern of the shape of the finished part which is also used to hold the components in position for gluing.
3. If the moisture content of the timber is acceptable, and the workspace temperature and humidity are correct, prepare the glue.
4. Fit the first laminate in the jig and secure it.
5. Apply glue to this first piece.
6. Put on the second laminate, glue it . . . and so on.
7. After the last one is in place, tighten close-spaced cramps, but not so hard as to press out all the glue.
8. Wipe off surplus glue, which must have oozed out all along the joins proving there are no dry joints between any two pieces.
9. When the glue has hardened and cured completely, remove the component from the jig and plane off the sides.
10. If two parts are made in one, they are now separated and the sawn faces planed up.
11. Test for final shape to make sure there is no significant spring-back after release from the jig. Where needed, trim to the final shape.
12. Bevel all edges which will stand out in the boat's accommodation.
13. Sometimes when a whole set of frames or beams have been made they will be varnished before installing. Laminated work is so prized and so attractive, it will be unusual to paint over it. Putting on even the first two varnish coats will seal the wood and help keep it clean.

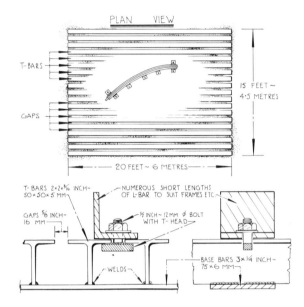

Laminating grid. McGruers, the well known yacht builders of Rosneath in Dunbartonshire, Scotland, do so much laminating work they are jokingly called 'McGluers'. They use this simple but effective base for laminating up every sort of component. It consists of a lot of metal T-bars welded to base straps of flat bar, all set carefully parallel and level.

Frames, beams, stems and skegs can all be laminated on this. The shape of the part is marked on the tops of the T-bars or a template is laid on them. Plenty of short lengths of angle-bar are quickly clamped to the T-bars, since each has a single T-headed bolt to hold it. If the curve is sharp an extra large number of these short angle-bar lengths is clamped down to the correct curve. Laminating proceeds in the usual way, and when the final laminate has been glued on it can be held in place by a further batch of short L-bars.

A base of this sort could be made using wood pieces, perhaps 4in moulded by 3in, bolted to a rigid base. Layers of polythene sheeting laid under each part prevent sticking. A wooden base should be less expensive for just one or two boats, and quickly dismantled afterwards.

All sorts of jigs are used for laminating. A primitive one can be made by nailing a row of blocks onto a workbench. Each block lies on the previously drawn curved line which will be the final shape of the laminated part. Almost always laminating is done from the inside, outwards. That is, the strip which will be on the inside of the curve is fitted onto the jig first, then the next one which is to a slightly easier curve, and so on. For a beam this means that the first layer to be fitted in the jig is the bottom one.

A jig must be rigid, so some builders use a section of the mould loft floor. Others have special laminating bases, made up of rows of vertical steel bars welded to cross-members. T-bars set with the T upright are popular as clamps can be hooked round the top of each T all along its length. Wooden chocks must be close enough together to ensure that the laminated piece follows the right shape. It is usual to have them 4in (10cm) wide, with gaps between the same size for the frames of a

30ft (9m) hull and two or three times that for one twice the length as the curve will be flatter. The corners of the chocks against which the first strip lies must be well rounded to prevent the laminated timber being dented by a sharp edge.

For beams, especially when made all with the same camber, a jig may be made up from two solid lengths of wood about 1–2in (25–50mm) thick, cut to the right curve. These two pieces are set down on the ground rounded edge up, with a gap between them of perhaps a foot or two, according to the number of beams to be made up at once. Flat pieces are now screwed across joining the two curved pieces, with gaps between them, making something like a hump-backed footbridge with ample gaps between the treads. Laminating is done on this former, and the gaps between the cross-pieces allow cramps to be fitted easily.

The cramping-up (clamping) of the glue-covered strips is critical. There must be enough cramps for the component to be held tightly together along its full length with no risk that any two laminates can spring apart. On the other hand

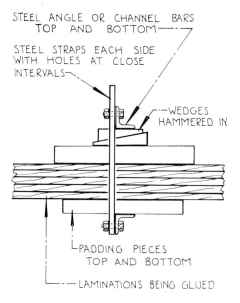

STEEL ANGLE OR CHANNEL BARS TOP AND BOTTOM

STEEL STRAPS EACH SIDE WITH HOLES AT CLOSE INTERVALS

WEDGES HAMMERED IN

PADDING PIECES TOP AND BOTTOM

LAMINATIONS BEING GLUED

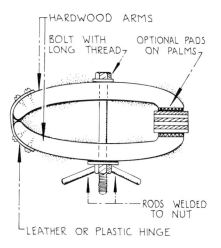

HARDWOOD ARMS

BOLT WITH LONG THREAD

OPTIONAL PADS ON PALMS

RODS WELDED TO NUT

LEATHER OR PLASTIC HINGE

There are many variations on this type of cramp, used to keep laminates together during gluing. For instance the angle-bar and the straps can be of wood, screwed or bolted together. A single wedge can be used, but generally a pair work better. The padding pieces can be long, extending from cramp to cramp. In some situations the bottom angle-bar and padding piece can be eliminated by using a flat workbench as a laminating base. Plastic sheet or newspaper to prevent the cramp sticking to the wood should be wrapped round before fitting it.

Cold-moulding often needs a lot of cramps (clamps), so some builders make their own. Pieces of hardwood are cut into a set of 'pincers'. The wood thickness should be four times the bolt diameter or more. The join is made from a short length of flexy leather or plastic or even woven webbing such as for dinghy toestraps. The bolt must have ample length of thread, with large washers at each end. These should ideally be of brass, lightly greased. The nut needs short rods welded on otherwise a spanner is needed for tightening. The palms may be padded with leather or a semi-soft plastic if softwoods are being worked.

the cramps must not crush the wood or squeeze out so much glue that there is a 'dry joint'. It is for this reason that wooden cramps are popular. They are made from two lengths of hardwood with two threaded rods working in recessed nuts to pull them together. This sort of cramp may be the 'enveloping' type, that is the tightening screws may be on each side of the set of laminations, or both tighteners can be on one side so that the cramp is 'overhung'. This is in many ways better as it is fitted and tightened up more quickly, and does not have to be dismantled and then reassembled round the work. One great advantage of these wooden cramps is that they can be home-made with threaded rod bought from an engineers' supplier, or lengths of $\frac{3}{8}$ or $\frac{1}{2}$in (10 or 12mm) rod threaded as needed. The ends of the rod must be bent 90° or have cross-pieces welded on as handles. On a frame for a 30ft (9m) boat the cramps will be spaced at about 5in (125mm), but when making a big backbone this gap may be more like 12in (30cm). The rule when clamping is: the more the better – there can't be too many and it doesn't matter if the clamps are touching each other. I've seen nearly a hundred lying in heaps in McGruer's laminating shop. Tighten them working from one end of the piece to the other.

Bolts as well as cramps are sometimes used to hold laminations together, especially in large pieces, and the bolts should go in before the glue has hardened. A backbone may have bolts through it for the floors. If these bolts have long threads they can be used to hold the backbone parts together, and later the nuts are taken off (not all together) to fit the floors. Bolting and cramping together is awkward, impossible without a sizable team. There are few tricks to speed up the bolting, which must be done after cramping. It helps if the nuts run easily on the threads, and this is a matter of careful and painstaking work when cutting the bolt threads. Some boatbuilders make their own bolts (I would not trust anyone else to make mine) and they test each nut, grease the thread and have bolts which can be tightened rapidly. To make sure there is no over-tightening use plate washers, not standard round ones. Grease on the bolt's shank keeps glue from sticking.

Laminates are all in one length from end to end when making beams, small frames, tillers and knees. If there have to be joins in the laminates they should be kept away from the area where the stresses are high, such as around chainplates or

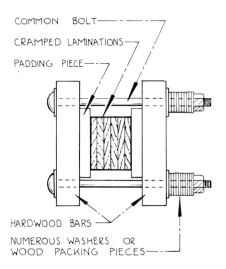

One of the most effective types of cramp is made up of a pair of hardwood bars, or steel angle can be used in which case the padding pieces are doubly important. The common bolts will not need large numbers of washers if the threading is run well up the shank; where lots of washers are not available, chunks of wood with holes through bigger than the bolt diameter can be substituted.

mooring bollards. If there are several joins they must be separated by at least three layers, and staggered so that no two joins in adjacent laminates should be within 3ft (1m) of each other. In big components with thick laminates, a backbone for instance, the laminates will be scarphed with a slope of about 1 in 8, and ideally 1 in 12. The scarph may not be easy to make from top to bottom of the laminate, in which case it should be made across.

For maximum strength the best wood is put in the two outer faces. Where strength is wanted but with the minimum weight, the enclosed middle layers can be of lightweight woods. In effect an I-beam is being built up, the outer surfaces being the flanges and the inner layers little more than spacers and tying the flanges together. This is an application of basic beam theory, which says in effect that for strength one goes for a deep beam with the strongest fibres on the outside. In practice it would be rare to have one strong laminate on each side. A more usual assembly would be two or three hardwood laminates, then three or four light ones, then two or three more hard ones.

It is important to know when not to laminate. A solid beam will be equally strong if it is made from

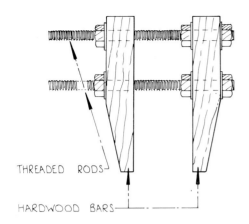

THREADED RODS

HARDWOOD BARS

Clamps are expensive because so many are needed, so this type of home-made clamp is popular. Threaded steel rod is not expensive, but some people prefer to get plain bar and put just as much threaded length on as needed.

Amateurs building just one boat might use bronze rod for the clamps, and later use the rod to make bolts to be used in her construction.

good, flaw-free hardwood and of normal camber. In fact, beams are a classic example of when laminating may well be unnecessary and wasteful.

To get even more strength, carbon fibre tows (ribbons) can be laid in between the laminates, if working from the inside out. Otherwise the ribbons will pull away instead of lying neatly along the previous laminates. (A later section covers carbon fibre.)

As each timber layer is put on it has to be held in place until the next one is on, and so till the last is in place and clamps can be applied. (It is also possible to stop halfway through building up the item, clamp it and leave it to set, then resume the job.) The first laminate can be tied or strapped

down or held by small clamps right on the end, or even nailed or screwed to the end chocks. The second laminate is held the same way, and the next. Alternatively the second and third can be held by barbed nonferrous nails, as few as possible. All laminated parts are made too long and both ends later trimmed off, so the nails can either be beyond the lines of the cuts or well clear of them nearer the middle of the component.

The first job after all the clamps are tight is to wipe away the surplus glue on the piece. The jig itself needs protecting with newspaper or plastic sheet, otherwise the waste glue will accumulate and make subsequent use difficult. Once glues are hard they are awkward to remove, being resistant to ordinary woodworking tools and as hard as stone. Surforms are effective, or the sides can be replaned; they should be made over-size to allow for the wood that will also be lost.

Any laminated work which shows should have the best possible finish, to get the fullest benefit from the fine appearance. So the exposed face of the last laminate should be hand planed; it may be machine planed first, but this will leave a subtle ripple. A single sweep with a well set hand plane is often all that is needed to give the final perfect finish.

The other side of the finished component will be against the boat's skin, if it is a frame, or against the deckhead if it is a beam. A finish off the planer saw or a power planer is adequate here. It is usual to complete a laminated part as much as possible before installing it: edges are bevelled off, knees bolted on, bolt holes pre-drilled, and so on. It is nearly always good practice to take any component as far along the road to completion as can be done while working on a good steady bench outside the hull.

Bending Wood

Wood bends easily to the curves found in boatbuilding without special equipment. If it will not effortlessly bend to the required shape, it is easy to thin it down until it will fit. The thickness, quality and type of wood determine just how small a radius it will take. The Bending Limit is defined as

$$\frac{\text{Radius of curvature}}{\text{Thickness}} \quad or \quad \text{R/S}$$

For wood in the natural state, and without heating or wetting it to improve bending, typical reliable R/S values are: African mahogany 110, agba 80, rock elm 70, iroko 150, makore 110, opepe 195, oak 100, scots pine 85, sitka spruce 115. These figures are normally safe and are for pieces over $\frac{1}{2}$in (13mm) thick. At about $\frac{1}{8}$in (3mm) the R/S ratio for a wide variety of species is likely to be around 50. The figure goes up fast between about $\frac{1}{8}$ and $\frac{1}{2}$in (3–13mm) thickness, so to be safe the best possible R/S figure should be multiplied by 3/2. If

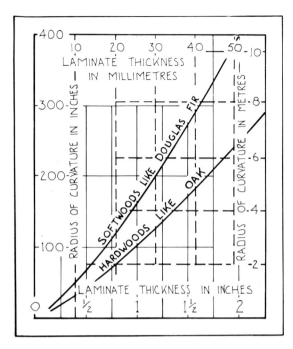

Graphs like this must be used with discretion. Wood varies greatly according to where it grows, how it was cut and dried, the method used for bending and so on. However, this graph is a good guide. The top and bottom scale are the laminate thickness. The right hand scale is the approximate bending radius in metres, the left one the same in inches.

If in doubt prepare a selection of laminates and experiment to see how the available wood bends.

there are faults in the wood, the same factor of 3/2 should be used a second time. This means that unless the wood is perfect, the best R/S figures should always be multiplied by 9/4. Even then the tightest radius should seldom be used, partly because of the risk of fractures, partly because wood is springy and it is not quick or convenient to work it near the limit, partly because the best R/S figures are the result of experiments and concede a 5 per cent failure rate, which most boatbuilders would consider a thundering nuisance.

Where the wood is not even 'medium quality boatbuilding' standard, or is over 1in (25mm) thick, the factor of 9/4 needs increasing. It is rare to use laminates 1in thick in boats, but the hog may be of this order and it is often bent in place.

For a part like a breasthook it is best to use thin laminations, around ⅛in (3mm) being typical. Where the finished piece is thick it may be possible to save time and glue by having thin laminations

on the inside of the curve and thicker ones near the outside, where the radius is larger.

Over-bending results in cracks on the outside of the curve and 'folding' or compression shakes on the concave side. The latter are not always easy to see, being quite subtle waves in the grain. Sometimes the wood splits down the grain on the inner side and a part zig-zags inwards, like an errant stream breaking off a main river which runs over flat soft ground. This dramatic indication of over-bending is found in stringy woods, whereas a soft wood like spruce gives the tiniest signs, which look like small distortions of the grain, hard to see but detectable as slight bumps by running the fingers gently over the smooth wood. Unless the laminations are very thin it takes quite an effort to get these ruptures, and in any case the rending across the grain on the convex side of the wood is a clear indication that over-bending has occured.

Well designed cold-moulding is nowhere near the bending limit: exceptions are expensive. If in doubt try bending sample pieces round a radius tighter than the sharpest curve on the hull. For a hog the wood should be used with the grain horizontal, since bending is easier this way than with the sections of the annular rings seen to run at or near the vertical, when viewed from bow or stern.

When choosing wood that will be bent, the Forest Products Research Laboratory who have been so helpful in providing much of this information suggest, as a rule of thumb: temperate hardwoods bend better than softwoods, and better than tropical hardwoods.

Once timber has been bent it is held in place by glue, fastenings or clamps, or a combination of these. After a time it 'sets' and will not spring back except a limited amount. I once had a dramatic experience of wood's ability to 'take a set', when building a cold-moulded boat with a shell thickness of ½in and working singlehanded. The boat was too big for one person and there was an 'incident'. A chock holding the hull up pushed the shell inwards too hard. What had been a slight outward bulge became an embarrassing inward dinge. It is a tribute to the toughness of cold-moulding that the planking did not rupture or split, creak or shriek. It just gave me a noticeable fright. When I'd wiped away the sweat, and crept closer to examine the trouble, I could see no defect apart from the gentle concavity. My heart stopped over-revving, I decided that suicide could be postponed, and I drove in a lot of extra props and shores round the hull. By then it was very late at night, I was tired, it had been a long hard day. It seemed a good idea to leave the problem till the next weekend, which was the first opportunity I would have to get back to reverse the dent. But the next weekend I couldn't work on the boat, nor the next. What with one thing and another I postponed taking the dent out for about eight weeks, and when I took the pressure off the dent refused to 'ping' out. It just stayed. I tried pushing by hand, but the wood had set almost solid. In the end I had to apply steam (from a kettle spout, carefully directed) and a little force.

Wood can be made easier to bend round a tight curve by steaming or immersing it in water, even cold water. A piece of timber left for twelve hours under water will be found to be noticeably more flexible, but the bendability will not improve much if the immersed time is increased over twelve hours. The trouble with cold water soaking is that it leaves the wood damp. This may not matter if one of those (less than ideal) glues which is mixed with water (or can work on wet wood) is used, but for epoxy resins it is totally unacceptable. Steaming pieces more than about $1\frac{1}{2}$in (4cm) thick is seldom practical. Allow about 45 minutes in the steam per inch thickness.

Once a set of laminations have been bent to a shape and glued up, they are left till the glue has completely cured. On release from the restraint of the jig the piece is likely to spring back. Just how much depends on the number of layers, the amount of curvature, the wood being used and so on. Thicker layers have more spring-back. A useful formula worked out by the Forest Products Research Laboratory is:

Spring-back as % of radius =
$$100 \times [1 \div (n^2 - 1)]$$
when n = number of laminations. Though this formula is approximate, it is valuable in two ways: it gives a working figure, and it shows that by having say nine or more laminations the spring-back can be largely eliminated. It also warns that frames and similar parts made and set up to delineate the shape of the boat will need checking on the scrieve board or mould loft after gluing up, and they are likely to need fairing after setting up.

Glues

Though expensive, the epoxy glues are by far the best for boatbuilding as they are water-resistant, fill gaps much more effectively than other glues and are strong. Using epoxy, two pieces of wood can be held together with a force of about 6000 kN/m^2. This is above the strength of normal commercial fibreglass or mild steel joins. In almost every case epoxy glue failures are in the wood and not in the glue line: the grain of the timber tears apart. The glue itself has strength, unlike other glues, so there is no weakness at small gaps which have filled. As long as they are in contact only with chemically clean and grease-free surfaces, tools and containers, epoxies are easy to use, especially after a little practice. They have a reasonable shelf life and are safe provided simple precautions are taken. It is probably true to say that the invention of epoxy glues has transformed all wooden boatbuilding, and made cold-moulding vastly more effective, stronger, long lasting and more reliable – a better race winner and a better investment.

Epoxy glues are made up of two main components; at 30°C the mix starts to harden in around thirty minutes, but at 5°C the time is nearer five hours. Varying the amount of accelerater alters the hardening time, so it is important to follow the maker's instructions. The glue is not fully hard until about three days have elapsed at about 30°C, or fourteen days at 5°C. Normally the glue is put on one surface, unless a lot is needed when both glued surfaces will be covered.

Tools and mixing equipment have to be cleaned before hardening begins, using solvents such as methylated spirits (methyl alcohol), cellulose thinners or acetone.

Because epoxy will not stick to polythene (polyethylene) this plastic can be used for spreaders or spatulas. Polythene containers are also recommended for mixing because once the resin has set the container can be flexed and the hard glue cracks out. One of the most popular mixing containers is a polythene child's potty because the handle is so convenient. Small beach buckets are also used but their handles tend to be somewhat in the way.

Epoxy resins and particularly their associated hardeners and accelerators have some toxic properties, though these are readily avoided. Skin sensitivity reactions on contact, inhaling fumes or dust from incompletely cured mixtures (as when sanding), and fumes from the solvents used for cleaning and degreasing are the main problems. To protect the hands, forearms and face a barrier cream such as Rozalex No. 8 or 9 should be used, and disposable thin plastic gloves such as those from medical suppliers. Rozalex Resin Remover and other proprietary products are effective in getting resin off skin.

Mixing must be done according to the manufacturer's instructions, followed very exactly when measuring amounts which may be by weight, by volume or both. Gently warming a thick resin before mixing makes it easier to handle, but as warmth speeds up setting once the two components come together this must be kept to a minimum. Large mixes give off enough reaction heat to affect the working time, and it is better to make up small batches the first few times, to avoid expensive waste and to get to know the material. Pot life of a mix can be extended by dissipating heat through increasing the surface area in a large flat tray, cooling the container or keeping to small batches.

As epoxy resin is a very good water barrier, it is logical to use it to cover and seal the outside of the wood. Dry wood is markedly stronger than 'green' uncured, moist wood, and also does not rot. Totally encapsulating every piece of structure and shell in a hull maintains its strength longer because water cannot soak into the timber; furthermore oxygen, as essential for rot as moisture, is also excluded, further protecting the strength and extending the life of the boat. However, effective use of the technique requires dry cured wood, and controlled temperature and humidity in the workshop and timber store.

The technique of using epoxy for a glue *and* a sealer has been developed with considerable success. A well-known name in the field has been the WEST System, which is the registered trademark of Gougeon Brothers Inc. of Bay City, Michigan. Other manufacturers, such as S P Systems, also make epoxy resin systems that are designed for boatbuilding in wood and various composites including fibre reinforcement. It is important to use those with allophatic (not aromatic) hardeners, to lessen the risk of dermatitis or other reactions, though the cost may be slightly higher. The low viscosity of proper marine resins gives easier working and better penetration of the wood, which enhances its mechanical strength. Clear epoxy surface finishes with ultraviolet inhibitors have also been developed, to counteract a tendency towards yellowing.

Aluminium powder may be used as a barrier against the sun's rays, as ultraviolet light is probably the main destroyer of epoxy resins, though to date there is not enough evidence to show just how long a life this relatively new material has.

Epoxies can also be mixed with microballoons to form a cheap filler which stands up to shaping with hand tools. Typical uses are to form a fillet between a fin keel and the main hull, or for fairing-in an external shaft log. Another type of filler is made by adding micro-spheres to resin. The resulting putty is very light, of the order of 12lbs/cu ft. Microspheres are like m-balloons, just tiny hollow balls, and they provide ease of use, cheapness, versatility and good adhesion.

Epoxy is compatible with carbon fibres (q.v.) and is used for holding them in place. Epoxy can be worked, but once it is fully cured it is not easy to abrade because it sets very hard. However, before the hardening is complete it is not difficult to work tools like a blunted (for finishing) Surform over it. Wood glued with epoxy is easy enough to saw through with ordinary handsaws.

Before epoxy resins, the two synthetic resin glues which could be relied on to give a long-lasting and watertight join were *resorcinol-formaldehyde* and *urea-formaldehyde* (e.g. Cascamite and Aerolite). They are cheaper and easier to mix than epoxy, but there must be no doubt in anybody's mind that they are much less effective even though they have done a good job over the years and lasted very well. They also have fewer toxicity hazards. One of the disadvantages is their limited gap-filling ability. An epoxy resin can be used to bridge small gaps with no loss of strength, but resorcinol or phenol glues are only suitable for gaps up to about 0.05in (about 1.3mm) and need near-perfect contact.

With urea glues the moisture content of the timber should be between $12\frac{1}{2}$ and 15 per cent, and with resorcinol glues between 15 and 18 per cent. Kiln drying is thus essential, the timber must be used without standing for long after the kilning, and it is important that it is transported and stored in truly dry conditions. To be absolutely sure of a good join the two pieces being glued should have the same moisture content. These percentages allow for slightly more moisture content than with West brand epoxies, where 12 per cent is the maximum and 7–10 per cent ideal. (Moisture content is the weight of the water as a percentage of the *dry* wood weight.)

Careful builders treat wooden boats with a preservative before painting or varnishing, and major components such as floors and beams before they are built in. One of the most popular is Cuprinol which is available in a colourless form for wood which is to be varnished, and as a green liquid. Because of Cuprinol's toxicity its use and sale are likely to be restricted in future, and substitutes developed. Whatever preservative is used, it should not be put on until all the gluing is complete.

The non-epoxy glues also involve mixing, and as soon as this has been done setting begins. Only a limited batch should be mixed at once, and as these glues tend to have a shelf life of about a year very large quantities should not be ordered at once.

Suppliers of these materials are very helpful with advice and recommendations (see Appendix). Four of the best known are Borden Chemical Co., Ciba-Geigy, Structural Polymer (SP) Systems, and Wessex Resins and Adhesives who are the appointed distributors for WEST System brand products. Bond strength and long-term performance depends on a number of factors and correct use is important.

Metal Fastenings with Glue

Perfect gluing requires no help, but because the glue is tucked between layers of wood, who is to say whether an area of gluing is perfect? A gluing fault may not show up until the boat is far offshore struggling for survival in frightening conditions. It is probably this danger factor which is the main reason why so many experienced boatbuilders use metal fastenings as well as glue.

Whereas airplanes stay up in the sky most of the time with factors of safety of the order of 1.25, it is more usual in boatbuilding to use factors of safety in excess of 3. For important and highly stressed areas such as the hull/keel join a factor of safety of 12 is not unknown. Part of the reason for this is that unlike airplanes, boats are not maintained or inspected carefully and continuously, by people trained at detecting growing troubles, and some crucial areas are out of sight.

Since laminated backbones and similar structures have to be held together while the glue is curing, there is a lot of sense in putting in bolts as well as clamping. Plenty of people do not have enough clamps, and alternate bolts and clamps are one solution.

A bolt can apply great local pressure so extra large washers are needed. For soft woods the washer area should be four times that of a standard washer, otherwise crushing of the fibres must occur when the nut is tightened. Any crushing is particularly serious because the weakness penetrates almost right through, as layer after layer of wood is forced downwards and sheared in line with the edge of the inadequate washer. Bolts also need staggering, otherwise the edges of the component may not be under anything like the same pressure as the centreline, and could even tend to open up (see sketch).

When bolts and clamps are used together some pre-planning is essential. It will probably be best to draw on the plans the location of each bolt, if it has not already been shown. Next, chalk on the gluing pattern the location of each bolt and each clamp; different coloured chalks or different symbols will avoid errors in the rushed period during the gluing up. Bolting only, with no clamps, is unusual partly because so many bolts are needed and it would be hard to get them in before the glue hardened. It is unusual to use bolts in beams and carlines and in minor items like laminated tillers (except onto the rudderhead fitting), but in some rugged and heavy craft bolts are used just about everywhere.

Up to now it has been assumed that bolting will be done to help the glue. Just occasionally screws

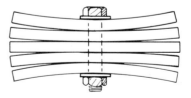

If laminations are held together by a row of bolts down the centre, this sort of distortion may occur. Though this is an exaggerated sketch, bolts which are not staggered either side of the centreline will often cause slight capping, and poor bonding along the edges.

are used, but they are much less effective. Nails, even the serrated type, are better than no metal fastenings, but only just. There are various types of serrated nails such as the Gripfast and Anchorfast, which have barbs circumferentially along their length and are non-rusting. They give a much better grip than ordinary nails, but they are just not as effective as screws; and they do not pull components together the way the screws and bolts do.

The sizes and spacing for fastenings is given below in the appropriate chapters for different parts of the boat. Safe bolt loadings and bolt strengths are given in *Boat Data Book* (Ian Nicolson, Nautical Publishing Co. Ltd). It is rarely good practice to use a single bolt on its own, particularly if there is a risk of reversing loads. Even just two bolts through a join is far from ideal because one may become slightly loose, leaving a single bolt to do the work. If a minimum of three bolts cannot be used, a combination of two bolts and four screws is sometimes almost as good.

Where weight-saving is very important, a join may be made with glue backed up by patterns of screws which are removed once the glue is dry. These screws will be of steel for strength, cheapness, to avoid breakages and because non-ferrous screws tend to burr at the slot for the screwdriver if used more than once. Screws are particularly useful where clamps cannot be used.

Preparation for Gluing

The best preparation of the timber is by planing, which takes off any surface contamination and gives a smooth flat face. At least, the surface should be flat: a badly set planing machine may give a series of ridges that result in poor wood-to-wood contact. As a rough guide there should be more than eight knife marks per inch (25mm) and the ridges should be very low, less than two-thousandths of an inch. Good hand planing will be better than machine planing though a good planer saw blade leaves the wood almost as smooth as a hand plane. Inspect for ridging and similar defects caused by machining.

Because wood left lying about collects dirt, dust and other contaminants the planing should ideally be carried out just before gluing, and certainly not more than two days before. If timber has to be planed well before gluing it should be carefully covered and sensibly stored away from contaminants and damp.

There are two completely opposed views about roughening the surface of the wood. The current scientific view is against any scratching or sanding, tooth planing or other form of deep marking or gouging a 'key'. Testing shows that scoring and scratching is likely to leave lines of bubbles, which weaken the glued join. Backwoods boatbuilders, and we must not disparage their many real skills and virtues, often take the opposite view: that gluing should be preceded by heavy scoring with a chisel or any sharp instrument in a criss-cross or diagonal pattern. The argument is that the glue then keys into the wood. This does not stand up to close inspection: if we were interested in a keying effect we would burrow into the wood and then turn at right angles so that the glue could literally hook onto the wood. But glue does not work like this, at least not to any great extent. The true strong bond is formed by a chemical reaction and this works best where there is an even smooth surface with no breaks, and certainly no lines of air bubbles.

'At least the timber should be sanded', the traditionalist might say. But here again the scientific view is not in favour. Sanding tends to scrape away the softer fibres leaving the hard summer wood as a series of ridges and valleys. Even more important, wood powder is left on the surface and this is a serious detriment to good gluing.

However, there is one situation where sanding is essential: if plywood is being used, and its surface has been pressure sealed by heavy steel plate clamps during manufacture, the outer skin of the ply is said to be 'case hardened'. This is a serious defect and results in poor bonding. The cure is machine sanding followed by very effective dusting off. It is not possible to detect 'case hardening' of wood by simple visual inspection: if in doubt the ply manufacturers, not the sellers, should be consulted. This is another good reason for using only the very best ply, and even then no one's word should be taken as a final guarantee. Some samples should be tested before starting the main gluing.

Just before gluing, dust the surface with a clean

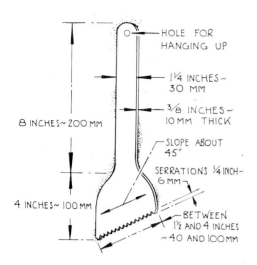

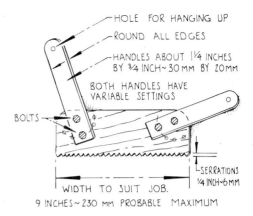

HOLE FOR HANGING UP

1¼ INCHES ~ 30 MM

⅜ INCHES ~ 10 MM THICK

8 INCHES ~ 200 MM

SLOPE ABOUT 45°

SERRATIONS ¼ INCH ~ 6 MM

4 INCHES ~ 100 MM

BETWEEN 1½ AND 4 INCHES ~ 40 AND 100 MM

An improved version of the usual type of small glue spreader used the world over. Most boatbuilders make up a batch of spreaders before starting on a job, and provided the surplus glue is wiped off after use they will last indefinitely.

HOLE FOR HANGING UP

ROUND ALL EDGES

HANDLES ABOUT 1¼ INCHES BY ¾ INCH ~ 30 MM BY 20 MM

BOTH HANDLES HAVE VARIABLE SETTINGS

BOLTS

SERRATIONS ¼ INCH ~ 6 MM

WIDTH TO SUIT JOB.

9 INCHES ~ 230 MM PROBABLE MAXIMUM

For extensive areas of gluing this large, cheap home-made spreader is useful. It is made up from scrap and used two-handed. To get the most comfortable grip the handle angles can be varied. It is essential that every part of the timber is fully wetted by the glue, which explains the importance of having glue spreaders.

rag. It is no good just splashing glue on: thorough wetting is really important, and achieved by energetically rubbing, scraping or rolling it onto the wood. Wherever possible both surfaces should be wetted, though with some glues the hardener is put on one surface and the glue on the other. A proper glue spreader is not just a help, it is virtually essential. If wetting does not seem to proceed easily then suspect the timber surface. The point of gluing soon after planing is to get prompt and efficient wetting, before moisture or dirt can get to the timber surface. Warmth helps, but it also speeds up drying or curing so too much heat has to

be avoided. Frost is fatal for Aerolite, and also to most people's concentration.

Wetting is so important that prior degreasing may be needed. Chemicals which have been recommended are furfuraldehyde and Teepol for resorcinol and urea glues. For epoxies the choice lies between acetone or methyl ethyl ketone (MEK). Check the glue manufacturer's recommendations as to the best degreaser to use with a particular glue, and at what concentration.

Here, as in so many other things, a little practice is worth pages of advice. The best procedure is to carry out some test gluing, then make up some unimportant components. Finally the important gluing can be done with experience and confidence.

Stapling and Strapping

To hold each thin veneer or plank layer down while the glue is setting, stapling is used. Staples are hard metal or plastic fastenings shaped like tiny goalposts, typically about ⅝in (16mm) across. The 'leg' varies according to the thickness of the laminates. Legs less than 2½ times the thickness of the wood might not hold tightly, and above all we want our staples to grip sensationally until the glue is hard, then come out easily and quickly. Stapling is always used with veneers but cannot be done with sawn laminates over about ¼in (6mm) thick,

for which pins are used; they too may be metal or plastic.

For a boat over about 25ft (7.5m) it is valuable to have two staplers because the work must be completed without delay, especially when the weather is warm and the glue setting fast. A single compressed-air driven tool can replace two hand-operated staplers, though few amateurs have air. (See Appendix for suppliers.)

Once the staples are in they should be tapped firmly in with a hammer, especially at plank ends,

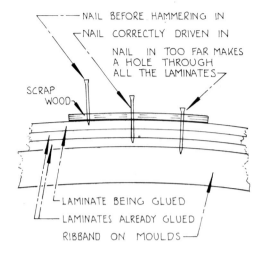

NAIL BEFORE HAMMERING IN

NAIL CORRECTLY DRIVEN IN

NAIL IN TOO FAR MAKES A HOLE THROUGH ALL THE LAMINATES

SCRAP WOOD

LAMINATE BEING GLUED

LAMINATES ALREADY GLUED

RIBBAND ON MOULDS

Instead of stapling, short lengths of any plywood, with three or more thin nails or pins driven through, can be used to hold the laminates down while the glue is drying. The nails are hammered just through the ply pieces, and then driven in just the right amount to grip into one and a half laminates. It may pay to punch the nails in slightly less, to avoid holes right through. The laminates need holding down tightly, but in the last one a lot of hole will need filling if this type of securing is used too enthusiastically.

The smallest nails which can be repeatedly driven should be used, so that the holes they make are small. The technique of using nailed strips is particularly useful if it is not possible to get good staples or a powerful stapler.

in hollows and wherever there is the slightest risk that the plank is not down tight. To hold a plank down well it may be necessary to space the staples very close. On an awkward curved stern of an IOR racer I have seen staples set $\frac{1}{4}$in (6mm) apart, over a length of 8in (200mm). In contrast I've seen staples spaced at 8in (20cm), but they looked a bit lonely and my inclination is to have them 4in (100mm) apart or less. Better too many staples than too few, and if the edge of a laminate is inclined to curl up a very large number of close-spaced staples, well hammered in, is what good professionals use.

Staples and staplers need to be powerful to be reliable, which is one reason why the domestic type of gun and fastening is no use for boatbuilding. But at plank ends even a lot of heavy staples lying shoulder to shoulder may be inadequate. Here thin nails are used. They are typically about 1in (25mm) long and $\frac{1}{16}$in (1.5mm) in diameter, but for a boat over say 45ft (14m) they would be more like

$1\frac{1}{2} \times \frac{3}{32}$in (2.3mm). Such pins are hammered in through thin pieces of scrap ply, in pairs or more, and not driven right home since they have to be pulled out when the glue has set.

Staples too have to be taken out once they have done their job, though some builders leave them in, to save time. There are snags to this: the hull has some extra weight which is hardly compensated by extra strength, the staples may not be fully countersunk so the next planking layer may not lie tight down which results in the worst of all faults, voids. If staples are left between layers repair work is likely to be more difficult, maybe much more. The metal used for staples has to be hard otherwise they collapse instead of penetrating: cutting through a lot of thin hard metal fastenings can make repairs slow, tedious and tool-blunting. There is yet another potential snag: some so-called stainless steel staples cannot be relied upon not to rust. If your super hull, built with so much care, work and thought, suddenly oozes rust from between the laminations there is just cause for suicide. Rust-weeping is a disease for which there is no cure. Once the hull starts to bleed horrid red marks it is almost bound to do so for ever more. Paint or vanish will only trap the rust for a limited time and over small areas. Bronze or nylon staples are a possibility where they are to be left in.

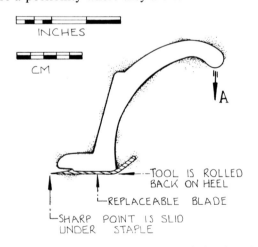

INCHES

CM

A

TOOL IS ROLLED BACK ON HEEL

REPLACEABLE BLADE

SHARP POINT IS SLID UNDER STAPLE

Taking out thousands of staples is speeded up by using a hand extractor, made by Rosetto. The sharp spike is pushed under the staple and the handle thrust down in the direction of A.

Another technique is to staple over string or tape. The end of the string or tape is later pulled firmly up and away from the surface, drawing the staples off successively.

Quick de-stapling is needed and one technique is to drive the staples in over cheap cotton tape, sheet plastic strips, thin nylon thread or banding strip. Pulling the end of the tape or thread whips out a whole row of staples. Alternatively the staples can be driven through wood strips, usually about $1\frac{1}{2}$ times as wide as the staples and about $\frac{1}{8}$in (3mm) thick. Ply or veneer offcuts, naturally very thin ply, are sometimes used instead of solid wood and give more protection to the surface, especially important on the final layer. Cardboard has been used, but it is a great nuisance when it tears instead of yanking the staples out cleanly. One of those claw-like jaws used in offices for extracting staples is a handy standby, but it is far too tedious to pull out thousands of well driven staples and may dent the wood. Strong webbing straps can be had for little or nothing from car scrapyards: seatbelts are hardly ever saved or recycled and are excellent and long-lasting for this job.

When a staple comes out it leaves a pair of tiny holes. These fill with glue if another layer of planking is being fitted, but not in the last layer. A technique for closing the holes is to make the wood swell by wetting it, ideally with hot water. My own inclination is to avoid this because the wood may not completely dry out before the paint, resin or varnish is applied. Better leave the tiny holes and let the finishing compound fill them.

Some professionals use an air-driven gun that punches in nylon nails, saving the time wasted in pulling out metal staples which sometimes break off. Nylon nails don't need to be removed, never corrode or otherwise misbehave, and a plane, saw or chisel can be used through them without damaging the cutting edge. It is important to first check with the adhesive manufacturer that the resin or glue is compatible with the plastic, and to get some practice. Nail guns and air compressors are usually considered too expensive by amateurs building just one hull, but they can sometimes be hired, possibly through a boatyard.

STEEL STRAPPING

Each layer of planking simply must be held tightly to the previous layer while the glue is setting and curing. It may be impossible to get staples, or the available staples may not be big enough, or it may very reasonably be considered that they are a nuisance, since they have almost always to be pulled out after use. The strapping technique was invented to avoid the use of staples. It consists basically of a wide steel or nylon strap, pulled down on top of a plank or planks and secured tightly. If only two or three planks are being put on at a time, as is very likely when an amateur is working for a short time in the evening, then only one strap for each plank is needed. The straps will be arranged to lie exactly along the run of the planks. But a more usual procedure will be to have ample steel straps laid more or less athwartships. As each plank is added another strap or two will be put on, lying diagonally across the planking if the latter is laid at 45°. As the glue sets the straps can be taken off and reused as new planking is laid.

Older glues might not adhere to nylon or steel, but with epoxies masking has to be done. The straps may be wrapped in plastic sheet or wax paper. A good case might be made for using strong webbing similar to that used for dinghy toestraps, though it might be harder to tension. However, the glue is likely to adhere and give a lot of trouble. The straps have to be truly flexible, and will therefore be about $\frac{1}{32}$in (0.8mm) thick by about $1\frac{1}{2}$in (40mm) or so wide, or more for a big boat. One end of the strap is fixed to the building base or the ground and the other pulled over the top of the hull and tightened down. Plenty of tension is needed so a tackle or similar device is used to apply firm pressure. If the tension is not strong enough the glue will not squeeze out along the plank edge for its full length both sides, and there may be voids. However, the steel straps should not crush or bite into the wood, and certainly not into the final layer. In way of hollows in the hull it is necessary to drive close-spaced wooden wedges between the straps and the planking to give the needed inward pressure.

In theory ropes and some sort of Spanish windlass could be used instead of steel straps, but I have never heard of it being done.

Because they give an even strong pressure over a long strip of the hull, metal straps are in some ways better than staples. But then staples put in close together give that powerful local grip just where it is needed. A combination of steel strapping and staples is probably best as it combines time-saving and reliability.

Metal Fastenings

BOLTS

Galvanized bolts are common even on expensive boats, though not on the very best. Ungalvanized steel fastenings of any sort are the greatest mistake, however, even on a boat built for a short life. Hot-dip galvanizing is the only sort which is any good afloat, all the electroplated or sprayed forms of protective coating being short-lived under the corrosive and rough environment that surrounds small craft. Galvanized steel rod can be threaded at both ends, a nut used for the head, and thus made up into bolts of any length.

Brass bolts are also commonly used for a variety of purposes, though brass is not a strong metal, a working average tensile strength being about 8 tons/sq in compared with 28 tons for steel. It is easy to cut a thread on brass rod, the metal resists corrosion so it is handy for general boatbuilding. However, brass bolts do not have good long-term resistance to corrosion, and the best boatbuilders are using them less and less. They should be kept well above the waterline. For craft up to about 35ft (10m) brass bolts ⅜in (9.5mm) in diameter can be used in many situations. For stanchions and similar jobs this size is rather large, but ¼in (6.5mm) diameter brass bolts are not satisfactory: they are too weak to stand up to enthusiastic

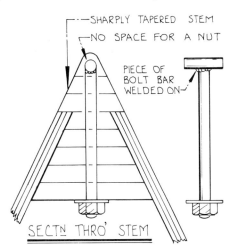

SECTⁿ THRO' STEM

—SHARPLY TAPERED STEM
—NO SPACE FOR A NUT
PIECE OF BOLT BAR WELDED ON

In some locations there is no room for an ordinary bolt head. A T-bolt is used here, the head being made of a short length of the bolt rod material welded on at right angles. A stem or sternpost which is well tapered away may require this type of fastening.

tightening, and they shear at the thread. They will not tolerate the hurly burly of life afloat, and break if used for stanchion bases. The alternative is to use bronze, or larger brass bolts.

Bronze comes in various forms, of which manganese bronze is one of the popular alloys for boatbuilding. It has a tensile strength of 28 to 33 tons/sq in, well up to steel, and rather better than phosphor bronze at about 15 tons/sq in. The combination of strength, resistance to corrosion and relative ease of working make bronze a good material for bolts, though it is more expensive than brass. (Metal fastenings are discussed extensively in the book *Metal Corrosion in Boats* by Nigel Warren, pub. Stanford Maritime.)

Stainless steel bolts are stronger than mild steel, and are used on stainless steel deck fittings. On no account should stainless be used below the waterline as it is subject to crevice corrosion, a particularly dangerous form of wastage which occurs in hidden recesses; it is intense and local, gallops ahead at a frightening speed, and is a most dangerous maritime malady.

It is not possible to generalize about bolt spacing as there are so many relevant factors, from the size of the craft to the stiffness of the materials being joined. To secure a cold-moulded hull to a grown or laminated frame bolts will be about 6in (15cm) apart in a 35ft (10m) boat, and 10in (25cm) in a 55-footer (17m). For watertightness, when holding together two flexible items such as a light low hatch coaming on a thin deck, the spacing must be surprisingly close to avoid leaks: in this sort of situation 2½in (65mm) centres are needed.

There are two basic principles of bolting which virtually always apply: 1. Never use less than three bolts on any side of any join. E.g. every knee should have at least three bolts in each leg. A doubler across a join in say a beam shelf must have at least three bolts each side of the join, and so on. If less than three bolts are fitted and one becomes ever slightly loose, the components pivot about the remaining tight fastening. What was a rigid join is now a moving one. With every wave, the loose join becomes looser. Water gets in, the wood swells, dries, moves more than ever. This is how boats deteriorate and leak.

2. Keep bolts well back from 'strapped' joins, otherwise the bolt hole in the strap will cause a

weakness near the break in the part being joined. An example of this is the beam bolted across the top of a ply bulkhead supporting a deck-stepped mast. This bulkhead often has a vertical join down the middle, below the mast step. To hold the two sides of the bulkhead together there is a strong beam bolted right across. If bolts are put through this beam near the vertical seam in the bulkhead the beam itself is weakened close by the point where the bulkhead needs all possible support in shear. The distance from the join in the bulkhead to the nearest bolt should be about two-thirds the normal bolt spacing.

SCREWS

Steel screws are not used for boatbuilding except very occasionally, and then only when galvanized. The standard of galvanizing on screws tends to be poor, so the thread should be dipped in anhydrous lanoline and the head covered with grease or well painted.

On any type of screw some grease or lanoline on the thread is a help when driving in the fastening the first time, and it makes it easier to remove it weeks or years later. (Don't use soap: it's corrosive in the long term and attracts water.) At most use enough grease to fill the bottom quarter length of the thread, and half this amount is often adequate. Any more grease will get onto the timber surface, prevent paint or varnish from adhering and show forever. It is particularly important to use grease on brass screws under 10 gauge as they are so easily broken when being driven.

Brass screws are the most widely used in boatbuilding, being of adequate strength for most jobs and fairly slow to corrode. Silicon bronze screws are used by the best builders because the price is reasonable and corrosion less likely. All bronze screws cost appreciably more than brass ones, but silicon bronze screws are the cheapest of the better-than-brass screws.

Stainless steel screws are not seen often in boats, partly because of cost, partly because their extra strength is seldom needed and where it is bolts are usually better.

The great majority of screws used will have countersunk heads, so to simplify purchasing, storage and avoid bin-ends it is no bad thing to avoid round-headed screws entirely. On the other hand for interior work a good case can be made for using raised countersunk screws with a dark copper-coloured finish. They look well and need no dowel or other treatment. However they only work well with polished furniture, not with varnish, since the copper finish comes off if sandpaper is used over it when preparing old varnish. These strong yet decorative screws can be used to hold bulkheads to frames or fillet pieces, to alternate between bolts joining beams and pillars to strength bulkheads, and to secure trim or edge mouldings, as well as in furniture.

Screws holding cold-moulded hulls to frames or stringers are not always put in under the last laminate, unless these members were installed over the moulds before shell layup began. Where screws are put in once the hull is complete a seal is needed over the countersunk head. Dowels should be used if the topsides are to be varnished, of the same hardwood used for the final laminate. To make the dowels a special cylindrical cutter is used, its inside diameter exactly the same as the outside diameter of the drill for the recess for the screw head. Dowels should be a firm push fit, glued in, with the grain running exactly the same way as the surrounding wood.

If the topsides are to be painted Mendex (see section on Sealants) can be used instead of dowels. It is a form of plastic wood made with resin and is put in so that it stands slightly beyond the planking, then smoothed down when hard. It can be used to seal over deck fastenings whether they are screws or nails, in a plywood or cold-moulded deck. Mendex is handy for all manner of filling jobs, but as it is a poor colour match for wood it is better under paint.

Screws are always put in first through the thin component, then on into the thicker one. Like bolts, they should be staggered, and driven so that the whole of the threaded part is in the thicker of the two scantlings. When fastening the plank edge to the hog, the screws should penetrate about three-quarters of the way through the hog. In a location like this the spacing must be of the order of 3in (75mm) centres in a 30ft (9m) boat and 5in (125mm) in a 50-footer.

For light work such as holding up furnishing a man's hand span is a good guide. It is about 9in (23cm) and even a beginner soon gets the trick of spacing the screws evenly so that they look shipshape, without wasting time with a rule.

NAILS

In modern boatbuilding nails are not much used except through ply decks, to hold laminates together before clamps can be applied, and in a number of minor parts. Nails are not strong compared to screws, and there are very few joins in a boat which can be less than rugged. If quite a minor part comes adrift it can have such dire consequences offshore that there is no justification for taking even a small risk.

Ungalvanized steel nails are totally unsatisfactory. Like other raw steel parts they quickly bleed ugly rust stains, start to disintegrate with ever-deeper corrosion, soften the surrounding wood, and introduce a trail of trouble. Galvanized wire nails tend to have an inadequate coating, but galvanized *boat* nails when properly made are hot-dipped. If the galvanizing is lumpy and rough with 'whiskers', the chances are the nails were hot-dipped. They may be used on a cheaply built boat, above the waterline, for jobs like securing down the deck or in furniture. But galvanized nails anywhere in a boat condemn her in the eyes of even inexperienced buyers and anyone who has any interest in her.

If nails are used, the type to buy is called a 'boat nail'. It has a square section and a slightly domed head, with a bluntish point. Round-section nails are much more easily available, but they should be avoided as they are made for house roofs and other sedentary jobs and tend to lose their grip. There is one type of round-section nail which is useful afloat, the barbed ring nail. In Europe the best known is made of silicon bronze and sold under the trade name Gripfast or Anchorfast in sizes from about $\frac{5}{8}$ to 3in long (15–75mm).

Nails, being less strong than screws, are spaced at about two-thirds the distance apart. The part through the upper (first) scantling does no real work, so the penetration and grip into the second piece of timber is critical. The length for a given job depends on all sorts of factors like probable loadings, the toughness of the wood and so on. A rough guide is: the length of the nail into the second (the thicker) item is about $2\frac{1}{2}$ times the thickness of the thin first layer. To secure $\frac{1}{2}$in ply a $1\frac{3}{4}$in nail would be used.

However, nails must not penetrate right through. If they come within about $\frac{1}{4}$in (6mm) of the far surface the chances of splitting the wood are increased, and nails which emerge so that their points protrude are a menace and reduce the boat's value.

Beddings and Sealing Compounds

When a part is put into a cold-moulded or strip-plank boat the builder's normal inclination will be to use glue copiously in the join. It serves the double function of giving strength and watertightness. Cutting away an area of deck for a forehatch results in a loss of strength: if the coamings are fastened and glued down all round, much of the strength is restored. The same applies to just about every part from cabin tops down to small mouldings on furniture.

However, there are places where glue cannot be used. It may be impossible to fit a part quickly and the glue would start to harden before the job was complete. This results in a join which lets in water and has no strength. To make matters worse, the hardening glue acts like an uneven rocky ridge, holding the two wood faces apart just where they should be tightly and continuously bonded. A good example of this difficulty is in the fitting of a big cabin top by a small team of men.

Then there are parts which have to be semi-portable. Over an engine space there is often a removable large panel which can be taken off without too much work or wood-wrestling. It cannot be glued down so some sort of semi-soft bedding is needed to keep water out, though it will not contribute any strength.

Most good bedding compounds remain flexible and semi-soft, so that they come and go with the wood's expansion and contraction, which can be 10 per cent of the plank width in extreme circumstances. To be any good over a period of years, bedding materials must neither deteriorate themselves nor encourage rot by losing their adhesion and contact. Though they should never go completely hard, they must not flow or ooze out of the join, even when it is vertical, even under the hottest sun.

Materials like Sealastik, though remaining flexy, have a firm skin on the surface after a few days, so paint can be applied and will stay on. The paintbrush does not stick to the bedding material once it has skinned over. Run a finger along the surface and provided nothing sticks to it, painting can be started. Seelastik is sold in tubes and cardboard cartridges which fit into dispensing guns. It comes in various colours, of which cream is the best since it blends well with many wood colours.

When bedding down a hatch, for instance, a continuous unbroken run of the sealant is laid on the deck right round the opening. In theory the hatch coaming will fit exactly on the deck, so only a thin line of bedding perhaps $\frac{1}{8}$in (3mm) wide is needed. If the builder has any doubts about the quality of the fit he will be more generous, making a run or two about $\frac{1}{4}$in (4mm) across. Round any flange of any fitting going onto the hull shell or deck it is usual to smear the bedding under the full width of the flange and about $\frac{1}{16}$in (1.5mm) thick, or even more if the hull has curvature and the flange does not. When a fitting with any bedding compound is secured tightly in place, it should ooze out along the entire join. Before the goo can stiffen the excess is wiped away.

In contrast, Sylglas must not protrude from the join line as it can't be trimmed properly. It is a comparable yet entirely different type of bedding, a tape or bandage thickly covered with a water-proof semi-soft sealant. As it has non-marine applications it is available from a great variety of shops and especially hardware stores. Sylglas is easy to use, being laid along the join line, normally in a single thickness; when one roll of tape runs out the next starts with a simple lap join. It is sold in different widths. If 1 in wide tape is in stock, and a piece of $\frac{3}{4}$in wood is being secured down, one can either fold the tape over at one edge or cut off part of the width before use. For a 1in wide join the tape should be $\frac{3}{4}$in wide, as it must not protrude.

One of the few disadvantages of Sylglas is that it tends to wrap round a drill and, less often, round a screw driven through it. To avoid this the fastening holes should be drilled first. After taping along the join line run a bradawl or similar tool along lightly to discover where the now hidden holes lie. Using the sharp point of the bradawl, the Sylglas is pierced and eased back round each fastening hole. Careful builders first mark where the holes are with a pencil tick, so that there is little time wasted probing with the bradawl to find the hidden holes.

Like all these tacky fillers, Sylglas stuck to fingers can be cleaned off with petrol, paraffin or white spirit. And like most of these compounds, it tends to stiffen and be less easy to use in cold weather. This is overcome by laying the sealant on a warm, not hot, radiator for three hours.

A contrasting form of tape is Inseal, which comes in various thicknesses and widths. The tape has no sticky material embedded in it and is made from closed-cell plastic foam material, each bubble being sealed and watertight from its neighbours. One face is tacky and it is a clean, quick, attractive material which is easy to use. It should not protrude from the edge of a join, but if it does it can be sliced away using a razor blade or Stanley knife. Perhaps the only disadvantage of Inseal is that a subtle green growth sometimes appears on it if it is left in damp conditions for long periods without painting. Like many good compounds it is not particularly cheap, but there is no wastage, it seems to have an indefinite shelf life, it is virtually impossible to make a mistake when applying it, and it is becoming a favourite in boatbuilding for jobs like sealing down winches, stanchion bases and so on.

Yet another different material is Mendex, which is a two-part paste for filling seams and gaps or for use instead of dowels. As soon as the two compounds are mixed they start to harden slowly, so only enough is made up for the job in hand. Mendex is a modern version of plastic wood, being wood flour and a resin. One tin contains the basic material, the other the hardener; different colours are available to match whatever wood is being used. Once hard, there is no difficulty in sanding, planing and generally working Mendex just like wood. It is not so cheap that it can be used casually for big filling jobs, nor is it the material to use as a bedding. Its great advantage is the ease which it fills irregular hollows, being worked in with a putty or palette knife or the back of a chisel.

Mendex is made by Alfred Jeffrey & Co. who also make a useful variety of other mixtures for filling, stopping and sealing. One of these is Jeffrey's Liquid Marine Glue, which can be described as industrial treacle! It looks like and feels like treacle, it pours like it and it can be messy in the hands of the clumsy. It is more a sealant than an adhesive, and is great for sealing two pieces of wood together in such a way that no water gets between them.

In contrast there is common builder's putty. There are no words to describe this, it is so bad. It has no virtues for the boatbuilder: it is not even cheap because it fails so quickly and as a result, even over two years, repairs and replacement are needed which puts up the original cost to a figure far above the first (and only) price of far better sealants and bedding compounds. Putty is made with raw linseed oil and powdered whiting. Put this paste between two pieces of wood and in no time the oil migrates inwards leaving the hard, brittle and crumbly whiting behind. In no time it falls out. Even if the oil doesn't soak into the wood the putty becomes compressed when the adjacent planks swell; as they dry and contract the inelastic putty does not follow, but leaves a gap on one wide or both. Water seeps into these gaps and leaks follow, with rot and all manner of other troubles close behind.

There are desperate situations where putty simply must be used, for instance when far from civilization and supplies of proper filling compounds. If putty has to be used in such crises, mineral grease (Vaseline is best) is added to prevent putty drying out. The formula is: to a handful of putty add a walnut-size piece of mineral grease. In practice this trick is still suspect because mineral grease will leak into wood eventually, but perhaps not so quickly as raw linseed oil. It's much better to use a good filler: it's cheaper in the long run, and in the short time-span too.

For sealing or bedding jobs where flexibility is needed one of the butyl rubber products such as Farocaulk is ideal. It is sold in tubes and cartridges and is a soft, sticky and tenacious material, not liquid enough to flow and capable of staying in a join which opens downwards. On exposure to air it hardens to a rubbery substance which not only excludes water but also gives a measure of bonding strength. It is available in white, grey, brown and black. For underwater use, as on keel/hull joins, two-part Farocure, a polysulfide, is recommended and provides some bonding strength as well as excluding water.

As sources of filling and sealing compounds the big paint companies have a lot of advantages. They will advise which materials are compatible with their paints, they sell in different sizes of container to suit the size of the project, they have a reputation to defend so they turn out good compounds carefully researched, and they are in touch with the boatbuilding industry. Firms like International Paints and Hempel Paints have comprehensive catalogues explaining how to use all sorts of complementary materials for sealing and bedding.

The manufacturers of bedding, sealing and adhesive materials are progressive and improvements are made every year. So it is worth: asking their advice and recommendations for particular jobs; carrying out small scale trials with any new compounds; making sure that the latest wonder material is truly better than an old tried and trusted one; and letting manufacturers know if their products are unsatisfactory. They want and need feedback from users.

PART 4

BUILDING THE BACKBONE AND HULL SHELL

Backbone Construction

The backbone of a wooden hull is that central 'spine' which both provides longitudinal rigidity and in cold-moulding takes the shell planking ends. Probably the simplest form of backbone is made from a single piece of bent oak, steamed and then curved and fastened down over the moulds from the stemhead to the base of the transom. However, except in small boats the structure is usually built up from several pieces of timber, and there is a considerable problem with the various names of these parts. In different regions a given part will have more than one name; sometimes it means one thing in one place and another a few dozen miles down the coast. Most people call the top part of the keel assembly, which extends amidships and takes the top face of the planking edge, the hog (see drawings), but I've also heard it called the keelson. For most people this is that inner member which is fitted late in the construction and goes over the tops of the floors, with

a gap underneath before the hog is reached. But the keelson can also be the doubler which extends over the lower stem (see drawing of *Myth of Malham* backbone).

The sketches show the nomenclature used in this book. Where the keel and hog are laminated into one solid unit, the assembly will be called the *hog*. That part of a sailing boat which extends downwards from the main hull and is principally to give stability and reduce leeway will be called the *fin*, or *fin keel*.

TYPES OF BACKBONE

The whole spine of a boat may be built up from glued laminations starting from the stemhead and extending right to the top of the transom, or the sternpost of a double-ender. However, a cold-moulded hull can be built using what might be called an old-fashioned backbone, made up entirely of solid timber. A third alternative, which is

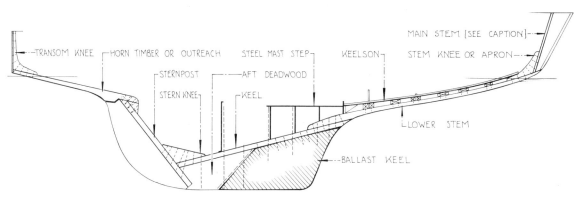

The terminology used in this book is shown in these drawings. This one, which shows the centreline structure of the famous racer *Myth of Malham*, is of special interest because it shows the use of the keelson, an extra member to give additional strength. As its name suggests it is commonly over the keel, and may be separated from the main part of the backbone by chocks or floors. Often it extends over the major length of the

vessel, but in this case it reaches only from the stem knee to the mast step. This yacht was built so that she could be lengthened, or altered forward, which explains the unusual inner and outer stem.

The dotted lines show the backbone bolts. Both the lower stem and the outreach (or horn timber) are tapered in moulded dimension towards the end, as less strength is needed there and to save weight in the ends.

usually the cheapest, quickest and often requires the least skill, is a combination of laminated and solid timber. Where there are bends, such as at the bottom of the stem as it turns into the hog, laminating makes sense. Where there is a long straight or slightly curved part, such as the hog or the upper part of the stem, there is seldom any need to go to the expense of setting up a jig and gluing. Wood can be bent to the necessary gentle curve or cut to the required shape quicker than laminating. When cutting out a part the grain should follow the final shape as far as possible.

Solid timber has to be selected with special care. As well as a close inspection along the whole length, preferably after planing off, it should be tapped for hollows. One reason why laminating is favoured is the guarantee that at worst any defect still hidden must be smaller than the cross-section of the individual laminates, and slicing up the timber will expose most significant faults.

If all-solid parts are used the building technique will follow tradition, except that instead of hook scarphs it is logical to use plain scarphs and epoxy glue, giving a strong join without the extra depth of timber and time-consuming work. The additional depth of a hook scarph makes it harder to find suitable timber with enough width. Plain scarphs will also be used when some components

are laminated and the others are solid timber. It is common practice, though not universal, to put some bolts in when using part-laminated part-solid timber, even with epoxy glues.

If the plans show the backbone of solid timber a skilled draftsman or naval architect will be able to change them to partial or full laminations. The more laminating used the lighter the spine can be. If the whole length of the backbone is laminated to best advantage it will normally be necessary to set up a jig which is slightly longer than the overall hull length. This may be expensive or inconvenient, so an alternative is to make up the backbone from parts which are small enough to laminate up on the same base or grid as is used for the frames, beams, coamings and so on. If the base is say 15ft (4.5m) square, as it will be in many yards, it may be hard to fit on a long sweeping stem. One answer is to extend a corner of the laminating base with a temporary table or a set of sawing trestles secured together with battens. The extension has to be the same height as the main base and secured to it very firmly.

DESIGN

All boats have to lift to on-coming waves: the lighter the ends the better they will respond to the seas. If there is weight right forward the boat will

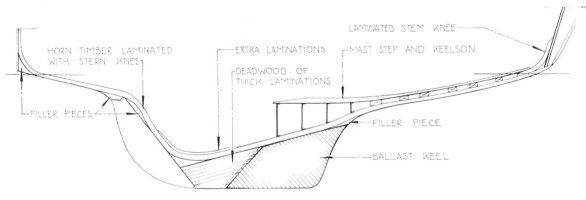

The traditional style of backbone made up of short lengths bolted together may be used for a cold-moulded or strip-planked hull, but to save weight and gain strength, also to reduce the chances of future leaks or rot, the centreline structure may be laminated. This sketch shows one way the laminations might be arranged, and should be compared with the previous one. Other techniques involve full-length laminations including the stem knee and stem. Taking the opposite approach, the straight pieces such as the keel may be of solid timber but the curved ones laminated, perhaps

recessed and glued into the solid parts. Where loads are high additional strength is easily worked in by adding extra laminates. The filler pieces are usually laminated by the best builders, otherwise they may expand and 'move' in a different way to the adjacent curved parts.

This laminated backbone shows how a 'traditional' one can be modernized. It is not the only way the job can be done, and because it will require a jig almost as long as the boat it is not necessarily the easiest. But the result will be light and strong.

pitch too slowly and be wet, and lose speed in bad weather. The same applies, usually to a lesser extent, to weight aft. To help reduce the weights at each end the backbone may be tapered, as is done in all types of high-performance craft. Some sailing boats need a reversal of the taper at the stemhead to give a strong anchorage for the stemhead fitting, but the main taper may begin almost immediately forward of the mast step, whereas the local thickening right forward will be quite short, and probably not more than 120 per cent of the length of the stemhead fitting.

On powerboats with widely flared bows the taper may have to be limited because a wide top of stem is essential for the planking. Here the designer may maximize the tapering of the moulded dimension because he has to enlarge the siding. Normally the taper at both ends can be in the moulding and the siding, and this is certainly usual in the lightest boats. There are snags to having any taper, and certainly to taper in both planes: it makes it hard if not impossible to finish the surfaces of the stem piece with a bench planer, though a hand-held planer may be used. Unless the boat is required to be a light as possible there are advantages in having long lengths of the backbone parallel sided. It is easier to laminate up, easier to cut the rebate, power sawing and planing are possible and normally easy, setting up is simpler, and so on. So if the designer has shown an awkward backbone, it may be worth altering this for simpler construction.

Except on small boats, laminated backbones have to have butt joins within them. These must be kept away from high stress areas, such as in way of ballast keels and mast steps on sailing boats, engine bearers on power craft and rudder stocks on all craft. The butts will not normally be shown on the designer's drawings; their location is planned by the builder once he has set up his laminating jig and got together the timber. He can then see how the individual pieces are going to fit together.

On the very finest and lightest craft a break in the strength of even one lamination is unacceptable, so the lengths of wood are diagonally scarphed and glued, using a slope of about 1 in 9. The scarph may be in the moulded or sided direction, and it may be necessary to use some scarphs even when fanatical weight-saving is not the aim; sometimes the available timber cannot be assembled without strong scarph joins. A rough rule of thumb is to have all butts at least 18in (50cm) apart, and $2\frac{1}{2}$ times this distance when they are in adjacent laminations.

When laminating there must be no sudden changes in thickness or direction. The sketch showing how *Myth of Malham*'s backbone might be modified for laminated assembly indicates one way of getting round an awkward curve smoothly.

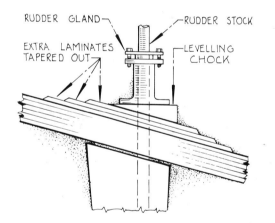

Where the backbone is weakened by drilling a hole for the rudder tube strength is restored by doubling up. The added laminations are tapered away to avoid hard spots at the ends. Each one is cut on the diagonal at its end, to give the best tapering out and to avoid end grain which holds paint poorly compared with the smoothness of side grain.

The doubler laminates help to contain the all-round forces on the rudder, which can be very large, for instance when the boat is driven astern with the blade hard over or when grounding so that the blade touches.

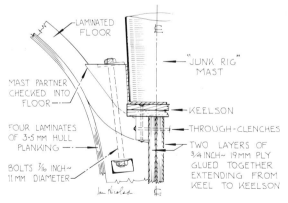

Galway Blazer II's masts are stepped down on the keelson. As they are for junk rig and have no shrouds, the stresses where the masts are in contact with the hull are unusually high.

Filler pieces are put in and the lamination is swept comfortably round gentle curves. Sudden changes of strength are avoided by 'tapering out', so that each successive lamination stops a few inches farther on (compare this with leaf spring floors).

Regardless of whether the backbone is laminated, solid or a combination of both, it should be kept as light as possible to avoid massive purchases of timber and to ensure that the boat does not carry around excess weight all her life, like an obese person. But of course if the parts are kept just strong enough any cutting away of the strength needs compensation, so in way of the stern tube and rudder tube there will probably (but by no means always) be doublers. They should be at least twice the cross-section of the cutaway timber, and should extend well beyond where the backbone is cut through. Doublers should taper out, and may be set on top of the backbone or on the sides and sometimes on both. (Various sketches in the text illustrate the principles of tapering out laminations and doubling.) However, if the designer does not show doublers in way of areas which have been cut away, it does not necessarily mean that the backbone has been made heavier than is essential.

A most important feature of a backbone is the landing of the plank ends and edges. The landing is by tradition twice the plank thickness, although we are not much concerned with tradition in cold-moulding: this method is characterized by thin planking, so it will be better to aim for a landing four times the plank thickness at least. This ideal may not be achieved, but it should be the goal because the landing provides the bond between the backbone and hull shell. The bond area not only gives the required strength, it also excludes the water along one of the most worrying join lines. It has to be admitted that the plank to keel (and to stem, sternpost, etc) join is one place where trouble is most likely to occur, and curing a failure here is not easy. The procedure will be to clean out the gap, possibly enlarge it a little, make sure it is dry (by applying a fan heater for some hours if necessary) and then run in epoxy glue. Before the glue has set a row of quite close-spaced screws are driven in. Clamps, shores or wedges may be applied too, though this can be hard if the two surfaces on which the clamp jaws or shore ends are lying are far from parallel. All this is a nuisance, and it is better to make the plank end landings perfect. One way is to ensure that the planks fair

exactly onto the backbone. If the designer has not provided a set of sections through the backbone it may help to do them on a special plan. It is almost always advisable to have full-size sections drawn out on the mould loft floor showing the precise angle where the planking comes into the stem, the keel, the sternpost and so on, every few feet. Only an experienced builder, working on the sort of boat he has built several times before, can safely omit this stage of the mould loft work.

These full-size section drawings have other purposes. They help when arranging the major bolts through the backbone, for the ballast keel, floors and so on. They show where side doublers are needed to prevent floors extending unsupported between planking and backbone. To an experienced eye they may show that the designer has been too rash in trying to save weight and has drawn in a main spine component which simply will not be man enough for its job in offshore conditions. (This presupposes that the builder is sufficiently skilled and has enough experience to detect excessive weight-saving in the wrong place.)

TIMBER

Hardwoods are used for backbones. A wood which is strong and glues well (see chapters on Timber) is needed. In the correct long-term view, the finest wood should be used for the backbone of a boat because it is the part which is hardest to repair and subject to some of the worst treatment. Not much of the planking lies under a constant puddle, but unless the inside of the boat is totally dry the backbone will suffer from long-term soaking. Even when a boat is laid up there is often at least a small puddle somewhere low down. Here no drying breezes nor even the enthusiastically wielded sponge of the keen owner can reach to remove the last drop of bilgewater. Planking is not too hard to renew, decks are easy, even a beam shelf does not always call for the most radical surgery.

As parts of the backbone are so very awkward to replace the logical wood to use is teak. However, it is so expensive and in some areas so hard to get that it is not much used except on the most expensive craft. Oak is good, but for weight-saving some of the better mahoganies and their cousins are popular. My own preference here and for many other jobs is to visit a timber yard specializing in boatbuilding woods and see what they have. Once the yard manager knows the

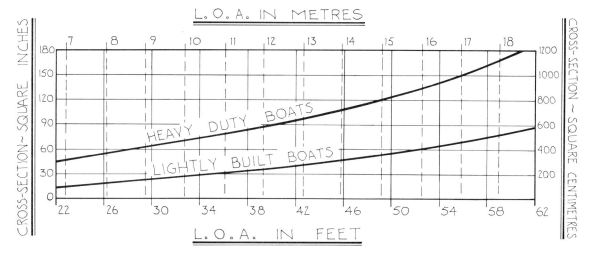

The dimensions of the boat's backbone are particularly important because lack of strength here is so hard to cure. If a backbone splits or becomes slightly rotten or is crushed, it is almost always expensive to repair. It is therefore logical to have a little extra reserve strength.

When a very light backbone is fitted there must be ample longitudinal strength in the rest of the hull, perhaps due to slightly over-thick planking, numerous stringers or an unbroken fully glued deck. Even the lightest backbone must have enough thickness for plank end and edge fastenings to grip: this limits its minimum thickness. The planks also need a good landing for their edges and ends, and this sets a limit on the minimum width.

These graphs must be used cautiously because so many boats are at least slightly unusual. For instance a boat which has to take the ground (dry out) regularly, or one which has a very heavy and highly concentrated ballast keel, should have an extra strong backbone. They are particularly useful during the preliminary design stage when weights are being calculated, or when the designer may be uncertain what final backbone size is going to be needed. But the figures given should be taken as a preliminary guide, and may need modifying as the design crystalizes. It is a measure of the approximate nature of these curves that 30 sq in is taken as equivalent to 200sq cm, a deliberate 'drift' of about 24 per cent.

purpose the wood has to fulfil he can go through his stock and recommend alternatives. If he has a lot of agba this may well be the cheapest, and it works well. For lightness one might go for a Honduras (occasionally called Mexican) mahogany where cost is not critical. I do not like the elms, though they are recommended in some books, as they are unpredictable and not consistent in the way they rot, and are hard to work.

To minimize the amount of laminating, the plies should be as thick as possible. It is fairly common practice to use $\frac{1}{2}$in (12mm) thicknesses for the hog, with $\frac{1}{4}$in (6mm) for the stem, larger stern knees, the apron, or to build up the stern log to take the shaft tube or a boss for the tube for a rudder shaft. Over tight bends it may be necessary to have very thin laminates, and a transom knee built up of $\frac{1}{8}$in (3mm) laminates is not uncommon. It is helpful to stick to multiples of $\frac{1}{8}$in because the inner layers can be made of thinner strips of wood than the outer ones if there is difficulty in building up a

component, yet the adjacent part can be blended in because overlapping layers will have the same thickness as two or four of the thinner size.

The hog is best if 'slash sawn', that is with the lines of the grain extending athwartships when viewed in section (see drawings). This makes bending easier and gives screws a better grip. Though wood bending tables are given in this book, wood is not consistent. So when in doubt get a sample of the timber to be used, take it down to the thickness which the drawings or your intuition suggests is correct, and try bending it round the sharpest curve on the jig. If it will not go round easily either select a different wood or reduce the thicknesses.

BACKBONE FABRICATION

Unless the builder is skilled and the boat remarkably simple, normal practice will be followed and the whole backbone will be shown on the mould loft floor. Full-size templates are made

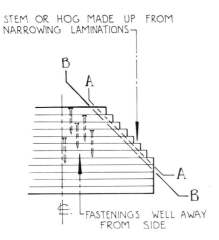

STEM OR HOG MADE UP FROM NARROWING LAMINATIONS

FASTENINGS WELL AWAY FROM SIDE

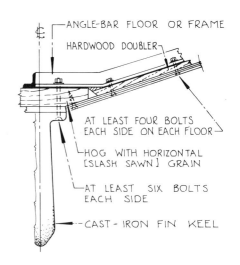

ANGLE-BAR FLOOR OR FRAME

HARDWOOD DOUBLER

AT LEAST FOUR BOLTS EACH SIDE ON EACH FLOOR

HOG WITH HORIZONTAL [SLASH SAWN] GRAIN

AT LEAST SIX BOLTS EACH SIDE

CAST - IRON FIN KEEL

Laminating the backbone. To save on timber and work, the outer laminations are made narrower than the first ones to get the correct final shape. Nails to hold each layer are kept well in towards the centreline so they will not interfere with the fastenings holding the ends of the planking laminates.

Saw cuts are made down to line A–A and the wood chiselled away to this line, unless a power planer, router or angled power saw can be used. If power tools are available they will cut the surplus wood down to A–A. The final finish to B–B is made with a hand plane.

using wood, card or paper. It used to be common practice to use scrap wood about $\frac{1}{4}$in (6mm) thick, often unplaned, for templates. Possibly only one edge of the template is cut to match the shape on the loft floor, though meticulous builders tend to make the template fit exactly over the full outline of the part being fabricated. If only one edge is shown there will be width dimensions marked boldly every few inches or feet. The waterlines and station lines or mould positions are also put on the templates.

Heavy, smooth surfaced paper can be used for templates. Some of my acquaintances use what they call 'building paper', which is a brown/orange, as thick as a thin card, dimensionally stable and stands up to splashes from coffee cups or minor roof leaks. Kraft paper, used for export packing, is another possiblity. Tracing paper has been used, and it is handy because it can be laid onto the mould loft floor and the appropriate line traced through. But it is too flimsy and is much affected by a damp atmosphere, in which it goes limp and changes its dimensions.

One attraction of paper templates is that they

A hog with the grain running across will bend fore and aft more easily, and hold fastenings through the plank edges better. The grain formation is called 'slash sawn', as opposed to vertical grain lines which is 'rift sawn'.

When a short deep fin is needed there is much to be said for using an iron or steel casting with a flange at the top. Only short keel bolts are needed, but there must be plenty of them and over the full length of the top of the keel. A steel floor in way of each pair of keel bolts makes sense, especially as the horizontal flange of the floor prevents the tightening of the nuts from crushing the top of the hog. Perhaps the only disadvantage of this configuration is that the ballast keel flange is a slight obstruction to a clear water flow.

can be rolled up and put into the back of a small car. Cardboard may break, and wood templates tend to be as handy as a frozen octopus, and too flimsy for lashing on a roof rack on a car. If solid timber is used for the backbone the way to get the best pieces of timber is to take the templates to the wood yard for trying on the available logs, so compact portable patterns are what we want. The template is laid on a likely piece and moved about till the grain runs round the curve as accurately as possible. The difference between the way the grain runs and the curve should not be more than about 20°. Where there are a lot of stresses the variation should be kept below 10°, but in practice this can be hard (which is, of course, one reason we go for laminated components). The template is moved round until it lies over a piece of wood clear of defects and with a suitable run of grain. If the buyer does not have a good bandsaw he may get the wood yard to cut the part out to the shape marked round the template. The saw cut will be outside the marked line by at least ⅛in (3mm) to allow for planing. The newly cut faces are carefully examined in case the saw has revealed a previously hidden defect. This is the time to reject the wood as unsuitable for this purpose and start looking for another piece.

Backbone assembly is done on the erected moulds unless the boat is so small that the builders can easily lift the whole spine after assembly. A light backbone can be put together on the mould loft floor using the lines as a guide, which saves a lot of checking. For a boat over about 25ft (7.5m) the moulds are used to support the backbone, and as there is bound to be a fair bit of heaving and humping of relatively large lumps of lumber they must be rigidly braced. Generally the hog will be laid on first, and it must be secured in such a way that it can be taken off the moulds, unless they are

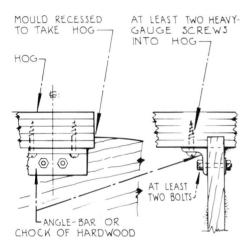

MOULD RECESSED TO TAKE HOG

AT LEAST TWO HEAVY-GAUGE SCREWS INTO HOG

HOG

AT LEAST TWO BOLTS

ANGLE-BAR OR CHOCK OF HARDWOOD

The hog is almost always recessed into the moulds. It must be held down while the planking is fitted, and after the hull has been turned over the moulds have to be released. If the holding screws are driven down through the hog when it is being put onto the moulds, they will normally be buried by the planking. So to get the moulds out is will be necessary to chop away the bottom of each mould, and even then the screws will be left protruding through the hog. The technique shown here gets round this problem. If metal angle is not available wooden chocks can just as easily be used, bolted to each mould and screwed upwards into the hog. If several boats are to be made from the same set of moulds the use of angle-bar is recommended.

The amount the hog is recessed depends on the thickness of the stringers laid on the moulds. The base of the hog must fair with the outer faces of the stringers, since the planking lies on both surfaces smoothly.

the final bulkheads in which case a permanent bolting arrangement can be used (see drawings). Ropes round the hog may be used at this stage, because once the full length of the backbone is fitted the ends can be very well secured down to the building base, and the ropes can be taken off.

Stage by stage the backbone is built onto the hog, each part being carefully aligned. It must be central, it must have its waterlines level, and its location marks (ensuring that it is correctly sited along the length of the hull) must come in just the right places. (Refer to the earlier section on Building Moulds.) Each part is clamped on first while the bolt holes are drilled, but no hole is made until the positioning has been checked and rechecked. The bolt holes should be at the very least three at every joint. It is better to have ample small bolts than a few large ones, not least because they make smaller, less weakening holes in the backbone and spread the clamping effect during gluing. As a crude guide, the bolts at backbone joins should be spaced at roughly one-eightieth of the boat's length, but a better guide is to study the drawing in this book and see how good designers fit in the fastenings.

If the backbone is partly laminated the parts which are so made are glued up just like frames. A rounded stem may want to spring open slightly when taken off the jig, and this can be stopped by fixing a piece of rod or rigging wire to the ends and straining it up, with a rigging screw or Spanish windlass, to get the correct shape. But normally there will be little spring-back if the laminations are chosen so that they bend in place without a lot of forcing and bad language.

During fabrication each part is planed clean and then has the centreline marked on the top and bottom faces, carefully aligned with the taut centreline wire stretched over the middle of the building base.

The stemhead will be bolted to the building base, the transom likewise. There may be struts down onto the hog from the overhead beams, and diagonal supports up to the stem and stern knees from the ground. It is common for the stem to be made too long, so that the top end (which is at the bottom while the boat is being built upside down) is used to help hold the backbone securely. Even if the stem should end 2 or 3ft clear of the ground, when the boat is built inverted, it is often extended this distance so that it can be bolted to a short length of anglebar secured to the floor. It may be

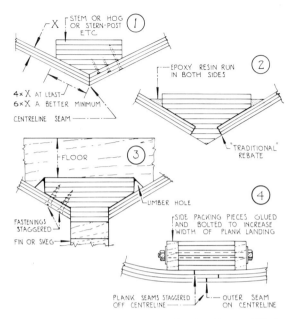

The lap of the planks onto the backbone (1) is important, a weakness here being hard to cure and likely to show up in bad weather. The lamination fastenings are shown on the right, light barbed nails through the first two laminates and heavier ones through the final layer. The nails must be marked through or set in a row measured from the centreline, otherwise the second set will foul the first ones. This shape of section is easy to make but the plank edge finishing needs care.

This section (2) of hog or stem is traditional but involves cutting a rebate. The angle of the rebate will change along the length of the boat and is taken off the mould loft floor. In theory at least, the chances of a leak here are minimized by the rebate, because water has to work in past a right angle. When the hull is upright and construction is almost complete, epoxy resin may be run in between the backbone and planking. This adds strength and reduces the chances of rot.

The hog (3) must be thick enough to take adequate fastenings through the planking. When an outer row of fastenings is being put in it should be staggered to reduce the risk of splitting and spread out the 'squeezing effect' of the screws. The limber holes in the floors are at least $1\frac{1}{2}$in at the minimum dimension, and the outer edge is angled steeply down to give the planking the maximum support, even though this means the top angle is a sharp one and looks like a weakness.

Where the hog is flat on the underside (4) it may be worth offsetting the centreline join of the port and starboard planks. On some craft it may be possible to carry the plank laminations right across, avoiding the centreline join entirely, at least for part of the length. The resulting increase in strength should be extremely valuable, though hard to quantify.

nailed down to a wooden building base or floor.

When a boat is built the right way up at least two diagonally extended pieces of wood are secured to the stemhead and up to the overhead structure of the building shed. Less often the transom knee is made over-long for the same purpose. Alternatively a pair or maybe three pieces of wood or metal bars can be bolted to the transom and the floor or overhead beams.

Most parts of the backbone take the edging of the planking, so there must be a properly bevelled edge or a rebate each side. It is easier to cut this bevel or rebate on each part before it is set up on the moulds. However, final fairing should be done *in situ* to get the plank landing exactly right. Cutting a rebate is a relatively slow job, even with a power saw, and most builders will prefer to avoid this job by having the planks lapped onto the backbone, where necessary planing the ends flush and adding extra backbone laminations on top.

Final truing-up of the plank landing is done after the battens or ribbands have been fitted over

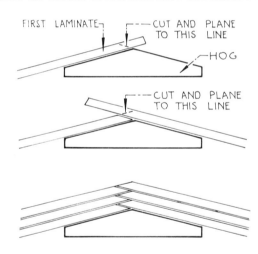

This method of ending the planks on the hog ensures that there is little chance of the water working in. It also makes trimming the ends easy, since each plank ,is merely run on over-length, then later (after the glue has cured) cut off close to the dotted line. A plane is run across to trim the planks. A row of several plank ends will be done at once. This way of criss-crossing the planks adds strength to what can be a weak point in a cold-moulded boat, especially if there are centreline bolts. Drilling holes for these bolts, for a ballast keel perhaps, may tend to force apart or split a long plain butt join.

Note that in this sketch the hog has been drawn undersize compared with the plank thickness, for clarity.

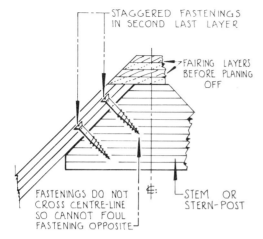

STAGGERED FASTENINGS IN SECOND LAST LAYER

FAIRING LAYERS BEFORE PLANING OFF

FASTENINGS DO NOT CROSS CENTRE-LINE SO CANNOT FOUL FASTENING OPPOSITE

STEM OR STERN-POST

Hood end fastenings. Even with the best glue it is usual to put in some metal fastenings, especially in critical areas such as at the plank ends. By setting the fastenings through the penultimate layer of planking the work of stopping in over their heads is eliminated and the planking looks better, especially if varnished. The fastenings should be long enough to get a secure grip into the backbone, but not so long as to come out on the inside, or to cross the centreline where they might foul fastenings on the other side.

The backbone is finished off with extra laminates to cover the plank ends, and a few fastenings might be put in on the centreline to secure them. These extra laminates will be planed fair and normally rounded at the edges.

the moulds. A piece of planking long enough to straddle several battens is laid diagonally across them so that its end lies on the backbone. It should just touch the plank landing area without being forced down onto the backbone. If the backbone causes this trial piece to lift off the nearest batten the landing should be carefully faired away. It is important to make this test on port and starboard over the whole length of the hull.

However, there is one case where this final test cannot be used: if the hull has what might be called a 'contrived' shape, that is a form which has a lot of curvature in an athwartships direction near the backbone, either concave or sharply convex, it will be necessary to make up templates for the final fairing. They are made from the mould loft floor and may be of scrap ply or template wood; the heavy paper or card used elsewhere for templates will seldom be satisfactory. One template will do for the port and starboard sides at a given point, and a different one may be needed for each station. The backbone is faired between these points.

SPACE-FRAMES

There is an unusual type of backbone that is entirely separate from the hull; the planks are not attached directly to it. Instead, the boat's outer shell is first made using a light, thin keel, stem etc which are just man enough to take the plank ends but not strong enough to withstand the major forces on a finished boat. The powerful stresses are handled by a special space-frame, which is a structure inside the hull designed solely for doing hard work and not for helping to keep out the water. The space-frame will often be built outside the boat and lowered into place before the deck is fitted.

On a powerboat the space-frame has to support the weight, torque and thrust of the engines. The engine bearers will be the major parts of the framework, and probably the earliest forms of space-frame were in fast double-diagonal planked high-speed motorboats built for racing, air/sea rescue work and similar jobs. Their engine bearers were carried right forward to stiffen the hull and cope with the pounding on the bottom. Aft extensions of the bearers took the A-bracket, rudder pads and so on. This just about sums up the jobs the space-frame in a power boat has to do, so it might be assumed that the whole framework was just a set of extra-long engine bearers. However, for maximum strength and minimum weight – which is the objective in using a space-frame – it is best to have the deepest possible structure: the way to get this is to have the top members up at deck level and the bottom ones as low as possible.

Coping with all the loadings on a sail-driven hull calls for the same basic approach, but there are more high-stress points. The down-thrust of the mast, the upward pull of the shrouds, forestay and backstays, and the massive load of the keel all have to be matched by parts of the space-frame. To make life more complex there are sideways forces on the keel and rudder, while the big loads on sheet winches and mooring strongpoints must not be forgotten. This is an area where, as so often happens, naval architecture becomes structural engineering. To get the most sophisticated space-frame, large-diameter thin-wall light aluminium tubes are sometimes used, joined together with big flanged brackets welded all round and peppered with lightening holes. This is not a cheap form of construction, though some money can be saved by using steel instead of light alloy, at the cost of greater weight however. A wooden space-frame

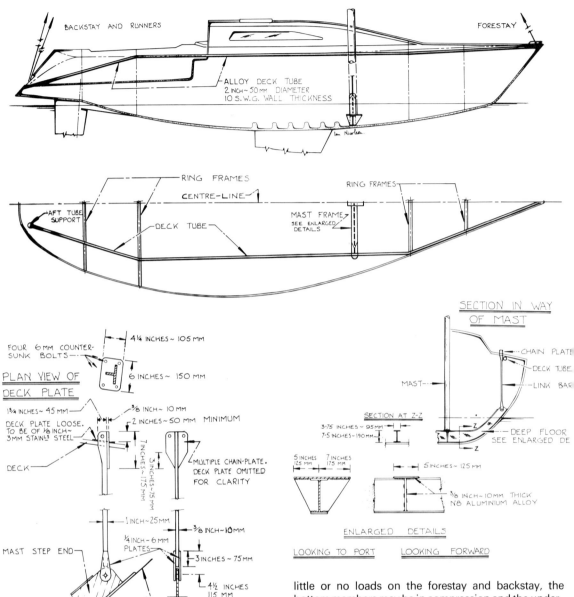

BACKSTAY AND RUNNERS

FORESTAY

ALLOY DECK TUBE
2 INCH ~ 50 MM DIAMETER
10 S.W.G. WALL THICKNESS

RING FRAMES

CENTRE-LINE

RING FRAMES

AFT TUBE SUPPORT

DECK TUBE

MAST FRAME
SEE ENLARGED DETAILS

FOUR 6 MM COUNTER-SUNK BOLTS

4¼ INCHES ~ 105 MM

6 INCHES ~ 150 MM

PLAN VIEW OF
DECK PLATE

1¾ INCHES ~ 45 MM

⅜ INCH ~ 10 MM

2 INCHES ~ 50 MM MINIMUM

DECK PLATE LOOSE.
TO BE OF ⅛ INCH ~
3MM STAINLESS STEEL

DECK

3 INCHES ~ 75 MM

7 INCHES ~ 175 MM

MULTIPLE CHAIN-PLATE.
DECK PLATE OMITTED
FOR CLARITY

MAST STEP END

1 INCH ~ 25 MM

¼ INCH ~ 6 MM
PLATES

⅜ INCH ~ 10MM

3 INCHES ~ 75 MM

4½ INCHES
115 MM

INSIDE OF
HULL SHELL

LOOKING FORWARD

LOOKING ATHWARTSHIPS

SECTION IN WAY
OF MAST

CHAIN PLATE

DECK TUBE

MAST

LINK BAR

SECTION AT Z-Z

3·75 INCHES ~ 95 MM

7·5 INCHES ~ 190 MM

DEEP FLOOR
SEE ENLARGED DE

5 INCHES
125 MM

7 INCHES
175 MM

5 INCHES ~ 125 MM

⅜ INCH ~ 10MM THICK
N8 ALUMINIUM ALLOY

ENLARGED DETAILS

LOOKING TO PORT   LOOKING FORWARD

little or no loads on the forestay and backstay, the bottom members may be in compression and the under-deck units in tension. All this has to be remembered when designing each component.

The pair of 2in (50mm) fore-and-aft aluminium tubes are joined to four athwartships strength members, of which the principal one is the mast support structure, shown in detail below. The mid-span of the fore-and-aft tubes is secured to the deck in three equally spaced places between the second and the third ring frames. Other materials including wood could be used. Because the space-frame takes all the principal loads normally imposed on the hull the shell can be made relatively thin and light, though it is thus more vulnerable to damage.

An example of a space-frame is seen in this drawing of a Rob Humphrey Half-Tonner. Many such space-frames have components along the bottom of the inside of the hull (to match the set under the deck), which help to contain the keel loads and act in tension when there is severe strain on the headstay and backstay. When the boat is supported by her keel, or when grounding, with

Aluminium space-frame in the 30ft light displacement *Alice's Mirror*, designed and built as a shorthanded racer by Adrian Thompson. The double-spreader fractional rig is supported on this frame: the tubing acts as compression struts joined at the ends by brackets incorporating chainplates for the rod headstay and shrouds, and shorter rods underneath connecting them back to the mast heel plate. The mast is stepped just forward of the athwartships tube and main bulkhead with the shrouds angled back 12°.

The hull was cold-moulded using SP Systems epoxy resins, from three 3.5mm layers on spruce stringers, 25 × 20mm for the hull and 20 × 15mm deck. Laminated ring frames at 60cm centres are spruce, Brazilian mahogany or American ash depending on position and function. Bulkheads and furniture are also designed to stiffen the hull, as is shown in the additional photos later in this book (page 173).

has the virtue of being cheaper still in most boatbuilding yards, and it can often be worked into the hull more comfortably, but again there is likely to be an increase in weight compared to aluminium.

A tubular metal space-frame is likely to end up making the inside of the boat look like the interior of a fighter plane, unless she is over about 45ft (14m) in which case it may be possible to blend all the tubes into the other structure and hide them below the sole and behind lining or bulkheads. But then of course space-frames are for out-and-out performance craft, so there is not likely to be much in the way of lining or bulkheads: in the end even the biggest craft which has a space-frame is likely to be somewhat harshly practical in appearance below decks. In smaller craft it becomes difficult to arrange a reasonable accommodation in and around the tubes. A boat less than 30ft (9m) overall with a full tubular space-frame is almost bound to be uncomfortable unless the designer is skilled and prepared to make an extra elaborate and expensive structure. Using wood may help, but above all the furniture has to be made to provide some strength, as bunk or galley fronts, cabin sole, and so on. Settee fronts may be run forward to form sail locker fronts, and run aft to become first the inboard vertical panel of the chart table and then the engine bearers. These fore-and-afters will be matched overhead by longitudinals possibly bolted to coachroof coamings and aft to the sides of the cockpit well. All the fore-and-aft members will be bracketed to bulkheads stiffened with pillars, pierced by small doorways with semi-circular ends, and there will be triangular brackets at many of the joins, even if these limit the length of the settees which can be used for sitting upon.

Where the scantling is in pure tension, such as from the deck down to the stem in way of an inner forestay, a length of high-tensile rod rigging may be used. But sometimes there are also upward loadings here, as in an offshore boat which pounds down into waves, or falls off the top of a crest and plunges towards the trough, or plunges at her mooring. So a large diameter tube is likely to be required even in places which at first seem to have no compression loads.

The main fore-and-aft members in a sail-driven yacht will usually taper and converge at the ends, to take the forestay and backstay chainplates. This tapering together is in plan and elevation. The extreme bow and stem are high-stress regions where structure does not obtrude into usable accommodation so vast brackets can be incorporated, to considerable advantage because the use of hydraulic stay tensioners results in some massive loads.

The design of a space-frame can in theory be done by anyone familiar with stressing calculations, but it is likely that the first attempt will not give the best strength/weight ratio which is the objective of all the work and no little expense. So it is best to use a computor to try out a variety of alternatives quickly, to see which is the most effective. There are technical organizations like the National Engineering Laboratory, East Kilbride, near Glasgow and Y-ARD (Yarrow – Admiralty Research Department) of Charing Cross, Glasgow which are practiced in this sort of technology. Other sources of help are the applied sciences departments of universities.

Where it is metal, the first inclination will be to use a large number of small bolts to secure the space-frame tube or flanges to the hull shell. If wood is the main material of the space-frame it will be natural to decide on epoxy bonding. My own inclination is to use glassfibre, glue and metal fastenings, though this combination is against the rules of pure mechanics. However, the sea is no respecter of theoretical calculations, and a great one for springing nasty surprises. Naturally the finished strength of the joins must be as great if not greater than the strength of the components linked together. For the strength of a join to be adequate its properties must be calculated at the same time as the space-frame. The bolted join strength is calculated at the same time. To avoid excessive costs and weight of materials, fastenings and so on, the fibreglassed join may be calculated with a factor of safety of 1, and the bolting likewise. The combined factor of safety will not be 2, but should be made well above 1.5.

Planking Dimensions and Direction

Though wide veneers make for quick laminating, narrow ones reduce the amount of fairing. Where the hull lacks curvature at right angles to the planks' length, the pieces can be widest. It is therefore logical to have different widths, as wide as possible on the flat areas and just narrow enough elsewhere to cope with the bold curves. When buying sawn planks it will be best to stick to one width to save money, but veneer arrives in different widths anyway. Once the planks have arrived from the mill some of them can be rip-sawed lengthways to half their width for the sharply curved regions. Or it may pay to rip them at one-third and two-thirds the width. For this sort of work a circular saw on its own bench is an asset, and the hand-held type less useful.

For a boat about 22ft (6.5m) long the planks will typically be about 3in (75mm) wide; a 45ft (14m) hull will probably be built of 6in (150mm) planks. Much will depend on the width of timber easily available. There is no point in selecting say $3\frac{1}{2}$in planks when the supplier has plenty of 4in timber which will conveniently finish off at $3\frac{7}{8}$in after machining. It is a mistake to go for very wide planks even if the laminates are only $\frac{3}{16}$in (5mm) thick, because it will not bend easily in two directions.

DIRECTION AND NUMBER OF LAYERS

The layers of planking can be laid horizontally or at an angle to the horizontal of usually 30° or 45°. Angled planks may slope forwards or aft. In practice the choice between 30° and 45° depends on the girth of the boat and the length of wood available. If wood can be bought economically to extend from sheer to centreline when laid at 30° to the horizontal, it is logical to select this angle. The longer the planks the quicker each layer is put on, the gentler the curves, and fewer planks are needed.

Running the planks horizontal on the outside and inside of the hull certainly gives the best appearance, especially if varnished. My own preference is so strong that I would rarely design a cold-moulded boat with diagonal planking on the outside, and only reluctantly with it visible on the inside. With the best will in the world and with the maximum skill, it is unusual for diagonal planking to give that perfect appearance of good horizontal

planking. However, diagonal layup is quicker and hence cheaper, so a compromise might consist of horizontal on the outside and 30° sloped planking on the inside of the hull with the hidden inner skins at 30° or 45° to the horizontal.

It is unusual to run two successive layers of planking in the same direction with seams staggered, though the idea has theoretical advantages. About the only time this is done is when only two skins are used and then they are usually both put on horizontally. A number of 6 Metre racing yachts have been built in the past using this technique but it is not recommended. It calls for an extra high standard of skill and seems to produce problems such as leaking in later years. It needs a fairly full set of frames, too.

If the *outside* planking is not horizontal it should slope from the sheer aft and down. It is bad enough when the seams or grain show through the

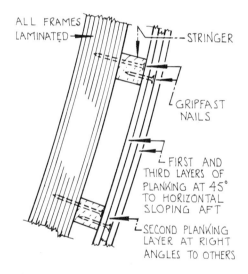

For minimum weight and maximum strength this planking/frame combination is hard to beat. Because boats (at least under 60ft or so) normally have ample longitudinal strength all the planking is laid diagonally. The stringers give ample fore-and-aft strength and the frames give athwartships rigidity.

Barbed (Gripfast) nails are lighter and cheaper than screws besides being quicker to drive, so they are used throughout the planking and stringering. As the heads are all covered, since the second layer of planking is nailed, there is no stopping or dowelling needed. The quality of the nailing must be perfect.

paint or varnish if diagonal outside planking is used, but if it is laid so that it slopes downwards and forwards the result is most unattractive, and detracts from the value as well as the appearance of the boat. On varnished hulls the forward downward slope of the grain is an irritating sight.

Three layers of planking is the most common, but for a boat working off a beach, where she is likely to be pounded, or in an offshore racing hull consideration might be given to five layers. A 50-footer designed for extended cruising might also have five layers since her planking could well be of the order of $1\frac{1}{2}$in (38mm) thick and each layer would be of the order of $\frac{5}{16}$in thick (7mm). This is too thick to be edge-trimmed with a knife but it is thin enough to work into a moderate reverse turn.

Summing up: there is a conflict between (a) a natural wish to keep down the number of laminates, in which case almost certainly three layers will be used, and (b) knowing that the layers should be thin enough to work easily, in which case the number will be built up to the required thickness using layers of wood around $\frac{1}{8}$in (3mm) thick. Some designers and builders like to compromise by varying the total thickness. They go for three layers over most of the hull area but fit an extra one or even two where the stresses are high, around the ballast keel in a sailing yacht or by the engine bearers in a powerboat. Generally, the additional layer will be put on inside once the main shell is complete. If it is laid on first and then other layers built up later, a rather special mould will be needed and there may be problems at the edge of the extra layer. My own view is that the extra laminate added locally is seldom as good as other methods of stiffening, such as the addition of 'leaf spring' floors (see later section on Floors) or extra framing and stringers. The extra layer is almost certainly more expensive and takes more time than

simpler local stiffening.

Up to this point, the discussion has been mainly from the designer's point of view, as he normally lays down the number and direction of laminates. If the plans are being adapted by a builder he is advised to get help from a professional designer who is used to altering construction plans from normal carvel to cold-moulded, though he may still want to state his preference, especially if he has a stock of timber to be used, or is short of help so that he cannot handle long floppy pieces of wood.

Very large numbers of layers seldom make sense. Even a 70-footer (21m) with planking finished to perhaps 2in (50mm) thickness will not have more than seven layers unless there are special circumstances, such as a quantity of timber cut thin and plenty of cheap labour. As with many things, a trial run is most valuable in helping to come to a decision. It is hardly possible to make the test on the boat to be built, but say a cold-moulded cabin top does not take long to put together and gives useful experience.

To sum up: three layers is most common, especially with boats under 40ft (12m), two thicker layers is rare but if there is to be Cascover sheathing it has advantages in minimizing the amount of glue, staples, timber wastage, man-hours and so on. Four layers is a good compromise and allows thin easy planking which can be trimmed with a knife if needed: four plies of $\frac{1}{8}$in (3mm) has been successful in ocean racers. By the time we got to five and more layers of planking either the boat must be big, say over 50ft (15.3m), or there most be a special reason for incurring so much work.

Other aspects of the subject of planking are covered in the earlier section 'How Thick, Wide and Close'.

Planking Procedure

As the majority of boats are built up with three layers of cold-moulded planking with the inside one laid at 45°, this sequence is described here. It needs the obvious modification if the middle layers is at 30° or runs fore-and-aft, or there are four layers.

The 45° angle is pencilled from the hog across the ribbands right to the sheer, starting amidships for the first plank; the mirror image line is marked

on the boat's opposite side. Check for direction: if there are to be three layers the inside one must run from the hog forwards to the sheer at 45° to the horizontal. The first plank is laid along this line, using the shortest piece of veneer which will extend from hog to sheer with just a little over for handling (this minimizes waste). Offcuts and short lengths are used at bow and stern where the girth is small, or for centre (buried) layers.

Some builders fit each plank in turn and glue it when it is fitted. Others fit a whole batch temporarily, number and remove them, apply glue and fix them all down as a group. Working on the first method, the first plank is glued and stapled to the hog, then pulled tight round the girth and secured near the sheer. A plank must never coggle (twist unfairly) or buckle (kink), so it is not forced to lie exactly along the 45° line. If it refuses to lie flat it is too wide: slice off a third of the width.

The sheer end is secured and surplus glue wiped away. Close alongside the first plank is set the second, on the forward or aft side: work in the easier direction first. It is held temporarily to the hog by clamps, two half-driven nails or weights, or by hand with more of the same at the sheer. With luck the new plank will lie exactly alongside the first one and can be promptly and finally secured in place with glue and staples. If it doesn't snuggle up with no gap between it and the first plank it must be fitted by spiling. This involves marking the edge of the second plank for trimming so that it will match exactly the first one. The second plank is taken off the hull and cut to the marked line, by saw if a lot needs taking off and here a bandsaw or sabre saw is a help. Thin veneers may be trimmed

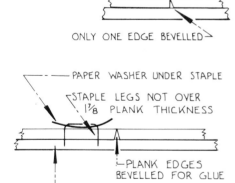

ONLY ONE EDGE BEVELLED

PAPER WASHER UNDER STAPLE

STAPLE LEGS NOT OVER 1⅞ PLANK THICKNESS

PLANK EDGES BEVELLED FOR GLUE

INNER PLANKING

Planking up: the second layer has been glued and stapled onto the first. Since in due course the staples will be removed thick paper or cardboard is put under them. Once the glue between the planking is dry all the staples are removed using either a special tool or a screwdriver of just the right width and sharpness.

Some builders bevel edges slightly so that glue is trapped in the recess. To save time there is no need to bevel both edges of both planks since the precise shape of the recess is not important. The top sketch shows only one plank edge bevelled.

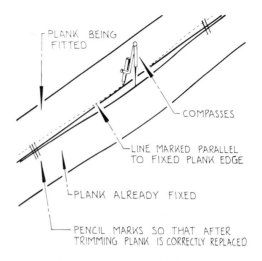

PLANK BEING FITTED

COMPASSES

LINE MARKED PARALLEL TO FIXED PLANK EDGE

PLANK ALREADY FIXED

PENCIL MARKS SO THAT AFTER TRIMMING PLANK IS CORRECTLY REPLACED

To get a plank to lie close to its neighbour without a gap it is planed along the edge to the correct curve. This curve is marked by spiling, which can be done with a set of stiff compasses. The spike of the compass is run along the fixed plank edge while the pencil marks the new plank.

If a saw, shears or a knife are used to trim the veneer a little wood should be left so that the final triming is done with a plane. The plank being fitted is held temporarily in place at the hog, where the end should first be cut to fit. As a check that the plank is correctly located when replaced after trimming, pencil ticks marks are made across the fixed and the new plank.

with a knife or shears. The cut must not be right up against the spiled pencil line; the final cleaning off is done with a plane to avoid a ragged edge. Where it meets the hog each plank has to have the end cut at the correct angle so as to lie on the centreline of the hog or tight into the rebate. The sheer ends are left rough and overlength for trimming later when all the veneers are on and the hull is the right way up.

The new plank is fitted back on and should be accurate to $\frac{1}{16}$in (1.5mm) or less if using epoxy glue and for middle layers. For other glues less than half that gap is acceptable, and whatever glue is used there should be no visible gap between the edges of planks on the outer and inner surfaces of the hull. The plank ends at the stem begin as on the hog. At the transom the plank ends are run on as at the sheer, for trimming off later.

If there are a lot of people available for planking four teams can work at once, two each on the port side and starboard side, one lot working forward from the first plank and the other aft towards the transom. This will give very swift work, but there must be plenty of communication! The planking everywhere must be tightly laid and pinned down so that no edge shows even the suspicion of a lift. With only one team it will be best to work over about a sixth or at most a quarter of one side of the hull and then go to the other. This will eliminate chances of distortion. If each layer is planked up in eight stages, starting amidships port then going to admiships starboard and so on there will be a neat balance of weight and tension. However, where the planking layers overlap the hog (see sketch) there will be a wait while the glue sets enough to allow the excess overlap to be trimmed off on one side before putting on the opposite layer.

If the planking is being laid at say 45° there may be a tendency for this angle to vary. When the planking does not show this does not matter much, but it should not be allowed to develop to beyond say 60° or 30°. On the outer skin the planks must be sweetly laid and not be allowed to vary much more than 5° to either side. Even such small variations should be gently phased over plenty of length, so as not to offend the eye.

If the outer skin is run horizontally it must be laid with a lot of care so that it looks sweet and fair. The greatest girth of the hull is measured and the plank widths divided into this. If the maximum girth works out at 8ft and the planks are 4in wide there will be 24 planks round the girth, assuming none are reduced at all. The girths are also measured at each end of the waterline and again halfway between the greatest girth and the waterline ends. All these girths are divided into the same number of planks as the greatest girth, which in our example is 24, so on this hull 24 divisions are marked round the girth at each measuring point and perhaps at some intermediate stations, and joined up to show the run of planking. If these lines are followed it will mean that every plank has a great deal of taper towards each end and many will have a lot of 'set' or twist. The planking is therefore rearranged so that the seams are fair and sweet over the topsides with a limited amount of taper. Below the waterline the planking is re-arranged so that it can be put in economically, with the necessary amount of taper. A few planks may be tapered away short of the bow and stern. Sometimes when planking fore and aft the top plank is parallel to the sheer and has no taper. If it does taper it should narrow towards both ends, and the widest part should be at or near the lowest

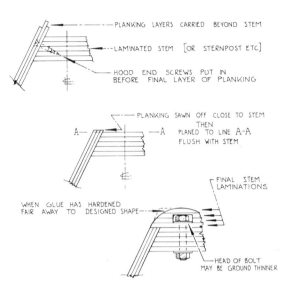

The fore-and-aft ends of the planks are called the 'hood ends'. One method of finishing them which is particularly quick and easy is shown here. The planks are run on, that is not finished neatly but left extending beyond the stem or sternpost. When the glued layers have cured and are all one they are cut back almost flush with the stem. A plane is used to make the ends exactly flush with the stem and extra stem laminations are added. Some bolts may already be through the stem, but others are added. The final layers cover the bolt heads, saving the need to dowel the holes. Surface damage to the stem is easily repaired by removing the outer layer and fitting a new one.

It may be necessary to grind the bolt heads thin, so that they are only as thick as one laminate. Notice how the hood end screws are put on before the final layer of planking to save dowelling or filling the screw heads. This gives a perfect finish with the grain unblemished and is particularly suited to varnished topsides.

point of the sheer; the aft taper will often be smaller than the foward one.

If the outer layer of planking is varnished it is important to match up adjacent planks for colour and tone. In fact all outer topside planks which are varnished should be made to match as closely as possible. If some are dark and others light it will be best to bleach the whole topsides and possibly stain them before varnishing. If this is not practical the darkest planks should be at the sheer on a horizontally planked boat and the rest gradually get lighter towards the waterline. With diagonal planking the darkest planks should be either at the bow, becoming progressively lighter towards the stern, or amidships with the change of shade blending gently towards bow and stern. Any change of shade should be slow and subtle. If a plank seems quite a different colour to others it may be sapwood, especially if it is lighter. Best reject this one, or if it is definitely not sapwood make sure it is used in hidden laminations. Burn sapwood before it is used by accident.

For the very best varnished topsides a wide piece should be selected and marked for cutting into numbered planks. They are then laid on in the same sequence as they were cut. The topsides will

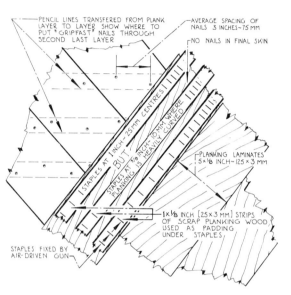

The last layer of planking on this McGruer built three-quarter tonner (approx 34ft or 10.3m) is being put on with close-spaced wood strips under heavy stapling. The man with the staple gun has to go mad in areas where the hull is heavily curved, to make sure the planking is very thoroughly held down until the glue has hardened. Staples must be very close wherever there is doubt about the planking lying totally flat.

The planking here forms a thin shell on a strong framework of stringers and athwartships frames. Grip-fast barbed nails into the permanent stringers are put through the first two layers of planking. Since the stringers are covered their location is marked on the first line of planking as it is applied. Then as the second layer goes on each piece in turn is marked with the lines of the stringers.

If by accident these pencil marks are forgotten, a thin hole may be drilled from the inside out, every few metres down the centre of each stringer. These holes are plugged with non-corroding nails after being joined by pencil lines which mark the location of the centre of each stringer.

appear to have been carved from a solid block of wood, the grain running continuously from bow to stern, as though the tree were cut and hollowed since there is no discontinuity from sheer to waterline. If .the log has colour variations the darkest part should be at the sheer. This is boatbuilding to a superlative standard and is prized beyond monetary terms.

There are quite a number of possible variations in planking procedure. For instance the inner and outer skins might be at 30° to the horizontal and the middle layer horizontal, making only a small change of angle between adjacent layers. This causes less tension if the planking gets wet and tries to swell. Fitting a middle layer fore and aft calls for little skill in the way of tapering out the ends, but it will still be necessary to make sure that the whole area is tightly covered and no edges stand up unfairly, especially on sharply curved or indented areas.

Another basic planking technique consists of laying alternate pieces, starting amidships and working towards bow and stern. Assuming the planks are 3in wide then a complete set is laid with a gap between adjacent pairs of just under 3in. These first planks are only secured in a temporary way. New planks are laid over the gaps and spiled on both edges, all the planks are very carefully numbered and marked for alignment, and all the spiled ones are trimmed to fit. There is now a complete set of fitting planks which must be carefully stacked in the correct numbered order. Plank up in the usual way, making sure that there is a surplus of glue at every join: everywhere glue is applied it should ooze out all round the join just to prove that there are no voids between plank faces or edges. *In this form of building there can be few more serious defects than voids or air bubbles in the glue.*

Securing the edge of the planking at the sheer calls for some thought. It can of course be fastened direct to the inwale if this has been fitted, but this assumes that the moulds are to be taken apart to get them out of the hull. If this does not suit the builder he may finish the edges of the planks, along the line that will be near the sheer, by securing them to the bottom riband. This will be farther down towards the floor than the sheer. Once the boat is the right way up the sheer is marked and the inwale fitted. The surplus top edge of the hull plus the top batten is then cut away. The idea here is to have a firm base which holds the staples in the plank ends. It does mean an extra 2 or 3in (50 or 75mm) height over the whole length of the sheer which is wasted, but against this it means that the top edge of the planking is almost certainly well made as the layers can be properly supported and held together for gluing.

Any plank may be butt-joined, provided care is taken to stagger the butts and locate them on ribbands when applying the first layer of planking. This prevents the plank ends sagging inwards. Butts on the outside should be kept below the waterline where they will not show. If the outer planks are scarphed up to make adequate lengths and are to be varnished it is best to use a colourless glue otherwise the fairing up of the scarphs will show a glued area which will not be elegant. A mild split along the grain in an inner layer of planking is not critical provided plenty of glue is worked in.

The job of cleaning off excess glue has to keep up with the fixing down of the plies. With epoxy glues there is a 'green' or semi-set toffee-like stage where the glue can be removed fairly easily, without sticking to everything else or pulling out of a seam. With other glues one may have to clean off earlier or later: this is something to work out when making up preliminary test pieces. Cleaning off the inside of the hull allows for tight-fitting stringers, etc as well as a far better appearance; cleaning off the outside of each skin after it's laid is necessary for the successive layers to fit tightly without voids. It may also be necessary to do a little smoothing off, using a long flexible sanding block after the glue has set and staples have been removed, before starting to fit the next layer.

Combined Strip-planked and Cold-moulded Construction

The use in combination of these two techniques is relatively new and further development is likely. It is attractive as a way of building up a substantial hull thickness without the need for normal carvel planking or very many layers of cold-moulding. When it comes to rough weather and hard driving ample plank thickness is an asset, and even more so if there is flotsam about.

Strip-planking is usually in one layer run fore and aft, and the timber is shaped differently from that used for cold-moulding. Strip planks are seldom more than twice as wide as they are thick, whereas cold-moulding veneer or planking is seldom less than eight times as wide as it is thick, i.e. comparatively wide and thin. If strip-planking is properly bonded with well fitted planks the resulting stiffness is equal to that of a cold-moulded shell, and the method is in theory quicker. However, its disadvantages are that all the seams run fore and aft and therefore any seam failure or damage is in the worst direction may 'travel' along the seam and can be difficult to repair. Probably the most worrying problem with combination planking is still the difficulty and awkwardness of repair. When only the cold-moulded layers are damaged it is not hard to make a good job of renewing the area using the usual cold-moulding procedures. But if a hole or other damage is deep or right through it could be a long job, especially if the seams in the strip-planking have been disturbed.

The techniques of strip-plank construction and repairing are discussed more fully in a later chapter: the following is concerned with the combined method.

For boats over about 40ft (12m) a combination of a layer of strip-planking followed by one, two or even three skins of cold-moulded veneers is worth considering. Below this size the advantages are not likely to outweigh the extra work; there is not only the need to master two techniques, but more tools and timber stock are required. For professionals this may not matter, but for amateurs building a single boat it will add cost and probably time spent learning new skills.

The building procedure starts as usual with setting up the moulds and backbone. If cold-moulding were to follow, fore-and-aft battens would then be put over them, close-spaced to take the first veneer layer. Instead, the inner shell of strip-planking run longitudinally is built on. Battens would be a waste of time, since they are not needed to support the strips and not part of the final hull unless left in as multiple stringers.

It is vital to clean off the strip-planking well and smooth any ridges at plank edges before putting on the veneer layers; but then this also has to be done for every layer of cold-moulding, and when the two are combined the chances are that the total amount of cleaning off is less than with pure cold-moulding.

I am not tempted to say that combining cold-moulding with strip-planking is any sort of a cure-all, or allows for a lower standard of work for either. If I did make some such suggestion builders would be less careful or try to take risky short-cuts. There is no substitute for doing the best possible work and this is what makes wooden boatbuilding so satisfying. But it may be whispered that a beginner can feel less worried if he makes little mistakes when using this combined method. The veneers help to 'bind' the strip-planking and the epoxy glue fills any tiny slits left in the seams. The cold-moulded layers also act as strapping over the strip-planking, giving important strength across the seams (just where the weakness lies) which will therefore not need quite so many fastenings.

As with all types of woodwork where there are hidden fastenings, planning is needed to avoid trouble during later stages of building. No-one cutting out a hole for a skin fitting likes to ruin the edge of a tool on concealed nails. So the location of all hull through-fittings should be marked at each stage of the planking, and the strip-planking fastenings kept clear.

If, as is likely, a fairly soft wood is used for the strip-planking, it may pay to substitute a hard-wood at the sheer, in way of chainplates and perhaps port-lights, maybe down at the garboards and by the floors, around the rudder tube etc.

One of the problems of normal strip-planking is the difficulty of dealing with an open seam. It is so hard to run in glue, which is the best cure, unless the boat is small enough to lay on her side so that the glue runs in under gravity. Coaxing glue into a horizontal seam is a slow and awkward job. It is a temptation to leave the gap, but a separation of one-thousandth of an inch is just as weakening as a half-inch gap: the join is broken and has no strength; it is also a potential site for rot. With the combined method there is little risk of the strip-plank seam opening farther, and even if it does there is a good chance the opening will remain sealed and secured across by the cold-moulding. But both types of skinning must be well done.

Frameless Construction

It is possible to build a boat which has no frames or stringers. The strength of the hull shell, made just from ample layers of cold-moulding veneers, is enough to deal with the stresses of weather, racing, bumping alongside quay walls and so on. The technique is simple and most commonly used for small, light boats such as tenders or sailing dinghies. In larger craft the hull skin has to be made with extra layers to take loads imposed by engines, masts, ballast keels and so on. For instance, there may be four veneers all over, but five from the waterline downwards, and a sixth over the middle third of the vessel for perhaps 3ft (1m) up either side. Other doubling or additional strengthening is put in way of the chainplates, around the rudder tube, perhaps in way of a mast step or bulkhead, and to take the local loads when on a trailer or cradle.

A frameless boat will almost certainly not be lightest possible one. She is, however, likely to be one of the best looking. The interior of a boat which has been superbly laminated with selected woods and then varnished is breathtaking. Lines of unblemished grain running through the accommodation need no further painting or lining.

It is also convenient to have no frames or stringers round which furniture has to be joggled. Cleatings to take furniture parts are glued on, perhaps with some screws, where needed. The time taken to make and fit furniture should be reduced, and there will be none of those infuriating slots at the backs of lockers where small objects can slip through and down into the bilge. Cleaning and varnishing or painting are easier in a smooth interior. There is also a tiny gain in space, since the boat will not have frames obtruding, so the available room will be wider by twice the frames' thickness, less the thickness of the additional veneers needed to make up the required strength. In a boat say 22ft (7m) overall this gain of perhaps 2in (5cm) is useful, but in a boat 32ft (10m) long the advantage is hardly worth considering.

When it comes to fitting an engine the frames can be a nuisance. They may force the designer to raise the engine higher than he would normally wish, and this can raise problems with the angle of the shaft. Engine makers specify the maxmim angle at which the engine can be installed; it is usually 10° though there are plenty of exceptions. So a lack of frames may be a help if the engine has to be well aft because it can be set lower. But under no circumstances can an engine be tight down onto the hull, not just because of vibration: the sump is full of oil which gets hot and if there is no circulation of air over-heating may occur, especially if no sump oil cooler is fitted. Also, even a small amount of bilgewater can reach the engine and cause damage or wet the electrics.

It is hard to say whether the total building time will be less for a frameless hull. If several boats are being built by professionals, it is likely that each one would be turned out quicker than if frames were fitted.

I have seen one or two yachts built with no frames and no sole in the fo'c'sle; the crew walked about on the inside of the hull shell. This is a subtle way of saving a little weight and building time as well as improving the headroom. I've seen the same idea carried further near amidships, with wide glued-in laminated floors carried well up the hull sides. Between the floors were solid chocks glued in to form a sole. This kept the crew's feet as low as possible so that there was full headroom with only a low cabin-top. Not so good is the total absence of space for bilgewater: even a little water inside then makes itself obtrusive.

The earlier chapter on calculating hull strength shows why a frameless hull has to be heavier than one with frames or stringers. A frame with the adjacent planking forms a deep T-beam section. Take away the frame and the vertical stiffener of the T-beam has been removed, so the 'cross-bar' (the planking) has to be a great deal thicker to make up for the lost strength. (Repairing a damaged frameless hull may necessitate adding some framing, possibly over quite a large area.) But hull weight is not the only consideration when building a boat, certainly not when the boat is something super-special. What may be more important is that surge of spirit which every right-minded person has who sees the interior of a fine cold-moulded hull. If the cabin stretches fore and aft unblemished, glinting with varnished golden-grained wood, it makes the blood pound faster. Visitors give a gasp of admiration. This is fine boatbuilding.

PART 5

FRAMES, FLOORS AND BEAMS

Turning Over the Hull

Often it is easier to build a boat upside down: almost the only snag is that she has to be turned over for completion. Inverting can be done a dozen ways and much depends on the gear and experience available. Professionals will have overhead lifting tackle; amateurs have to use their ingenuity and whatever help and equipment are at hand.

I once built a boat in Nova Scotia and when I wanted to bolt on the ballast keel we picked the boat up by hand and laid her on her side! She was 30ft long, planked with $\frac{7}{8}$in fir, with a heavy cabin top and a stout backbone: she must have weighed about $1\frac{1}{2}$ tons. I have to admit I was helped by a boatyard full of shipwrights, a storeman, some fitters and so on. Not ordinary people, but Nova Scotians. These men, each with a lifetime spent among boats, had an uncanny understanding of the problem. They just stood round the boat in a cheerful crowd, shoulder to shoulder. At a given word they all lifted in unison with little apparent effort. The ground had been prepared beforehand with a double layer of old mattresses and similar padding. The men lifted only a little at a time, and no unnecessary height. They set the boat down gently, with a remarkable mixture of strength, skill and timing.

After I had bolted on the keel the process was reversed. The boat was stood 'on her feet' by hand without the aid of a single piece of mechanical lifting tackle. A few beams slid in athwartship were used to give everyone a good grip. It was a remarkable demonstration of that innate ability which good shipwrights seem to posses. I thought it was most unusual, but recently I heard about a 36ft cold-moulded hull weighing about 1700lbs (770kg) being turned over by a mixture of professional and amateur muscle-power. This must be about the top limit, and it is far better not to use this technique except for light hulls about 20ft (6m) long, unless everyone concerned is experienced in the problems involved.

It may be necessary to know the weight of the boat at the turning over stage, and the designer will be able to calculate this. There are normally three elements in the weight to be lifted: the bare hull shell, the moulds and the stringers or battens. It is sensible to add 20 per cent to the total, and the lifting tackle should have a factor of safety of 3. When summing the weights some parts of the lifting tackle may have to be included; for instance when reinforcing rafters over the hull, the weight

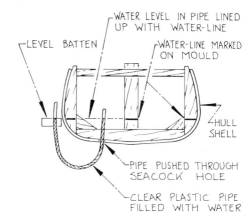

The construction moulds will have the boat's waterline marked on them, taken from the loft floor. Once the hull is level in all directions, transfer the waterline to the outside of the upright hull by using a piece of transparent plastic hose filled with water as a level. The hose is pushed through a hole in the hull, such as is left for a seacock. Hold one end up inside and lift the other till the water level inside is in line with the waterline marked on the moulds. Using a spirit level or batten held in line with the water level on the outside of the hull, make a pencil mark on the hull. Repeat this mark all round, port and starboard, at about 1ft (30cm) intervals, and also transfer the waterline to the inside surface in a few places. Join up the marks with a smooth curve.

It may help to stain the water in the tube with ink or dye, to make it easier to see. This job needs two people, one to watch the level inside and one on the outside.

of chain blocks has to be supported by the rafters.

The weight of a cold-moulded hull with no framing or stringers at the turning over stage will be roughly:

Length in feet × mean girth × hull plank thickness × 5 = approximate weight in pounds.

The mean girth is found by measuring the girth at six equally spaced distances along the full length of the hull, adding these together and dividing by 6. Take eight stations, no. 1 at the transom, no. 8 at the stemhead, and use the middle six measurements only.

The weight in pounds of the moulds may be found by multiplying the number of moulds by 50 for a 30-footer (9m), by 100 for 40ft (12m) and 150 for 50ft (15m).

The weight in pounds of the stringers or battens will be:

$\frac{1}{3}$[Total no. of stringers × average length (in feet) × cross-section area (sq inches)]

The average length of the stringers for this purpose can be taken as 95 per cent of the hull's overall length.

To save making these calculations one might go on the assumption that *lightweight* hulls are about: 750lbs for a 30-footer, 1750lbs for 40ft and 3750lbs for 50ft. This is of course at the stage when no beams or decking have been fitted. These weights could be doubled to give a rough guess at the total 'turn-over' weight including moulds etc if a crane is being ordered. Allowances should be made if the boat is not a light type, or if the building base cannot be separated from the moulds before turning over, and so on.

Cranes are handy for turning over, and if one cannot be brought to the building site it may be possible to manoeuvre the upside-down hull onto a trolley and tow it to a crane. If a mobile crane is ordered, take care about local regulations: in Britain the person who hires a crane is liable for any damage or injury it causes from the moment it leaves its base. This calls for some rather well thought out insurance and a written agreement free from loopholes. The crane driver must be a man sympathetic to the whole operation: no horny-handed metal basher should be allowed near the crane controls.

Turning over on the building site without a crane is not difficult and need not be expensive, but it should not be rushed. 'Goalposts' have to be rigged over the boat. They can be made of timber, scaffolding or even Dexion. I have seen the strong steel uprights that supported a shed's roof used, but they were large, free from corrosion and there was no wind loading on the roof at the time. Scaffolding, Dexion, straps, props, jacks and chain hoists can be hired and sometimes steel beams too. They can also be bought second hand, through trade magazines like *Machinery Market*.

Boats up to 30ft (9m) need only two goalposts; over 50ft (5m) it is a brave man who uses less than four. They need supporting fore and aft with diagonal struts or wires, as well as diagonal stiffeners at the top corners. Stays, or wire or wood from the top of each post, outwards and downwards steady the supports and prevent collapse inwards.

I have turned a 40-footer over singlehanded, and in some ways this is ideal as there is no doubt who is in charge, no shouting or distractions, and if someone has spent the previous year building the boat his mind will be wonderfully concentrated. I used the wooden beams of the building shed. Stout wooden pillars were trimmed to the precise length and driven in under the beams, as close as possible to the boat, so that their unsupported length was as short as possible. Just enough room was left between the pillars for the hull to rotate. Wedges were driven in under the pillars and nails through the wedges ensured that vibration would not loosen anything. The pillars were also secured to the beams with a few nails.

My own view is that the goalposts should be all too plainly up to their job. But if the equipment to make them has to be specially bought it will be worth working out the minimum size which will be thoroughly adequate, to save overspending. It may then pay to call in an architect or engineer to make a few calculations.

To save time there should be a lifting tackle on each side of the boat at each goalpost. Sometimes the boat's running rigging and blocks can be used as some of the lifting gear, or chain hoists will give good mechanical advantages with ease of use. If there is a shortage of blocks one side can be designed for lowering only: ropes over the top of the goalpost beams are made fast to the hull and taken to large cleats. Though no lifting can be achieved with these ropes (unless the hull is very light and there is a crowd of assistance) this does not matter, as this is the side which is lowered, all the lifting being done on the opposite side.

The boat is moved in short, slow, gentle stages. Up she goes on one side perhaps 6in (15cm).

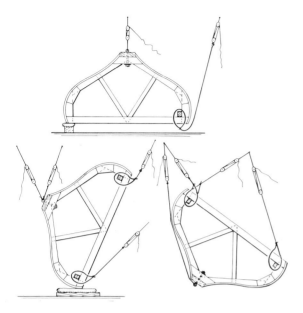

One way to turn over a hull is shown here. Eyebolts through the keel (in holes later used for the ballast keel bolts) take vertical tackles, or they may be secured to a steel bar fastened to the keel. A beam is secured near the sheer onto several moulds, to take the turning tackles, seen on the right of the top sketch. The lashings round this beam and the one later put in opposite are drawn as if they were slack, for clarity. The boat is lifted slightly off the ground and the turning tackle(s) tightened.

Extra tackles may be needed to prevent movement sideways. In the second sketch (bottom left) the weight of the boat is on two tackles (or sets of tackles) and the turning tackle(s) cannot exert much more rotating force, so a second beam is put in at the lower sheer and well fastened to several moulds, to spread the load. A tackle on this (or several tackles on a larger boat) continues the turning, and at the same time those holding the keel are eased away. In time the whole load of the boat is taken by the beams secured to the moulds. By slacking off the high side and tightening in on the other side the hull is levelled up, and the keel lowered onto blocks clear of the lifting eyebolt(s). Before slacking the tackles at least three props are secured on each side to prevent the hull tipping.

Chocks (more than two) are put under so that she cannot fall back. The other side is now lowered a similar distance, down onto prepared chocks. Up the first side again. Any tendency to slide sideways is checked with ropes made fast to the hull and passed round strongpoints (dead men) buried in the ground. These ropes are eased out slowly. They must not be round the goalposts but should be taken round anchors dug into the ground (outside the shed perhaps), or round the supports of the building *if* these are deeply cemented in.

Sacks stuffed with straw or sawdust, or old sails or mattresses, or rolls of old carpet are used to rest the hull on while the tackles are repositioned, and as the hull reaches the stage when it is lying on its side. Try to locate the resting points close by moulds, and make sure the weight is spread over three resting places at least. If old car tyres are used, cover them with cloth or plastic sheet to keep black marks off the hull.

When the boat is lowered so that she rests on her side she will have a tendency to roll, and it may be best to fix some tackle onto the verticals of the goalposts instead of the cross-beams. Slacking off any tackle is done slowly, so that any tendency to roll or get out of control will be seen before trouble can develop.

Securing ropes and lifting tackle needs thought. The chainplates of a sailing yacht are fine when the load is in the same direction as the rigging will extend. A length of angle or channel bar can be bolted where a chainplate will later be fitted, if there is a chance that the pull of a lifting tackle will bend the chainplate.

Ropes, or better straps, right round the hull both keep the shell tight onto the moulds and give convenient joining points for lifting tackle. However the lifting tackle will slide along a girth rope unless a rolling hitch or similar securing knot is used.

A T-bar or a pair of L-bars secured back to back may also be used, bolted to the backbone or the topsides. So that it spreads the load it should be about 8 per cent of the hull length with at least six through-bolts. Once the job is completed the bolt holes are plugged, but T-bars along the sheer are very useful for holding the top of props when the boat is upright. The usual props under the bilge are important, but they often have a tendency to slip out when work causing vibration is going on in the hull. The T-bars must have holes in the upstanding flange to take shackles for the lifting tackle.

If the rudder tube or stern tube holes have been drilled padded wire strops can be passed through to take lifting tackles. Eyebolts are suspect unless tested, but when turning over a boat weighing less than about 2 tons all-up, steel eyebolts through the stem or keel, or even through a well doubled part of the transom, might be used provided no more than one-quarter of the total weight is put on each one and the eyebolts are at least $\frac{1}{2}$in (12mm) thick. It needs a 2in (50mm) square plate washer to spread the load and avoid crushing the wood.

The hull must not deflect, not even slightly, when being turned over. Normally the moulds will make sure the hull does not distort, but a very light hull might first be given additional stiffening such as temporary beams between each of the moulds, over the middle half of the hull's length.

Before turning the boat over, if the rudder or fin have been fitted they should be taken off, as they protrude and make inverting more difficult. Any other weight which can be removed should also be taken off.

The whole job is done slowly and gently, with one person definitely in charge. The team should be small, dedicated, sober until the work is complete, and interested. No-one should be allowed beneath the boat, and that means that no-one stands with his feet under the hull. This is no situation for spectators, even though it is an exciting and dramatic event. Children, dogs and other extraneous animal life must be banished during the operation.

The lifting equipment must be above suspicion. One reason why chain blocks or chain hoists are favoured is that they are 'self-holding' and safe to use: when released, even when heavily loaded, they do not run back. The load is held precisely, there is not even half an inch of drop when the hoisting chain is let go. Yet moving the load a fraction up or down is easy. If ropes and blocks are used they should be new, properly secured, and the ropes ends taken to bolted cleats or tied round the whole tackle with a pair of clove hitches.

Turning a boat over is basically a matter of simple, careful preparation and observation. If anything creaks it is overloaded: spread the load, or lower back down and enlarge the lifting gear. If, as the boat is lowered onto her side, the sheer is seen to cave in, lift again and arrange more padding so that the hull weight is spread over a greater length, and at the same time leave some of the load on the lifting ropes or wires.

All along thinking is compulsory. And safety factors should be twice the number you first thought of.

Bent Framing Timbers

The lightest cheapest form of framing a boat can have is made from bent timbers. Scantlings are given at the end of this chapter. A complete set can usually be made and fitted by even a fairly inexperienced team in a weekend, more or less regardless of the size of boat. Once the completed hull shell has been turned right way up and trued up, the procedure will be something like this.

Light up the steam box to start it getting hot.
Meanwhile, the timber is cut, planed and the inboard edges (corners) bevelled.
The first batch of frames is put in the steamer. While they are heating, the inside of the hull is marked very clearly, so that in the flurry of fitting the hot frames no-one has any doubt as to where each one goes.
The first frame is taken out of the steam box and rushed to the hull, where it is fitted. First the bottom end is located, then the frame forced into place up the hull. The top is secured with a clamp while the bottom is being held with two or three nails or screws, or wedges.
Holes are drilled in the frame, from the outside through those already pre-drilled in the shell.

The fastenings are put in; there may not be time for them all, but at least every other one is driven home.

Because of the need for speed, pre-planning is essential. Two people can do this job, and one skilled man alone might succeed, but the best team is three or four. On boats over about 45ft (13m) there is more space inside and the team could be five or six. Working on smaller boats, a team of five or six is sometimes a great success if one person concentrates on keeping the steam box hot and full of timbers, another on the fastenings, and another may concentrate on preparing the timber. For the actual fitting it is a help if one person, wearing gloves, takes the hot timber from the box to the hull, where the crew inside wait to take it and secure it in place. The men inside the hull may wear gloves or have pieces of folded cloth in each hand like pot-holders.

Bent timbering is normally begun from amidships and worked towards the ends of the boat, port and starboard together. There are several objects in mind here. A few frames will break as they are forced into place: with luck a broken one can be cut down and used right forward or aft where the girth is much less, so there is no waste. Also, amidships there is more space for working, the inside of the boat is more nearly level, and it feels right to start there.

In a way this nebulous 'feel' is wrong, in that there is more curvature amidships and frames there are more difficult to force down onto the hull. For an inexperienced team it is worth first trying two or three pairs of frames right forward, where the hull has little curvature. Here they should go in with the minimum of forcing. Once say three pairs have been fitted, the team can either go on working progressively aft, or revert to convention and continue from amidships. On no account should the port side be done, along the whole length, then the starboard side: this is the way that subtle and irreparable changes of hull shape occur.

It is rare to put the bent timbers in until the hull shell has been completed and turned the right way up. In theory they could be put onto the building moulds and stringers, then the hull laminated over them. In practice the nature of bent timbers is against this procedure; they are uneven, do not lie precisely and uniformly, tend to coggle slightly in the best built boat and are altogether unruly.

There is not much choice of woods when it comes to making bent timbers. One hears of beech being used, but the practice is rarely seen in Europe. Ash is occasionally found, but it is not widely available. One of the past favourites has been Canadian rock elm, a wood which certainly does bend wonderfully when properly steamed. However, it is not resistant to rot; on the contrary it seems to make a special effort to get rotten, and positively revels in the disease once caught. In a few months the rot travels up the length of the timber, which thoughtlessly shows few outward signs of trouble. A lot of leaking and too much flexibility of the hull are sometimes the first signs of trouble. I'm not in favour of this wood.

A wood which is fairly widely available, bends properly, is tough, puts up a good fight against rot, and can be recommended is oak. It stains badly and steel must be kept away from it, but it takes fastenings well and is not too hard to work. When buying wood for bent timbers a quantity allowance of 10 per cent or more must be made for breakages.

If there are sharp turns at bilge and garboard the required size of frame may refuse to fit round the

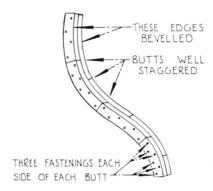

The neatest grown frames have double futtocks, made in the form of two grown frames with staggered butts. The grain in each futtock follows the curve of the hull so careful selection of the timber is needed. Ideally the futtocks should be glued together, but whether this is done or not there should be at least three staggered bolts on each side of every join. Countersunk bolts must be used if a bulkhead or furniture component is to be fitted onto the forward or aft face of a frame.

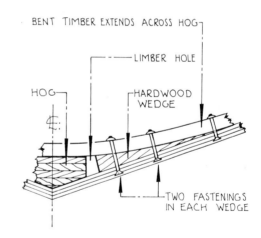

Where possible bent frames should be run across the centreline to back up the floors and help tie the shell planking to the backbone. Because the hog stands up above the planking wedge pieces must be put under the timbers, otherwise they will be unsupported and weak. The wedges should be of rot-resistant hardwood since they are right in the bilge. Limber holes at least $1\frac{1}{2}$in square are left between the wedge and the hog.

To be sure the wedge cannot twist sideways and come out from under the frame there must be at least two fastenings through. Clenches are shown but screws are sometimes used, and on craft over about 45ft (13.5m) bolts might be used.

curve. A longitudinal saw cut from the bottom end up round the sharp curve makes the job easy, but it leaves the frame much weakened, harder to fasten strongly, and in the long slit rot spores and moisture can easily accumulate. Ample Cuprinol or a similar rot preventing fluid is needed here. Use the colourless version if the wood is going to show and be varnished, but otherwise go for the stronger types which are more toxic to rot organisms.

Slitting the frames should only be done sparingly. In some respects a better technique is to plane away a little of the frame's thickness just along the sharpest part of the bend. Some compensation may be put in such as a few extra frames locally. Where the sharpest turn is at the garboard, another approach is to put in deep floors which extend up beyond the bold curve and secure the timbers to the floors.

A trick which may help bending is to increase the amount of wood taken off the inboard corners when bevelling. Normally about one-eighth the width is planed away, but this can be increased by about 50 or even 80 per cent just at the sharp bend.

It is good practice to carry the bent timbers right across the backbone where possible. Forward and possibly right aft the hull shape will usually be too veed, so the port and starboard frame feet will meet in a butt or land on a floor. But where the hull is flat-floored one frame is twisted slightly forward and carried across the centreline, the opposite one worked aft, so that along the middle of the hull over the backbone the frames lie adjacent for 2 or 3ft (60–90cm). To work this twist, and to force any frame which needs some sideways set, some boatbuilders make up a special tool. It is like a set of bicycle handlebars with a plate in the middle; in the centre of the plate is a square hole the same size as the frame. For the best grip the handlebars stick out each side and do not curl back. To force a frame in place the tool is slipped over the timber and twisted. This naturally works much more easily at the top, clear above the sheer, than at the bottom.

Bent timbers are put in over-long, and when cold the tops are cut off either about $\frac{1}{2}$in (12mm) below the sheer, or so that the beam shelf fits tight on top of them. Years ago there used to be a practice (not often seen now) designed to protect the frames against rot: before the upstanding ends were trimmed off each one had a vertical hole drilled down from the top. This hole would be an inch or two deep and about half the cross-section of the frame; it was filled with whatever concoction the foreman considered most efficacious and left as long as possible, the theory being that the liquid would seep down the length of the wood and later prevent rot from entering. As oak is made up of tiny tubular cells which run down the grain, this trick is founded on logic.

It is usual to copper-clench bent timbers using square-section copper boat nails and rooves. The principal disadvantage of clenches is the presence of the rooves all the way down on the inside of the timbers. These little metal molehills are obtrusive, they prevent stringers and furniture lying flush on the timbers, and even when well finished they tend to be rough and likely to catch on clothing or sailbags.

Screws are used as an alternative, but they are a much less efficient form of fastening in this situation. They do not pull the frame tight to the planking in the same way, they are less reliable, mis-drilling is easier, they need closer spacing by 15 per cent or more, and they tend to be less easy to fit in the hurly-burly of timbering up.

Whatever form of fastening is used, the holes through the hull shell are drilled and countersunk

PRELIMINARY GUIDE TO BENT TIMBER SIZES
Suitable for costing, preliminary weight estimating etc

Boat Length		Frame Spacing		Light				Medium				Heavy			
ft	m	in	cm	in		mm		in		mm		in		mm	
25	7.5	6–8	15–20	$\frac{3}{4} \times \frac{3}{4}$		19 × 19		$\frac{7}{8} \times \frac{7}{8}$		22 × 22		$1\frac{1}{8} \times 1\frac{1}{8}$		28 × 28	
35	10.5	7–10	17.5–25	1 × 1		25 × 25		$1\frac{1}{4} \times 1\frac{1}{4}$		30 × 30		$1\frac{1}{2} \times 1\frac{1}{2}$		40 × 40	
45	13.5	8–12	20–30	$1\frac{1}{4} \times 1\frac{1}{4}$		30 × 30		$1\frac{7}{8} \times 1\frac{7}{8}$		50 × 50		$2\frac{1}{4} \times 2\frac{1}{4}$		60 × 60	

Note: steamed timbers over about $2\frac{1}{4} \times 2\frac{1}{4}$in (60 × 60mm) are hard, sometimes impossible to work.

before the frame is put in. These holes are made from the inside outwards, once the frame position has been determined and marked. As soon as the frame is fitted in and secured at top and bottom it is drilled from the outside through the holes in the planking. If the boat is to be clenched the copper nails are driven home, but often not clenched over until all the frames are in place: the inside of the boat is then like a hedgehog turned inside out, all inward-facing spikes.

Laminated Frames

These take quite a long time to make, which means they are costly in labour; also material expenses are high since glue is not cheap and plenty of it is used for frames. But when a boat is to have a high standard of reliability, strength and appearance laminated frames are hard to beat. Because of the glue water absorption is limited and rot unlikely provided the correct wood is used. Of course puddles, neglect and bad ventilation will cause rot in the most perfect frames, but laminated ones will hold out longer in adverse conditions. Laminated frames carefully made also say quite clearly that the builder is a cut above the average, a man of skill, discernment, pride in his work, an artist. Do I begin to sound just a tiny bit biased? I cannot recall ever seeing this type of frame in a poorly built boat.

Laminated frames can be tapered towards the top so that there is just the right amount of strength where it is needed. Tapering cuts down the top weight and marginally increases the amount of room inside the boat. Then again the laminations can be swept around at the top into beams or half-beams combined with hanging knees. Complete hoop frames can be made including not just the side frames but also the floors and beams, possibly with extra stiffening to support a mast step or chainplates or both.

Frames have to be glued up on a jig or laminating board. Since the curve of the port and starboard frames at any one section are the same, the two can be made at the same time as one lamination and then sliced in half longitudinally. Apart from the saving in time, the planking timber can occasionally also be used for the frames, though normally it would be too wide and require slicing lengthwise.

Laminated frames require bevelling on their outboard face, to fit the curve of the hull. A time-consuming job, it can be speeded up by cutting the bevels with a bandsaw with a tilting table. Three people are needed for this, one at each end of the frame and one to work the tilt. It may help to have a fourth, so that one person can adjust the tilt mechanism and his helper can check off the tilt angle from a bevel gauge. (A bevel gauge is just a piece of wood with the frame bevels marked on it, these bevels being taken off the mould loft floor.)

Small frames, for boats under about 35ft (10m), can be bevelled by one or two people on a bandsaw which has no tilt table. The amount of wood to be cut off is nothing at the aft outboard edge (for frames forward of the widest part of the vessel), and it varies at the forward outer edge. The amount to be cut off is therefore clearly marked on the forward face of the frame by a continuous line. The frame is held at the correct angle and run through the bandsaw slowly and carefully. To do this the frame has to be held at the correct angle, which explains why it can only be done with small frames, large ones being unwieldy and hard to hold.

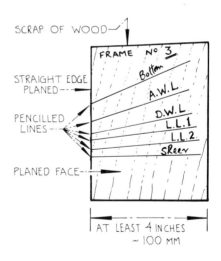

Bevel board for putting the bevel onto frames. The bevels are taken from the loft floor using a bevel gauge and marked on the board with a pencil line. When transferring the bevels to the frames it is essential to remember that a port side frame has the opposite bevel to the starboard one!

A portable circular saw which has a tiltable base can be used for cutting the bevels, but if the frames have much curvature a series of runs have to be made. The frame should be held very securely if this technique is used, but it only needs one pair of hands to wield a portable circular saw.

Whatever technique is being used, the saw should not be taken up to the finishing line: a plane must be used for the final trimming. Where power saws are unavailable or not suitable the frames will be bevelled by making a series of saw cuts across and chopping out the surplus wood with a chisel.

Laminated frames are faired up using battens or ribbands. If a ribband does not lie fair it is easy to pack out or fair off a laminated frame. Provided the mould loft work has been done carefully, trimming off should call for no more than a few strokes of a plane.

Though it is quite usual to laminate in floors *in situ* after completing the hull planking, it is unusual to laminate whole frames in place. Making a very neat job is difficult. Even working outside the hull, laminated frames are a mess after assembly, with glue spewing everywhere and the adjacent layers not perfectly aligned. The forward and aft faces are planed off smooth down to the correct siding, and this means that the frames have to be made about $\frac{1}{8}$in (3mm) over-size in the fore-and-aft dimension. After planing the rough faces,

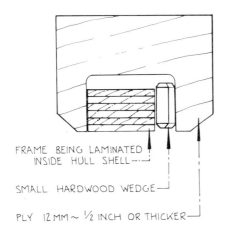

FRAME BEING LAMINATED
INSIDE HULL SHELL

SMALL HARDWOOD WEDGE

PLY 12 MM ~ ½ INCH OR THICKER

When laminating frames or floors inside a hull, using it as the mould, it is important to get the strips of wood carefully aligned or the finished appearance will be poor, though there will be little loss of strength. A batch of ply C-shapes can be cut out and used with small wedges as cramps across the frames, spaced about 12in (30cm) apart.

the edges are 'broken' (the shipwright's term for planing off). Rounding the edges takes longer, especially if done accurately. My own view is that it looks better than a flat bevel and is worth doing sometimes if the frames show boldly, in the main saloon for instance. Only when lining is to be secured to the face of the frames are the edges left sharp.

Frames made up off the loft floor are laminated on a jig. Its shape is taken off the loft floor and some builders use the scrive board (which has the body sections all marked on it) as a jig base, to save drawing out each frame shape twice. The main argument against using the scrive board as a jig base is that the glue may soil it, but this is circumvented by spreading polythene sheet over it.

One of the attractions of laminated frames is their versatility: they can be increased in siding or moulding in way of the chainplates to take the high loadings; they can be made up of three laminates of a hard wood, then three of a light wood, then three more of the hard, darker wood to give a decorative finish.

There is another procedure for building with laminated frames. I have met it only once and it was devised by my partner, the late Alfred Mylne, for two amateur builders who were constructing a 36-footer. It may be unique, though in boatbuilding there are so many inventors across the world dreaming up ideas that I hesitate to claim it has never been used, except in Scotland. It involves using thicker veneers for the hull shell as they are only supported by the frames and not by ribbands.

Moulds are made, screwed or bolted together for easy dismantling. They are sized to fit inside the ribbands, which in this method will be *inside the laminated frames*. So the moulds are made up to the full finished size of the hull minus: plank thickness + frame thickness + ribband thickness. Thus the moulds are smaller than usual.

The moulds are set up in the usual way, then the backbone secured to them, again all as usual. Ribbands are fitted, again in the usual way. They will be about 5in (125mm) apart on average, and perhaps 7in where the frames run straight or on a boat over 45ft (13.7m). This spacing shows a timber saving compared to some methods, but on the other hand they have to be thick enough to resist the pull on the frames. The ribbands are secured to just a few moulds as they press on them and only need a little restraining athwartships. Securing is by screwed or bolted short lengths of angle or wooden chocks on the inside, so that after turning the hull over the ribbands can be freed easily from the moulds for dismantling. Cover the moulds and ribbands (but not the backbone) with plastic sheet.

The frames are laminated up over the ribbands, which act as their jig. Great care is needed to ensure that all the surplus glue which oozes out is wiped off before it hardens. Try to pre-plan the clamping points to employ the moulds as well as the ribbands, to resist the straightening-out tendency of the frame laminates.

Care is also needed in aligning successive layers so that they all have flush sides. This means using lots of plywood guides, made U-shaped like thick-sided goalposts, to slip over the part-completed frame to keep all the layers in line. One way of getting over the problems of surplus glue and side alignment is to make the frames up quickly and without taking a great deal of trouble. When the glue is thoroughly hard they are taken off the skeleton of the boat and run through a planer or hand planed on both sides, to clean them up completely. The frames need to be made about $\frac{1}{8}$ or even $\frac{1}{4}$in (3–6mm) oversize to compensate for this if the final siding is critical, as for instance in a boat built to a scantlings rule.

The first frame laminate to be laid needs its inner edges chamfered or rounded before it is put in place. If this is not done the chamfering may be done later using a drum type belt sander or spokeshave when the boat is upright.

The advantage of this whole method of laminating the frames up on the male mould is that no jigs are needed. Frames can be glued up quickly, whereas with a single jig only a limited number can be made at once. The frames must be spaced close enough to avoid sagging of the first veneers and in the case of the 36-footer mentioned the frame spacing was 12in (30cm) for the initial skin laminate of $\frac{5}{16}$in. Of course with 2in (5cm) frames spaced at 12in centres there is only a 10in (25cm) gap between each member, and it is not asking much of a $\frac{5}{16}$in laminate to bridge that without drooping. To make the stapling coincide with the frames, mark their position on each layer.

Frame ends at the sheer are left too long and trimmed off when the boat is the right way up. Bilge stringers and sheer stringers or beam shelves may be fitted over the moulds and prior to the frames instead of some of the ribbands. First, it is easier to bend them in place onto the outside of the

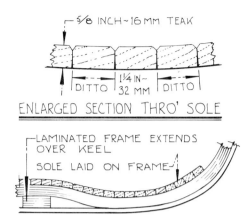

ENLARGED SECTION THRO' SOLE

A simple technique used on a 40ft racer to get the maximum headroom forward of the mast and to save weight. The cabin sole is made up of $\frac{5}{8}$in (16mm) teak strips set close together and resting on the frames which are spaced about 20in (40cm) apart. The bevelled top edges are important to give a good appearance and make the sole less slippery when wet. Carrying the sole up the sides makes life aboard more comfortable when the boat is well heeled.

structure, rather than into the cramped, curved hull shell. Second, their fastenings can be put through the frames during laminating, which helps keep the frames clamped tight with no gaps between layers. If heavy screws are used no fastenings are seen inside the completed boat where the frames cross the stringers – a neat touch. Third, these longitudinals take the place of some ribbands; being wide, each stringer will probably replace two ribbands. (Check for fairness.) Also the frame head (the bottom end when the boat is upside-down) can be well and truly screwed or bolted to the beam shelf. Finally, when the hull is being turned over the whole structure will be extra strong with its permanent stringers already fitted and joined to the framing.

Laminated frames are screwed or bolted to the shell planking. Bolting is stronger, screwing far neater as the screws do not show inside. The best job is often a compromise: bolts below the cabin sole and along the sheer where the stresses are higher, and screws where the frames show, might be the basic plan. In way of a mast or where extra stresses are expected the screws or bolts might be brought in from a normal spacing of say 1/120 the boat's length down to half that distance. Or bolts might be worked in where they will be hidden under furniture or lining.

Steel Frames

It is fairly rare to find steel frames in cold-moulded boats, and very rare to find them in craft under about 50ft (15m) overall. But as suitable timber becomes scarcer, and as so many places have steel-working facilities, a good case can be made for using this relatively heavy material. The weight of the frames does not form a great proportion of total displacement, but steel frames are often secured to steel beams, and virtually always to steel floors. So the total weight of steel can become significant. (This figure and its percentage of the whole displacement should show up in the designer's preliminary calculations.) Craft built down to a minimum weight will not be found with much steel inside.

As a rough guide, steel is ten times the weight of a hardwood, but it is used in the form of angle-bar for frames so the weight of one steel frame may not be much more than one stout wooden frame. It is common to see frames with both flanges the same size, though this is not the most efficient use of material. The flange against the hull is only needed to take the fastenings through the planking, and the main source of strength is the athwartships flange. So it is logical to have a narrow flange fore and aft, the largest depth athwartships. As ever, plenty of other considerations intrude, though. A deep athwartships flange takes up extra space in the accommodation; unequal angle-bar is less widely available; it is not so easy to bend; it may spring back more when it is bent or when it is galvanized, and so on.

Before considering steel frames it is essential to investigate cost and availability. Most boatbuilders lack facilities for dealing with steel frames. Some who do have bending slabs will take on a contract to supply a set of frames, and a few shipyards (i.e. builders of craft over 100ft (30m)) are prepared to do this work for other firms. Costs will vary enormously. In any case a fixed estimate should be obtained before placing the order, and the quotation should state the conditions, if any, under which the final price may be higher than the quotation. In some regions a fixed quotation means what it says, and come hell or high water the price charged will not be varied. Other regions (or trade customs) have a more flexible attitude towards pricing. All this is important when buying anything for a boat, but it is especially relevant when it comes to steelwork, which may well include beams, floors and other parts.

As a very crude guide, it is likely that steel frames will be more expensive than wood for boats under about 60ft (18m), but much depends on the quality and finish of the timber used, whether the steel frames are galvanized, transport costs, also factors like handling, finishing and fastenings. The cost of steel frames may be minimized by using very few of them, interspersed by strength bulkheads, and in conjunction with strong, thick moulded planking. Indeed, when cold-moulding was in its infancy it was widely argued that one of the special advantages of the system was the need for very few frames, and this remains true in principle.

Steel frames were formerly bent after heating in a furnace, in the manner of blacksmith work. Modern frame bending is done cold for the most part. A scrieve board is needed, and this is normally provided by the loftsman, who also makes up a bevel gauge. Steel frames need to have their flanges opened apart so that the athwartships frame is exactly across the vessel even though the planking is at an angle to the centreline. The flanges are always opened, never closed, to cope with this bevel, otherwise it would be difficult in places to fit the planking fastenings. So frames

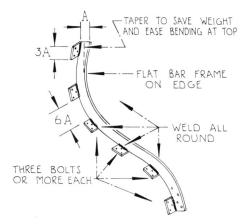

This form of flat-bar frame is much lighter than the conventional angle-bar type. It is often easier to bend, but it is hardly attractive and should be hidden by lining or furniture. Hot-dip galvanizing after drilling and edge bevelling or fairing are recommended. The bottom will almost always be bolted or welded to a steel plate floor.

forward of amidships 'look' (open) aft, and those aft of amidships look forwards.

It is common sense to drill metal frames before fitting them, making an excessive number of close-spaced holes, but by no means universal practice. All drilling should be done before galvanizing otherwise every time a fastening hole is made the galvanizing is broken and rust must start. Holes are made $\frac{1}{16}$in (1.5mm) oversize to allow for the layer of zinc in the hole, otherwise fastenings will chip out the galvanizing as they are driven through. Holes must also be made in the athwartships flange for furniture, bulkheads, stringers, floors, beams and so on; a few extra holes are put in by wily boatbuilders to allow for contingencies.

If the frames are galvanized they are likely to change shape slightly in the process: the more bend in a frame, the more it is likely to wrack in the bath of molten metal. So every frame has to be re-checked before fitting. When galvanizing is not used painting must be thorough, and this too should be done after all the holes have been drilled, again oversize.

Fastenings are commonly galvanized bolts, and here as elsewhere hot-dip galvanizing is the only reliable type, other forms varying from moderate to super-lousy. For boats around the 25ft size $\frac{1}{4}$in (6mm) diameter bolts are used; around 32ft (10m) they will be about $\frac{3}{8}$in (10mm) in diameter; and from about 45ft (14m) upwards they will be $\frac{1}{2}$in (12mm) in diameter.

In the best boats the fastenings for steel frames are bronze bolts, which are sensationally expensive. They need insulating washers and sleeves under the hard washers, which are used to prevent the nuts from tearing the galvanizing as they are tightened, and to isolate them as an anti-corrosion measure. For the same reason the frames and fastenings should be painted. (Suitable combinations of metals for frames and fastenings, and corrosion prevention methods, are discussed in *Metal Corrosion in Boats* by Nigel Warren, published by Stanford Maritime.)

The feet of steel frames are joined by steel floors. They ought to be at least 'one size' thicker, because the floors are constantly wet and corrode away all day every day. Just how 'one size' is interpreted depends on the projected life of the boat, the availability of material, whether weight is really being saved, and so on. Floors are sometimes made of the same angle-bar as the frames but more often steel plate is used. For $\frac{1}{4}$in (6mm) frames one would certainly go for $\frac{5}{16}$in (8mm) plate floors and in most situations $\frac{3}{8}$in (10mm) would be a far better choice. The floors should be flanged and bolted or welded to the frames. Welding is only appropriate if the frames are only being painted, unless the galvanizing bath can accommodate a complete frame hoop, or the galvanizing team are prepared to take several dips to get the whole cumbersome unit immersed. Bolting will simplify later replacement or repair.

Logically, steel frames are secured at the top to steel beams, with steel knees. Wooden beams may be used instead because they look good whereas steel beams demand an under-deck lining to hide them from view in anything except commercial craft. The beam knees will be made from angle-bar the same size as the frames, or flanged plating. The knees can be one thickness lighter than the frame, except in way of masts or by heavy beams or deck fittings.

Stringers are commonly joined to steel frames by short steel flats welded to the athwartships frame flange. Where welding is not convenient a short length of angle-bar is bolted on, being just about as long as the stringer is wide. Bolting on short lengths may be done regardless of the facilities available, if the exact location of the stringer is not decided until construction is well advanced. Some builders put stringers along the line of least resistance, not following the planned line exactly. This is fine if the builder is in consultation with the designer, and if the stringer does not have some critical position.

Where an extra strong frame is needed a steel inner angle-bar may be bolted, riveted or welded to an ordinary frame, making a Z-section frame. An alternative, seldom used because it does not make the best use of the material, is to fix two frames back to back. It might be thought that this would be impractical, because one of the angle-bars will be closed, to get the correct bevel, and there would be trouble getting the fastenings in. However, extra strong frames tend to be near the middle part of the ship, where there is little curvature and therefore little frame bevel.

Steel frames are convenient for taking the outer edges of bulkheads. Before the finally shaped frame is put into the hull it should be laid on the ply and a line drawn round, so that the precise shape of the bulkhead is quickly marked without the time and trouble of drawing offsets or making templates.

Suitable for costing and preliminary weight estimating, etc

Boat Length		Frame Spacing		Light		Medium		Heavy	
ft	m	in	cm	in	mm	in	mm	in	mm
25	7.5	10–14	26–36	$1 \times \frac{3}{4} \times \frac{1}{8}$	$25 \times 20 \times 3$	$1\frac{1}{2} \times 1 \times \frac{1}{8}$	$40 \times 25 \times 3$	$2 \times 1\frac{1}{2} \times \frac{1}{8}$	$50 \times 40 \times 3$
35	10.5	11–15	28–38	$1\frac{1}{2} \times 1 \times \frac{1}{8}$	$40 \times 25 \times 3$	$2 \times 1\frac{1}{2} \times \frac{3}{16}$	$50 \times 40 \times 3$	$2\frac{1}{2} \times 2 \times \frac{1}{8}$	$65 \times 50 \times 3$
45	13.5	12–16	30–40	$2 \times 1\frac{1}{2} \times \frac{3}{16}$	$50 \times 40 \times 5$	$2\frac{1}{2} \times 2 \times \frac{3}{16}$	$65 \times 50 \times 5$	$3 \times 2\frac{1}{2} \times \frac{1}{4}$	$75 \times 65 \times 6.5$
55	16.5	13–17	33–43	$2\frac{1}{2} \times 2 \times \frac{3}{16}$	$65 \times 50 \times 5$	$3 \times 2\frac{1}{2} \times \frac{1}{4}$	$75 \times 65 \times 6.5$	$3\frac{1}{2} \times 3 \times \frac{1}{4}$	$90 \times 75 \times 6.5$

Like laminated and solid wooden frames, steel frames may be fitted before or after planking. Unlike them, steel cannot be easily trimmed with a swift swipe of the plane or Surform, so steel frames must never be oversize. If one is a little bit skinny wooden packing can be added so that the planking lies smoothly. It is a waste of time, and not always a simple job, to add the necessary thin slivers tapering out top and bottom and it therefore behoves the frame-maker to be skilled, careful and knowledgeable. Such people tend to be rare, pricey and much in demand. Before specifying steel frames it is vital to get a guarantee that they will be available, accurately made, at an economic price and on time. Plenty of boatbuilders will scornfully say this is asking for a miracle.

Aluminium Frames

For a given strength, aluminium is expensive but light. The people who sell it boast that aluminium sections and plates are one-third the weight of steel but have two-thirds the strength. This is a handy rule of thumb, though it can be 20 per cent or more inaccurate. Aluminium comes in a variety of alloys so the obvious approach is to buy it from one of the suppliers specializing in marine grades. They should be told exactly and in writing what the material is to be used for so that they, not the designer, can specify the correct alloy and confirm its suitability.

Aluminium frames are used in racing craft and wherever high speed or weight-saving is more important than first cost. Where the life of the boat is expected to be limited the metal can be left unpainted. This saving is welcome, because the material is remarkably expensive when compared with other boatbuilding materials. The price varies a lot, but a crude guide suggests that an aluminium bar will be five times as expensive as a steel one of equivalent dimensions, and even ten times the cost is not unknown.

It is logical to link aluminium frames to floors and possibly beams of the same material. Engine bearers, support plates for a deck-stepped mast or a mast step straddling alloy floors are all normally linked with aluminium frames. To save money and simplify ordering it is best to make all these components out of one size of extrusion (usually angle-bar) and one thickness of plate. However, anyone using aluminium is almost certainly aiming for a light structure and so either the design is likely to work out as a time-consuming operation involving concessions and compromises, or else no concessions are made and the material is bought in small amounts of different sizes, which puts the price up viciously. So in practice it may be best to subcontract the aluminium work to a specialist firm which carries stock. Considering that aluminium is not hard to work, the subcontract price is likely to be high due to the cost of the material and the absence of repitition work.

Apart from cost, the main disadvantage of aluminium is the tendency to corrode. It can do this without actually getting wet; the salty atmosphere inside any boat afloat or even in a boat shed is enough to start the trouble. However, sufficient experience has been gained for the corrosion problem to be overcome with good design.

Metallurgical analysis is used to distinguish one aluminium alloy from another. This makes life awkward for the boatbuilder, who cannot tell one type from another when he handles it in the course of his work, since extrusions and plates made from ten different alloys all look alike. The current British Specification for boat-building aluminium is BS 1470. For extrusions the ideal grade is NE 8, but this tends to be hard to find so more often HE 9 or HE 30 is bought. For sheet, NS 8 is normally best but HS 30 is used more often because it is less difficult to buy. In the U.S.A. the specification for general boat construction is alloy 5086, or the slightly less attractive 5083. Where extra strength is needed the one to select is 5456.

Stockholders have a disconcerting habit of sending big catalogues to anyone interested in buying aluminium for boatbuilding. The list of different sections and the numerous sizes of many of these suggests that the designer's problems are half solved, since there seem to be shapes to suit everything. Inquiry of stock-holders and even manufacturers is likely to turn up a very sad situation: few of the listed extrusions are available and many can only be supplied after a long wait or in quantities which are often too vast for boat-builders to buy at once. So one's first move must be to find out just what is available, and then reserve it so that stocks are not sold between the design and ordering stages.

For the strongest, lightest structures welding should be used to join components. Aluminium welding has made considerable strides in the last few years, but it is still not as easy as steel welding. Craftsmen who can make fine welds in mild steel are not always able to show the same virtuosity with aluminium. This is another reason for subcontracting the work. Welding has the virtue that it is fairly quick, but one does occasionally see otherwise well built craft with a disconcerting number of weld failures. These would probably be eliminated if the complete hoop unit, consisting of port and starboard frames, floor, beam and hanging knees, was assembled flat. Each weld should normally be full and continuous, run right round the end of the frame where it meets the hanging knee or beam, and continuously round the other side. If the welder is not skilled and careful there may be some distortion. Provided the distortion is 'inwards' some wooden packing can be fitted outside to make up the want. But if the frame or beam stands out beyond the fair line of the hull its end join has to be severed and remade. Any defect wastes time and increases the already high cost, so welding designed to eliminate distortion should be used.

Its promoters defend aluminium on the grounds that weld fractures are often very tiny; this ignores the fact that a gap of one-thousandth of an inch is still a total break and just as significant as if it were one inch wide. The strength has disappeared, and the very tiny fissure is more serious because it may not be detected.

For joining together a limited number of aluminium parts, for repairs or where there are limited facilities, bolts are best. Although not the lightest method nor always the cheapest, they are often the most convenient and in the long run give least trouble. They allow components to be assembled inside the hull, and to be taken apart for repair or replacement. The bolt thickness should be at least that of the thicker of the two parts being joined and up to a maximum of three times that of the thickest part. Spacing is at about four times their diameter, which gives a watertight joint. Zinc chromate should be used as bedding and on the faying surfaces. Fastening holes should be set in twice their diameter from the edge of the pieces. Finally, aluminium and its alloys react with anything containing copper, so brass and bronze fastenings are totally unsuitable.

Much that has been said about steel frames applies to light alloys. Normally the frames will be of angle-bar with one flange bolted to the planking. The bolt spacing will be about 1/150 of the overall hull length. They may be put in before the final laminate is put on the hull, to cover the head and give the hull a perfect finish without any dowels or stopping.

Joins of frame heads to beams need some form of bracketting except perhaps right forward and aft, over say one-fifth the forward and aft lengths of the hull. A cheap handy bracket may be made from a piece of beam or frame extrusion set at 45°. If the familiar hanging knee or web made from a flanged triangular plate is used it should be pierced with holes for piping and wiring, and perhaps a lightening hole, before being fitted.

To simplify ordering and to reduce the cost of the metal it may be decided to use the same extrusion section for the beams as for the frames. This is likely to give a beam which lacks adequate strength, so a little cunning is applied. For instance two bars may be fastened back to back, making a wide-topped T or a Z-section. The unsupported beam span can be reduced by using extra large knees each end, or fitting pillars of aluminium, steel or wood. In way of bulkheads or in lockers the knees can extend well inboard and well down the frame without intruding on the accommodation. The resulting extra strength will more than compensate for the extra weight.

Limber holes at the bottom of frames and floors are even more important with aluminium than with steel; the latter turns red with rust giving everyone fair warning that trouble is brewing.

Curved frames are made using hydraulic rams or hand-levers. For a limited number of curves two strong vertical pillars, suitably padded, have been used and so have pipe benders. When bending aluminium it is important to make the curve once, positively, with no reversals or alterations; because the metal work hardens the minimum amount of bending is essential.

Instead of bending angle-bar to make frames, plate can be cut to the correct shape. The inside cut of one frame will almost form the outside edge of another, so in theory a little trimming of the plate after making one frame will provide another frame nearly adjacent. However, frames made from flat plates need stiffening and also flanges to bolt onto the planking. The flanges need not be continuous, and if they are in quite short lengths, perhaps just enough for two or three bolts, they can often be uncurved. The inner edge of the frame may be kept straight, then it can be stiffened by a straight anglebar or welded flat bar. Flat bar, being easily bent, can be used for the outboard or inboard edges, intermittently welded. Using plate for the frames makes it easy to have deep-section extra

strong frames, in conjunction with stringers which can be of wood or aluminium. This is the strongest form of framing for a given weight, and the relatively few transverse frames may form the building moulds.

At temperatures above 150°F stress corrosion can occur in all aluminium alloys. For this reason engine exhausts and silencers, stoves and cabin heaters should be kept away from aluminium parts. Where it is hard to keep the source of heat and the metal components well separated, there should be lots of ventilation and copious fire proof insulation.

PRELIMINARY GUIDE TO ALUMINIUM FRAME DIMENSIONS

Length overall		Frame size (angle-bar)		Frame spacing	
ft	m	in	mm	in	cm
24	7.3	$1 \times 1 \times \frac{1}{8}$	$25 \times 25 \times 3$	12	30
30	9.1	$1\frac{1}{2} \times 1\frac{1}{2} \times \frac{3}{16}$	$40 \times 40 \times 5$	14	35
40	12.2	$2 \times 2 \times \frac{1}{4}$	$50 \times 50 \times 6$	15	38
50	15.2	$2\frac{1}{2} \times 2\frac{1}{2} \times \frac{1}{4}$	$65 \times 65 \times 6$	16	40

Note This is a basic guide. For heavy duty craft the spacing will be reduced or the frame size increased, or both. For high-performance vessels the scantlings may be reduced. The outer flange bolted to the hull may be narrowed without great loss of frame stiffness when its strength is combined with the hull shell.

Stringers

Structural members which extend fore-and-aft rather than athwartships are called stringers. They are in several respects better than ordinary frames not least because for a given full strength they are lighter. They may also be cheaper and easier to fit as they don't have to be forced round the sharp turn of the bilge. They may be spaced widely over the topsides and high up, where the deck edge provides a lot of stiffness and local strength is not needed so much. In contrast, the tops of athwartships frames do little work and can be classed as excess weight. It is usual to have wide-spaced deep-section athwartships frames (sometimes called web frames) in association with stringers; this form of frame resists racking strains whereas ordinary frames are not good at this. Often

strength bulkheads take the place of web frames.

Stringers can often be put in faster than athwartships frames because they need less bending to fit. However, there are situations where stringers are awkward or ineffective. A canoe-sterned boat with a tight turn at the deck edge and at other level lines can be the very devil to frame up with horizontal stringers, so it may be worth having vertical frames over the aft few feet with stringers elsewhere. To make building even easier, these vertical frames may be set at right angles to the planking, in a fan shape when seen from above. Set this way they are called cant frames.

Stringers obtrude into the accommodation no more than frames, so far as athwartships thickness is concerned. With careful planning and packing

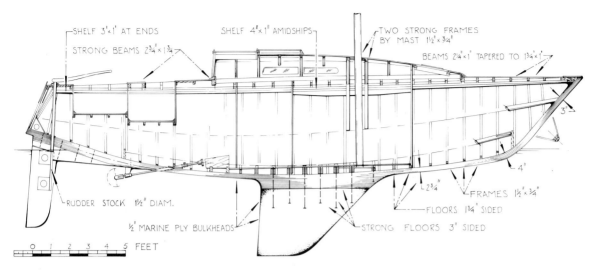

SHELF 3"×1" AT ENDS
STRONG BEAMS 2¾"×1¾"
SHELF 4"×1" AMIDSHIPS
TWO STRONG FRAMES BY MAST 1½"×¾"
BEAMS 2¼"×1" TAPERED TO 1¾"×1"
3"
4"
RUDDER STOCK 1½" DIAM.
½" MARINE PLY BULKHEADS
L 2¾"
FRAMES 1½"×¾"
FLOORS 1¾" SIDED
STRONG FLOORS 3" SIDED

0 1 2 3 4 5 FEET

Buchanan designed 30ft (9.1m) racer. Of special interest is the way the backbone laminates are increased in number at the top of the fin keel and by the skeg, as well as at the curve of the stem.

An unusual feature is the twin bilge stringers. A single one has often been criticized because it tends to be near the neutral axis of the hull, and so does not make the maximum contribution to longitudinal strength. Here the lower stringer runs along the tops of the floors and the upper one along the bottoms of the hanging knees by the mast.

pieces they can be used to support the berth bases, chart table tops, and other horizontal surfaces. Engine bearers, rudder tubes, transom knees and other structural parts are joined to stringers too.

Any good grade strong wood which is available in long lengths free from knots, preferably with a grain which runs true and straight, is worth considering for stringers. It is usual to select a wood which is resistant to rot, not only for the obvious reasons but also because it is hard to replace a defective stringer. Water tends to lie on top of stringers unless special precautions are taken. Stagnant water is the great breeder of rot, so woods like oregon pine should not be used even though it has the other desirable qualities. Spruce used to be a favourite but it is hard to buy in many areas. However, it may in time become more easily available; for years in some countries it was

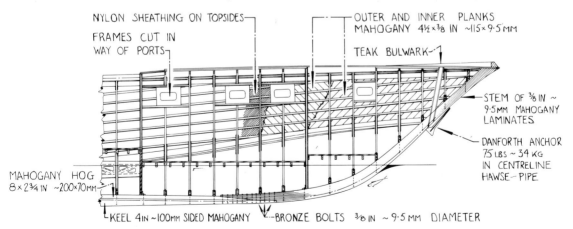

NYLON SHEATHING ON TOPSIDES
FRAMES CUT IN WAY OF PORTS
OUTER AND INNER PLANKS MAHOGANY 4½×⅜ IN ~115×9·5MM
TEAK BULWARK
STEM OF ⅜ IN ~ 9·5MM MAHOGANY LAMINATES
DANFORTH ANCHOR 75 LBS ~ 34 KG IN CENTRELINE HAWSE–PIPE
MAHOGANY HOG 8×2¾ IN ~200×70MM
KEEL 4IN ~100MM SIDED MAHOGANY
BRONZE BOLTS ⅜ IN ~ 9·5 MM DIAMETER

Derek Haswell is well known for his fast strong power cruisers. This 61ft (19m) boat has longitudinal stringers and ample deep frames, with each bulkhead very much a strength member. For additional strength and to minimize maintenance the topsides and bottom are sheathed with nylon cloth set in epoxy resin.

impossible to find pitch pine worth having but now it seems to be easily available. Spruce and pitch pine with their favourable strength/weight ratio, ability to hold fastenings well and resistance to rot are good choices. That grade of larch called 'boat skin' is also suitable, but other qualities of this wood have too many knots. Where the wood is good apart from the knots it does not involve too much work to make up stringers from relatively short lengths by gluing up scarphs provided a scarphing jig is set up.

There is another useful trick when the available wood is in rather short lengths: stringers are put in from forward to just aft of amidships, so that those from the bow overlap those from aft by about 10 per cent of the boat's length. No stringer runs horizontal, every one slopes down from the end to the middle of the boat, ensuring that any water caught on top of a stringer drains down to amidships where it runs off the stringer end into the bilge. Another way of ensuring that water does not lie on top of a stringer is to cut limber holes. These have a bad habit of getting bunged up with dirt unless they are at least $1\frac{1}{2} \times \frac{3}{4}$in (40 × 20mm) and this is large compared with the thickness of stringers in boats less than about 35ft (10m).

Stringers may be tapered in moulding and siding at the ends of the boat. Where weight-saving is critical the aft third of the hull can have stringers reduced by about 30 per cent of the cross-sectional areas, except in way of powerful engines,

or by a big mizzen mast or some similar source of large strains. Forward, the reduction might be the same provided the stringers converge together, as they will tend to because of the reducing girth of the hull. The deck stringer will normally only taper in the moulded dimension as the deck edge is secured down onto it and the width of the landing cannot be reduced without risk of leaks and weakness.

Motor boats with large transoms will probably not have their stringers tapered at the aft end, especially if there are more brackets holding the transom onto the shell than the usual quarter knees and stern knee. These extra brackets may be seen when the engine is linked to a Z-drive or outdrive through the transom, particularly if the total horsepower is high. Also engines right aft against the transom linked to V-drives need ample strength round them, so here again extra brackets between transom and stringers make sense.

Stringers are glued or clenched or nailed to the hull planking just like athwartships frames. The planking is glued to the backbone and it is not usual to fit breasthooks between the stringers and the backbone except on very strong boats.

To save time stringers are fitted in single lengths. Unless the boat is short and the available timber is long, scarphing up is needed. A scarph of about 1 in 6 and in high-performance boats 1 in 8 will be used. Glue them together well before they are needed, so that the glue has ample time to cure; when the glue has set plane all round, then the scarph is almost invisible and no rough edges can be felt.

The inboard edges of stringers are chamfered or rounded. If the work is done by hand chamfering is quicker, but if the edges are cut with a spindle it is better to use a round-section tool. It gives a more regular finish, one which is not likely to vary along the length of the wood, and it looks more modern, suggesting that a great deal of trouble has been taken with the finish. It holds paint and varnish better too.

Scarphs should be perfect glued joins, but just to be safe they should be kept away from the high-stress areas. No two adjacent scarphs should be within about 5ft (1.5m) nor should any two scarphs be within 3ft (1m). The usual boatbuilding rules concerning the staggering of joins apply.

A stringer which is the length of the hull needs several people to handle it. To get it the right length it has to be made slightly too long and then

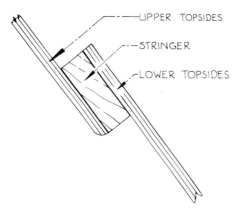

A stringer sandwiched between upper and lower parts of the topsides gives extra room inside, a degree of extra flare, helps keep spray and solid water off the deck, adds strength, and can be used to add interest to an otherwise high-sided ugly boat. It can also be used as a chine between the topsides and the bottom.

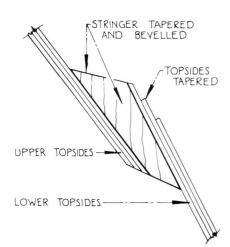

STRINGER TAPERED
AND BEVELLED

TOPSIDES
TAPERED

UPPER TOPSIDES

LOWER TOPSIDES

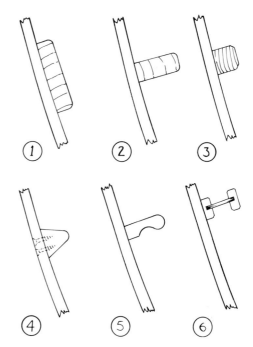

① ② ③

④ ⑤ ⑥

A more sophisticated version of the previous stringer. The siding has been tapered to give a more pronounced flare to the upper part of the topsides, and both top and bottom edges are bevelled to avoid a hard line. For the same reason the lower part of the topsides are tapered out. This can also help simplify fabrication and possibly save some time in finishing off the top edge of the lower topsides. It may be necessary to laminate, to get round curves and build up sufficient thickness and depth.

cut exactly when it is fitted. Some builders taper stringers right away at the ends and make them an inch or two short, to speed up fitting. Others join the stringer parts by butt straps, short lengths of stringer timber glued and often screwed as well to the top or bottom faces, bridging the join. The butt strap is seldom put on the inboard side because it would obtrude into the accommodation. Besides, setting the strap against the planking above or below gives two glued faces, against the planking and on the stringer. Very strongly built boats have butt straps in pairs, above and below the join but not the same length, otherwise there will be a 'hard spot' at the strap ends. For the same reason, the best built boats have butt straps which taper at each end. Butt straps on top of stringers are liable to cause puddles, and this is not the ideal location for limber holes, so it is better to put the strap under the stringer. It is good practice to hide butt straps behind furniture, in which case the strap might be put on the inboard face of the stringer and the two ends left an inch apart to form a drain slot. However, this calls for an extra strong butt strap and it loses the advantage of two glued faces.

The precise line the stringers run may be shown on the drawings. It is hard, especially without a lot

Alternative types of stringers. (1) is simple to install and secure; the ends can be tapered substantially. (2) is stronger than (1) but more difficult to fit. Large puddles will lie on top unless drains or limber holes are made. These holes are easier to make and keep clear than in (1). (3) is a good compromise between strength and easy fitting. Being square in section speeds up machine planing and generally simplifies cutting and finishing. The grain should be parallel to the planking (as shown) if a sharp bend has to be negotiated.

(4) is an elegant compromise giving ample strength, ease of fitting and a good appearance. Puddles will not lie on top except where the stringers are set low down on a part of the hull which is about 30° to the vertical or flatter, where drain holes are needed. Can be useful for securing berth tops, furniture etc. (5) is a more complex version of (2), being strong but light with a good gluing and screwing face, plenty of strength and a sophisticated appearance. (6) is the Herreshoff stringer, complex and costly but light and strong. (5) and (6) are possibly worth two seconds a mile in a race if the opposition can be lured on board beforehand to see the emphasis on weight-saving.

of experience, to get the best run, ensuring that they are put in without awkward twists. A designer may specify the spacing and leave the builder to work the stringers in the easiest way. Some may have to pass through particular points or along specified lines, to fit in with other structural members or the furniture, so they will be the first stringers to be fitted.

Stringers may be put on over the building moulds, so that the hull planking is built up on them, or they may be fitted after the hull shell has been completed and turned over. In the first method the stringers have to be held temporarily to the moulds and permanently to any bulkheads that are used as moulds. Plank fastenings will probably be put in before the final skin is applied, and the run of the stringers has to be drawn in on each successive layer of planking.

When putting stringers into a completed shell, the line of the first pair is first marked in pencil. It is important to work port and starboard together. If the lower ones, port and starboard, are put in first they will give a foothold when working the higher stringers. The top edge is pencilled in, then the stringer moved away so that screw holes can be drilled from the inside out.

Screws are driven from the outside and used to pull the stringers into the planking while the glue sets, whereas barbed nails may be used if the planking is built up on the stringers. Screw spacing varies enormously but a man's hand span of around 9in (23cm) is a fair working average for a great variety of boat sizes and types. Countersinking on the outside is needed, and it should be slightly overdone so that there is no risk that a screw will stand out and prevent the final layer of planking fitting well.

Clenches can be used instead of screws, or a few bolts among the screws help if the building team is small or inexperienced. Bolting the whole length is liable to be expensive in time and materials, but for boats over about 38ft (12m) the need for extra strength justifies bolts all along, especially in stout heavy craft.

Before gluing in the first stringer a dummy run is worth the time it takes. As the stringer is pulled in place by the screws the glue should spew out all along. Screwing can be from the middle towards the ends, or from one end to the other, but not at random nor from both ends together. The aim is to pull the stringer in tight against the planking along its full length and this can only be done if the progression is as recommended.

Wooden Floors

'LEAF-SPRING' FLOORS

These look something like the car springs of the same name. They are laminated but each piece is shorter than the one beneath so that the thickness and strength taper away towards the end. This type of reinforcement is extremely popular in cold-moulded boats; it is easy to fit and uses relatively short pieces of timber. However, they must be continuous from end to end and free from serious knots. It is normal to build these floors directly into the hull after planking, though they are occasionally made up off the boat like laminated frames. They are seen in way of ballast keels, engines, mast support structures; even as engine bearers, certainly for units under 10 hp.

The width of the floors should be at least four times the diameter of any keel or other bolts which pass through. Bolting should be carried one-third of the way up the hull, and ideally considerably farther. The side bolts should be staggered, and will normally have countersunk heads outboard. A hardwood is best and offcuts can be used, particularly for the top laminates which may be quite short. The ends of each layer should be at least partly rounded for good appearance, or at least the corners should be taken off.

Where there is a big jump from the top of the hog to the planking some form of chock should be fitted and a through-bolt here is desirable. If no chocks are fitted, or chocks are fitted but no bolts, with a heavy keel it is likely that some flexing will occur in this area. This is most likely in bad weather when the skipper will have much on his mind. Leaks between the planking and the hog are difficult to seal up.

Guidance for the spacing of floors is given in the later section on Metal Floors, but because leaf-spring floors are large in siding they can perhaps be set farther apart. It is hard to set a standard for moulded thickness, but a rough guide might be:
for inshore craft: about $3 \times$ plank thickness
for coastal craft: about 4 or $5 \times$ plank thickness
for highly stressed craft: about 6 or $7 \times$ plank thickness.
The siding must be enough to leave at least three-quarters of the wood intact after the bolt holes have been drilled. A siding $1\frac{1}{2}$ times the moulding is fairly common; this may seem illogical because the loadings are best carried by a maximum moulded depth, but space in the boat may be

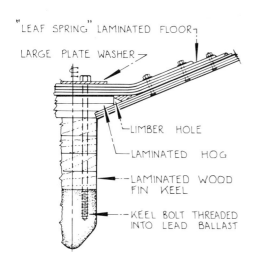

"LEAF SPRING" LAMINATED FLOOR

LARGE PLATE WASHER

LIMBER HOLE

LAMINATED HOG

LAMINATED WOOD FIN KEEL

KEEL BOLT THREADED INTO LEAD BALLAST

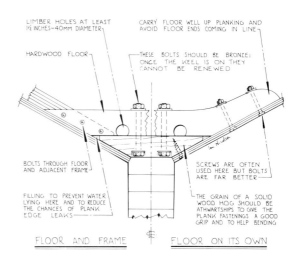

LIMBER HOLES AT LEAST 1½ INCHES—40MM DIAMETER

CARRY FLOOR WELL UP PLANKING AND AVOID FLOOR ENDS COMING IN LINE

HARDWOOD FLOOR

THESE BOLTS SHOULD BE BRONZE: ONCE THE KEEL IS ON THEY CANNOT BE RENEWED

BOLTS THROUGH FLOOR AND ADJACENT FRAME

SCREWS ARE OFTEN USED HERE BUT BOLTS ARE FAR BETTER

FILLING TO PREVENT WATER LYING HERE AND TO REDUCE THE CHANCES OF PLANK EDGE LEAKS

THE GRAIN OF A SOLID WOOD HOG SHOULD BE ATHWARTSHIPS TO GIVE THE PLANK FASTENINGS A GOOD GRIP AND TO HELP BENDING

FLOOR AND FRAME   FLOOR ON ITS OWN

Keel bolts of bronze may be tapped into a lead keel, provided the keel has been hardened by the addition of antimony. Keel bolts need exceedingly large stiff washers under their heads to prevent crushing down into the hog. In way of the ballast keel there must be plenty of floors, which may be of metal, or laminated wood as shown here. These are 'leaf spring' floors as each laminate is shorter than the one under it. This avoids a high stress area and carries the torque of the ballast well up the sides of the hull shell. The gaps at the side of the hog are almost filled with hardwood wedges, just enough space being left for the bilgewater to flow through. Ample countersunk bolts hold the floor to the hull shell.

limited, so the siding has to be put up to compensate for the restricted moulding. Also, a large sided dimension allows the bolts through the planking to be well staggered, a most desirable refinement. It is rare to see too many leaf-spring floors, or to find them too large. Where they are fitted next to bulkheads a little extra moulded depth makes sense so that fore-and-aft bolts can be put through to hold the bulkhead.

It is usual to have flat plate washers across the full siding of the floors at each ballast keel bolt. This may have been adequate years ago, but modern boats are so hard driven, very light, and have such highly tensioned rigs that flat washers are no longer adequate. They should be in the form of inverted metal channels, straddling the wooden floors and at least three times as wide athwartships as they are fore and aft. To avoid having to make massive washer plates it may be worth using fairly light channel section with a large round washer on top. When channel cannot be obtained angle-bar might be used. All wooden

A simple floor (left) made from straight-grained hardwood and bolted fore and aft to a laminated frame. This is a cheap, easily made structure which needs a fairly deep floor to be fully effective. Ideally the floor should be glued as well as bolted to the frame. Common to both sides are the bronze bolts through the hog, into the floor. Except on boats under about 25ft (7.5m) there should be two bolts through the hog into each floor. A single washer plate can be shared by both.

The floors here are rather shallow in moulded depth, so they should be at least as large sided as moulded. The limber holes take out just about as much strength as can be allowed, but they must never be smaller than the size shown regardless of the size of boat. The right side shows the floor tapered off, again a skimped floor suitable for a lightly stressed boat not over about 30ft (9m). For larger boats or hard use the floor should extend farther, taper more and have four or more bolts.

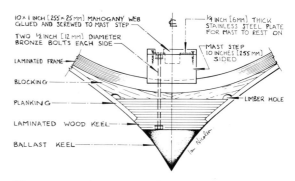

10 × 1 INCH [255 × 25 MM] MAHOGANY WEB GLUED AND SCREWED TO MAST STEP

¼ INCH [6MM] THICK STAINLESS STEEL PLATE FOR MAST TO REST ON

TWO ½ INCH [12 MM] DIAMETER BRONZE BOLTS EACH SIDE

MAST STEP 10 INCHES [255 MM] SIDED

LAMINATED FRAME

BLOCKING

PLANKING

LIMBER HOLE

LAMINATED WOOD KEEL

BALLAST KEEL

The area round a mast step is one of the most highly stressed so it is worth studying the way Holman & Pye have designed the floors to cope with the loadings. The yacht concerned is 41.5 × 30 × 11 × 6.8ft. There are packing blocks under a laminated floor, with limber holes so that no water is trapped forward of the mast.

floors carrying massive keel or rig loads need these sophisticated 'washers' for the bolts.

Care is needed to get the forward and aft faces smooth, with each laminate lying exactly on top of the one below. Chocks of wood wrapped in plastic can be clamped on each side as guides. Another technique is to use pieces of metal channel or plywood which fit over exactly, as guides. Standard metal channel is best, so to be sure that it slips neatly onto the floor the timber is given a sided width which suits the available section. A few fastenings, either silicon or phosphor bronze screws or non-corroding barbed nails, are put into each laminate to hold it till the next one is fitted. When all the laminates are in place, but before the glue has hardened, bolts or clenches (or more rarely screws) are put through to clamp all the timber layers and the planking together.

PLYWOOD FLOORS

In so many ways ply floors are God's gift to boatbuilders: they are light, cheap, quick to make and fit, don't corrode and can be made from offcuts. Only marine ply can be used, but there is usually plenty of that about in every boatbuilding shop.

To join the ply to the hull glassfibre and resin may be used, epoxy resin being much the best. Glassing on both sides is essential, and should ideally cover the whole floor. If this is done the floor should not have a top stiffener, as it is difficult to get the cloth to lie tight where there is a flange. A minimum of three runs of 1½oz chopped strand mat strips is used, of the heaviest weight that can be applied and adhere in the 90° angle between the floor and the hull. Ideally there should be fillet pieces up each side of the floor so that the glassing never has to fit in an angle of more than 45°, but such fillets are seldom used so the glassing has to be worked into 90° interior angles. Each strip of glassfibre is wider than the one before so as to overlap on both edges. The glass must be worked in so that limber holes are left, and a short length of non-ferrous tube is sometimes pushed through a hole at the bottom of the floor so there is no chance of the limber hole being bunged up with glass and resin.

Ply floors may also be secured to the forward or aft faces of frames, using bolts and sometimes glue as well. The shape of each floor may be taken from the mold loft or off the hull on a cardboard template. Where there is little hull curvature an

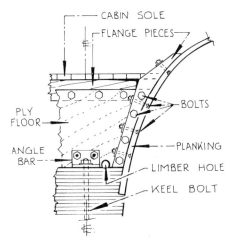

Plywood cannot be screwed into its edge, so there must be flanges. The top flange is not essential, but it makes the floor stiffer and is shown here supporting the sole. Flanges may be glued and screwed, or bolted on. The side bolts are drilled from inboard, but it may not be possible to get the drill into the lower part of the bilge. Once the top hole has been drilled the lower ones are carefully lined up with it. The limber holes on each side are drilled before the floor is fitted. Where there is no keel bolt the angle-bar should have two vertical bolts through the keel, or even three for a wide keel.

ordinary angle gauge is all that is needed to get the angle between the top of the hog and the inside of the planking.

Where there are few or no frames the floors can be made with wooden or metal flanges for securing to the planking and the hog. The side flanges will need bevelling to suit the angle of the planking, and be curved to follow the hull shape, but the inboard sides of wooden flanges need not be curved. Wooden flanges will be screwed or bolted and probably glued to the ply. Another flange, across the top, makes a lot of difference to the strength of the floor, since it eliminates bending of the ply.

The bolts up each side will be spaced at about 3in (75mm) centres in boats up to about 30ft (9m) and at about 6in (150mm) in boats up to about 50ft (15m). Where possible the fastenings through the hog should be bolts rather than coach-screws. In way of ballast keel-bolts, angle-bar may be bolted to the ply by its vertical flange and the keel bolt passed through the horizontal flange. The top flange or stiffening piece can be positioned so as to act as a sole bearer. If the edge is kept well below the sole, with a clearance of perhaps an inch, the stiffener can be added at the precise height after the floor is in position. The doubling piece need not extend right to the planking at each side.

In a cabin, the forward and aft stiffeners are put in at the correct height. A straightedge is laid on them and the other stiffeners fixed so as to touch it exactly. In this way the whole row of sole bearers cum stiffeners is precisely aligned.

At bulkheads floors may not be needed, since it will often provide adequate strength. But where the bulkhead is much thinner than the floors a doubler may be added. Its top edge can take the sole. When fitting a doubler, or when making up ply floors from two thicknesses (in order to use offcuts), there must be very copious glue or bedding between the two pieces. This is always the rule, but it is extra important down in the bilge.

Lightening holes in floors are a waste of time unless weight-saving is up to fanatical levels. Any lightening holes should leave about one-quarter the floor's depth at top and bottom. Limber holes are essential, however, and should be about $1\frac{1}{2}$in (40mm) square regardless of the boat size if they are not to get blocked.

Ply floors should be $1\frac{1}{2}$ times the hull shell thickness for light fast boats and 3 times for stout craft. The flange pieces will generally be square section and about three times the thickness of the floors. At bow and stern plywood cross-members may be fitted horizontally, to act as stowage shelves or berth ends. Short bulkheads, to serve as sail lockers or berth supports, are valuable as they are much deeper and therefore much stronger than ordinary floors. Being so deep, they can be half or a third, or even a quarter, the thickness of other floors.

Metal Floors

These are usually of galvanized mild steel, though at greater cost they may be of a stainless steel or bronze compatible with keel bolts and other fastenings, and certainly these materials extend the life of the vessel besides reducing her corrosion troubles.

Simple metal plate floors have a flange at the bottom bolted or (much less effectively) coach-screwed into the hog. Up each side is a flange bolted through the planking. Sometimes the side flange is made in short lengths but this may not be fully effective. There should be at least four bolts through the planking on each side and where possible they should be staggered. The vertical plate of the floor should be flanged across the top for stiffness. Flanging is not always easy and in some cases flat bar is welded along the top instead or angle-bar may be bolted or welded on. Lightening holes in the main vertical plate are useful not only to save weight but also for pipes and electric cables, although to be sure electric cables should if possible be kept out of the bilge.

Angle-bar floors are made from lengths of standard rolled section. As always, the designer should find out what is available locally before specifying. One piece extends across the top of the hog with lengths up each side of the hull. These side pieces may need bending to fit the planking but if this cannot be done conveniently wood packing is put in. Again there must be at least four bolts each side, fairly commonly countersunk. As with other types of metal floors the fastenings should be of the same material, though if the floors are of ungalvanized steel the bolts should still be galvanized. It is a false economy to do without galvanizing on steel floors, taking just a five year view: in the long term unprotected floors are invariably expensive. Unless the boat is extremely light there should be a good allowance for corrosion if steel is used, as the floors are subject to corrosion more than almost any other part. Since they are so important, it is serious when they become weakened by wasting. They should all have good limber holes ($1\frac{1}{2}$in) and as much protection from moisture as possible.

Flat-bar floors are seen quite often, but they are not fully effective because they are too whippy. They can be improved if they have a cross-bar set on edge vertically about halfway up; this will also strengthen an ordinary angle-bar floor. Flat-bar floors can be improved by tapering their ends so that their strength does not cease abruptly at the top corners.

All metal floors should be designed so that their upper corners do not end in a line along the hull, otherwise there will be a weak ridge each side along the whole structure. Generally metal floors are fastened to frames, but if the frames are spaced

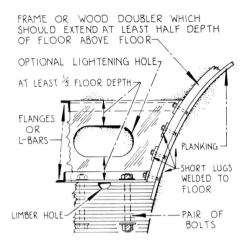

FRAME OR WOOD DOUBLER WHICH
SHOULD EXTEND AT LEAST HALF DEPTH
OF FLOOR ABOVE FLOOR

OPTIONAL LIGHTENING HOLE

AT LEAST ⅓ FLOOR DEPTH

FLANGES
OR
L-BARS

PLANKING

SHORT LUGS
WELDED TO
FLOOR

LIMBER HOLE

PAIR OF
BOLTS

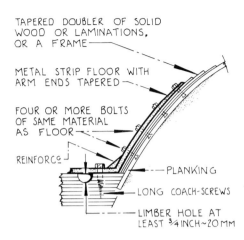

TAPERED DOUBLER OF SOLID
WOOD OR LAMINATIONS,
OR A FRAME

METAL STRIP FLOOR WITH
ARM ENDS TAPERED

FOUR OR MORE BOLTS
OF SAME MATERIAL
AS FLOOR

REINFORCe

PLANKING

LONG COACH-SCREWS

LIMBER HOLE AT
LEAST ¾ INCH~20 MM

Steel plate floors need a flange across the top for stiffness, but when no flanging facility is available angle-bar can be rivetted, bolted or welded across. Alternatively a less stiff flat bar can be welded across. The flange is shown facing away and the bottom flange facing this way, so that the top flange does not interfere with fitting the vertical bolts.

If the hull planking runs straight in way of the floor the sides can be flanged to take the side bolts, of which there must be four or more each side. Where the planking is curved the side flanges must be shaped, but this may be awkward so short lengths of plate are welded on (as shown) or short lengths of angle-bar rivetted or bolted to the main plate.

The limber hole is a groove chiselled in the wood under the floor, which avoids weakening the floor by cutting away some of the bottom flange and plate.

Metal strap floors were in the past forged, and this allowed extra thickness at the elbows with plenty of taper towards the tips. Nowadays it is usual to weld up lengths of flat bar, so there should be some reinforcing at the corners. The ends may be tapered by grinding away, and perhaps by reducing the siding as well as the moulding. As with all floors, there is some form of doubling or padding between the planking and the metal, to prevent the floor crushing the wood, to compensate for the local loss of strength caused by the bolt holes in the wood, and to make it possible to fit the floor exactly if it arrives from the fabricator slightly misaligned in any plane, by fairing away the doubler.

Though coach-screws are shown through the base, bolts are better. If coach-screws are used they should be as long and as thick as possible, at least two in number and accurately fitted with particular care being taken when drilling their holes.

well apart there will have to be more floors than frames. When it comes to deciding how many floors to fit, apply Nicolson's law, which is: 'Think of a high number. Then double it. And for long range sailing or a highly stressed boat, double it again.' This may seem flippant, but it is my observation (as a result of surveying a lot of boats) that builders save money by cutting down the number and thickness of floors. They reckon that few owners will query a technical matter of this sort, and not many even haul up the floorboards and examine the structure below critically. For anyone unable to apply Nicolson's law, a rough guide to floor spacing might be: 'In way of stressed areas fit a floor every 12in (30cm); double this distance for a quarter of the boat's length beyond the close spacing; at the ends of the hull the spacing can be doubled again.' The stressed areas are near masts, keels, centreboards and engines. It may seem odd to suggest a fixed spacing figure

regardless of the craft's size, but stresses go up steeply as size increases. The loading that bolts in wood can take is limited by the strength and hardness of the wood, so large craft need floors spaced as closely as smaller ones.

The scantlings of the floors can be taken from Lloyd's Rules. However, in saving weight the tendency will be to use a metal that does not corrode, and have lots of depth with the minimum possible dimension at right angles to the direction of load. This means that the moulded dimensions are generally increased as much as possible and the siding is made just large enough to take the fastenings. For the very highest standard of weight-saving the floors will be designed on aircraft principles and the stresses calculated. It is likely that they will be linked to the mast step or engine bearers, to shroud plates and other critical strength members. For anyone involved in this

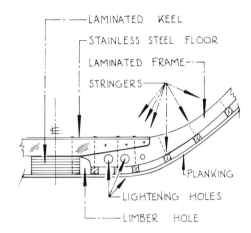

LAMINATED KEEL
STAINLESS STEEL FLOOR
LAMINATED FRAME
STRINGERS
PLANKING
LIGHTENING HOLES
LIMBER HOLE

The steel floors of this Three-quarter Tonner built by McGruers are flanged and bolted both vertically and horizontally. It is only when building expensive racing craft that a builder can afford such details as lightening holes. Each stringer is bolted through at each frame, the bolt head being covered by the cold-moulded skin.

level of design work who wishes to subcontract the stressing, help can be obtained from such organizations as the Wolfson Institute of Aeronautics and Astronautics at Southampton University in England or the National Engineering Laboratory, East Kilbride, Glasgow, Scotland.

Whatever metal is used, it is rare to specify a thickness for plate bar or strip under $\frac{1}{8}$in (3mm) even on small boats. For galvanized mild steel this thickness should be considered a minimum because galvanizing does not last forever. To help the zinc galvanizing stand up to the rugged conditions of the bilge of a boat, where there is a swirl of abrasive muck and corrosive salt water, floors should be painted before they are fitted. Holes for fastenings need to be drilled doubly oversize, to allow for the galvanizing and paint; that is, the drill size should be $\frac{1}{16}$in (1.5mm) larger than the bolt. Degreasing before painting is important, and the paint should be renewed as soon as it is damaged. Only hot-dip galvanizing is worth using. If mild steel floors simply have to be used without galvanizing, the scantlings should be increased by 50 per cent and the painting should be scrupulous; also the limber holes ought to be extra large so that there is no chance of puddles lying beside the floors.

In flat bar floors the bolt holes must not remove more than a quarter of the cross-section of the metal; in angle-bar floors the flange must not be reduced by more than a third. These figures give an indication of minimum floor size, especially when it is remembered that the floor fastenings should be at least 30 per cent larger in diameter than the plank frame fastenings.

Beams

Typical beam sizes are given at the end of this chapter, as well as in drawings throughout the book. Most beams are of ordinary timber because this is cheapest. For lightness spruce is used; for strength and long life oak used to be popular, but because it is now hard to find iroko is widely used. Where extremely long life is required and price is no object, also where maintenance may be minimal, teak is used, but it is unusual.

Solid wooden beams need the minimum timber and labour, especially if they can be cut from a wide board. The saw line along the top of one beam is the underside of the next, assuming they all have the same, or nearly the same, camber. A very bold camber, something more than a rise of 1 unit for a full beam width of 20 units, usually means 'short grain' beams, resulting in weakness at the ends because the grain cuts at a sharp angle across the member instead of following the curvature. Unless timber can be found that has the correct run of grain, laminated beams are needed.

One good application is when the beam and the knees at each end are combined in one strong unit, for example at cabin-top or cockpit ends, by masts and in way of powerful winches. Even better from the point of view of strength, continuity and appearance is the single 'hoop' frame, right round the boat, in the form of a single strong fabrication of laminated frames, floor and beam. This looks elegant and saves space, reduces weight and has no hard spots such as are often found at the join of a floor to its frames.

Because there is no risk of an internal fault in the wood, a laminated beam can be 5 or sometimes 15 per cent smaller in sided dimensions than a solid one. It is rare to reduce the moulded depth, because a small change makes a big reduction in strength.

For all sizes of craft this minimum deck beam spacing is usually at 12in (30cm) centres. Closer

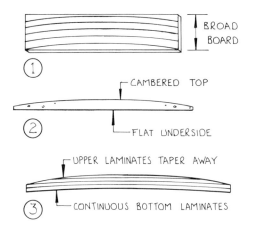

① ⟦BROAD BOARD⟧

② CAMBERED TOP / FLAT UNDERSIDE

③ UPPER LAMINATES TAPER AWAY / CONTINUOUS BOTTOM LAMINATES

The economical way to make beams (1) is to cut them from a broad board so that the top cut of one forms the under side of the next. Another time and money-saving approach (2) is to camber the beams on the top but not on the underside. This gives a slight loss of headroom, but narrow pine pieces are cheap to buy. Knots should be kept away from the middle where the highest stresses are. The most sophisticated beams (3) are laminated and taper towards the ends. The upper laminates are the ones which should be faired away, so the curve of the jig should fit the underside. The laminates are built up on this, then the top camber is cut and finally the top planed smooth.

than this and fitting becomes tedious and expensive. The maximum spacing, on a boat of about 60ft (18m) overall, will seldom be much over 1ft 8in (50cm). More than this gives the deck unsupported panels which are too large: flexing becomes noticeable unless the deck is made thicker.

It is a mark of good building that the beams are close together. Since virtually all the load on a beam is vertically down, depth matters, and fore-and-aft width needs to be little more than enough to take the deck fastenings. In practice beams tend to be about 1½ times as deep as they are wide. This narrowness can be turned to great advantage when making laminated beams; a wide beam is made and sliced up into two or more, which is a great saving of time and allows the wide boards prepared for cold-moulded planking to be used without further machining. Beams are made like any other laminated component, on a jig. It is obviously a help if they all have the same camber. Even where the full-width beams are laminated it is rare to laminate half-beams, except those which will be exposed and are a decorative feature. Half-

beams are often made from straight parallel sided pieces of solid timber, with the camber only put on the top face.

When laminated beams are required with more thickness at one point, it is usual to have the bottom laminates running through the full length and the upper ones tapered out. A set of very light beams would be thicker in the middle than at the ends since this gives the greatest strength from the least material. They would be made up with parallel top and bottom faces, glued up to the correct curvature in the usual way, but the *bottom* of the beam will be to the desired curvature and the top flatter than the final camber. When the glue has set the top of the beam will be planed off at the ends to the correct camber.

All this takes time, which explains why solid wood is favoured so often. Because of the shortage of spruce, which used to be very popular, many boats are built with pine or larch beams. These woods need careful selecting otherwise there will be too many knots, or the knots will be too large –

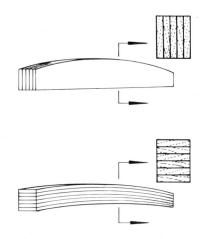

Occasionally laminations are set at right angles to the curvatures. The top sketch shows a beam with camber on top but a horizontal and straight underside. For supporting deck-stepped masts this sort of high-strength beam has advantages. The lower sketch shows the more usual way of arranging the laminates, with the planks laid round the curvature. Most frames, beams, backbone structures and in fact the vast majority of glued-up sections are built this way. It tends to be more economical in labour and timber, and though the scantling may be more flexible this is not always a disadvantage.

Sections through each beam are shown enlarged, the upper one having vertical laminates and the lower one horizontal.

so we come back to laminating, as a sure way of getting rid of such weaknesses. One problem (if that is the right word) about building a cold-moulded boat with such attractive features as laminated frames is that every part of the boat must be made to accord. If solid unlaminated larch or pine is used for beams the builder who wants a fine-looking craft will take trouble to put the worst wood at the ends of the boat, where no-one will see it; against bulkheads or in lockers.

Cold-moulded hulls tend to be unusually strong yet light, so a special type of beam with this characteristic is worth considering for a racing boat, or one which has to be carried on a trailer, or wherever weight must be pared right down. Web beams are made from marine ply, with spruce or perhaps the cheaper Douglas fir in upper and lower flanges. The ply is set on edge, often with the bottom edge straight to save work and give depth on the centreline. There may be lightening holes in the web. Along the top and bottom edges are the flanges, which are often made from square section timber glued to the two faces. These flanges give the beam great strength, since they make it like an I-beam with much of the material located as far as possible from the neutral axis. The flanges also supply a ground for the deck and for fastenings.

Another variation is a box section: the top and bottom flanges form the upper and lower sides of the box, and there are two identical ply verticals which form the other two sides of the box. The flanges are again glued on, perhaps with some screws or barbed nails. It is particularly advisable to have lightening holes in this enclosed type of beam to give ventilation. Holes are always kept away from the highly stressed areas such as the middle and the ends. This type of beam will be made from $\frac{1}{8}$in (3mm) marine ply for boats up to about 30ft (9m) and of about $\frac{1}{4}$in (6mm) ply for boats up to about 45ft (14m). Such astonishingly thin ply can be used because the beams have great depth, 6in (15cm) being quite usual on a 30-footer and 10in (25cm) on a 45-footer.

At each end of any deck opening such as a hatchway, cockpit or coachroof it is good practice (not universally followed) to put extra strong beams. Thicker beams are also located under big sheet winches, anchor winches, by masts and mooring points. Strong beams are roughly 25 per cent deeper and wider than standard beams, and occasionally 50 per cent larger. Increasing both the siding and depth is not convenient however, for

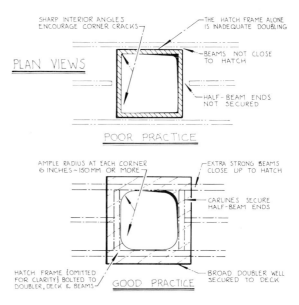

PLAN VIEWS

SHARP INTERIOR ANGLES ENCOURAGE CORNER CRACKS

THE HATCH FRAME ALONE IS INADEQUATE DOUBLING

BEAMS NOT CLOSE TO HATCH

HALF-BEAM ENDS NOT SECURED

POOR PRACTICE

AMPLE RADIUS AT EACH CORNER 6 INCHES ~ 150MM OR MORE

EXTRA STRONG BEAMS CLOSE UP TO HATCH

CARLINES SECURE HALF-BEAM ENDS

HATCH FRAME (OMITTED FOR CLARITY) BOLTED TO DOUBLER, DECK & BEAMS

BROAD DOUBLER WELL SECURED TO DECK

GOOD PRACTICE

Deck strength is reduced, sometimes seriously, when it is cut through for a hatch, cockpit well or skylight. It is not enough to make a rectangular hole and bolt a hatch in place, unless the deck is unusually rugged and also not going to be seriously stressed. The aim must be to put back round the hole all the strength which was taken away by cutting the aperture. Shearing and bending forces have to be met and one of the best solutions is to fit a thick doubler. Circumstances alter cases, but a doubler twice the deck thickness and having a width ten times the deck thickness often looks right and gives adequate strength for a limited weight. But for an exposed mooring or where severe weather may be expected these figures might be doubled without the reinforcement looking grotesque. To be effective a doubler must also be well fastened.

Half-beam ends almost always need proper securing to carlines so that the whole opening is ringed by beams and carlines, all closely knit and close to the opening.

instance when running the beams through a thicknesser the machine has to be reset. When ordering the timber two sizes are needed. If the boat is built with the beams set on top of the beam shelf (i.e. if the shelf is not tight up under the deck, but lowered by the depth of the standard beams) the extra deep ones will not fit. So some people just increase the siding or moulding but not both. Keeping to the same moulded depth also ensures no lost headroom. Another trick is to put in a hardwood beam for extra strength where the majority are softwood.

At the top of each bulkhead a beam should be put in. Ideally there should be bolts at about 6in

(15cm) centres staggered through the bulkhead and beam, though most builders use screws. Bulkheads, especially ply ones, cannot hold deck fastenings and so the beam both stiffens the bulkhead and takes a row of fastenings along its edge.

A deck member seldom used except on ultra-light boats is a fore-and-aft 'deck stringer', though in some areas this term is used for the beam shelves especially if they are right up under the deck and right out against the planking, like chines at deck-edge level. Longitudinals particularly suit decks which are very heavily cambered because little shaping is needed and there is less work and waste. The top surface may need bevelling, and trans-verse supports in the form of bulkheads or a limited number of deep athwartships beams are still essential. A disadvantage of this form of structure is that it does not prevent the boat being crushed, say when lying with other craft alongside a harbour wall, and strength bulkheads are required for athwartships stiffness. Longitudinals must be of clear-grained timber such as spruce or a fine pine with faults (like knots) which take away no more than 20 per cent of the cross-section at the very most.

Because all beams are more vulnerable than most scantlings to rot, they should be treated with Cuprinol even if other parts are not. Rain coming in through hatches, leaks in the deck or via stan-chion bolts which work slightly loose are just some of the ways beams become saturated. The anti-rot fluid should be applied to the beam shelves, carlines and other associated parts before they are fastened in.

The bottom edges of all beams should be 'broken', that is rounded, or bevelled (the quickest and cheapest), or recessed with a cove (groove) put in with a spindle moulder or router. Laminated beams are usually either bevelled or rounded, and only to the depth of the bottom laminate; the carlines (fore-and-aft pieces) should match them. Edge treatment is omitted if a lining covers the beams.

Where bolts are put through beams in such a way that the beam strength is seriously reduced, some sort of doubling is needed. If the bolt diameter is one-fifth the beam siding it is time to consider reinforcing, and if it is more than one-third full doubling up is important. The doubling may be a strip of the same or a harder wood glued along one side of the beam and extending at least

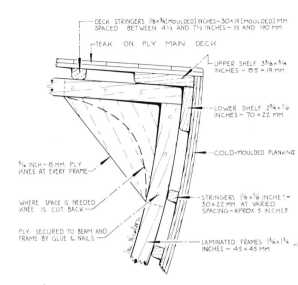

A section through the deck edge of a McGruer built 32ft (10m) yacht shows one of the strongest techniques where light weight is required. The hull and deck planking are supported by numerous light stringers so that the shell keeps the water out and the internal framework holds the structure together. But this is only half the case since the shell also gives part of the strength and the stringers together with the planking are massively thick.

The beams and frames can be made up as complete strong hoops, with the frames extending across the hog (or stem, up forward). This gives a wonderful structure because the potentially weak corners at each beam end are stiffened by glued ply webs. While the glue is setting they are fastened by bronze barbed nails. By bunks, especially pilot berths which are right outboard and usually fairly high up under the deck, the webs are cut to a curve on the inboard edge. This does not weaken them much but it gives valuable extra room.

eight times the beam moulding, in way of the bolt. Or in a laminated member enough extra layers to make up the lost strength can be applied.

Beams are put in as soon as the boat is turned the right way up, and before the moulds are removed. Normally they are fitted working from amidships towards the ends, leaving out enough to make it easy to get in the engine, tanks, furniture and other parts. The short end beams may be made from the offcuts or smaller pieces left over from the long beams.

A great deal of trouble should be taken fitting the first beam to make sure it is exactly athw-artships. The correct location on one beam shelf is marked, and the beam laid in place. A large set-square is put against the beam and against the centreline wire to make sure it is precisely at right angles to the ship's centreline. The beam end position is marked on the other shelf and the second, third and fourth beams can then be marked from the pencil lines for the first. But after two or three have been taken from the first one an error may creep in, so at the third or fourth a further check should be made against the centreline. As a second check, or where there is no large reliable set-square, measure from the centreline right forward, first to the beam face on the port side, then the starboard, at the shelf. These diagonals should be of equal length: if not,

either something is not at 90° across the centreline or the hull is no longer symmetrical.

Once the beams are in they may seem flexy, and this is not unusual. However, when the deck has been laid and fastened the beams work together and with the decking, so there should be no more than a slight sensation of give, and then only on lightly built high-performance craft. It is no good copying that outrageous sponginess which some factory built pseudo-boats have. If the deck seems to lack strength when complete, as it may even when plans by good designers are followed, the addition of hanging knees and perhaps at least one pillar will make a lot of difference.

PRELIMINARY GUIDE TO BEAM DIMENSIONS

This table must always be modified to suit individual craft. It assumes high quality wood and a high standard of workmanship.

Length overall	Light duty			Medium duty			Heavy duty craft			
	mould'g	sid'g	spac'g	mould'g	sid'g	spac'g	mould'g	sid'g	spac'g	
25ft	$1\frac{3}{4}$	1	11	$2\frac{1}{4}$	$1\frac{1}{2}$	11	$3\frac{1}{4}$	$2\frac{1}{4}$	12	in
7.5m	45	25	280	57	38	280	85	57	305	mm
35ft	$2\frac{1}{4}$	$1\frac{1}{4}$	13	3	2	14	$3\frac{3}{4}$	$2\frac{1}{2}$	15	in
11m	57	32	330	75	50	355	95	65	380	mm
45ft	$2\frac{3}{4}$	$1\frac{3}{4}$	16	$3\frac{3}{4}$	$2\frac{1}{2}$	17	$4\frac{1}{2}$	3	18	in
14m	70	45	405	95	65	430	115	75	460	mm
55ft	$3\frac{1}{2}$	$2\frac{1}{2}$	20	$4\frac{3}{4}$	3	21	$5\frac{1}{2}$	4	22	in
16.5m	90	65	510	120	75	535	140	100	560	mm

Notes Beam ends may be reduced to 60 per cent of the middle moulded dimension, or made the same dimension as the siding; e.g. a beam $3\frac{1}{2} \times 1\frac{1}{2}$in in the middle may be $2\frac{1}{4} \times 2\frac{1}{4}$in at the ends. Spacing refers to distance between centres.

Extra strong beams are often fitted at each end of hatches, cabin tops etc. The strong beam dimensions may be taken from the 'duty' column next on the right of the ordinary beams being used, i.e. if beams for Light duty are specified the strong beams will be taken from the Medium duty column.

This table is only a preliminary guide. It will in particular be usual to reduce the beam spacing if the deck thickness is not commensurate with the beam dimensions. In a vessel with no strength bulkheads or pillars, or with above average beam, the scantlings must be increased.

PART 6

FROM DECK TO KEEL

Plywood Decks

The majority of boats now built in wood have decks of ply. The speed at which the deck goes on, the absence of leaks and its strength all make ply popular. Because ply panels are rigid across the plane of the material, no lodging knees are needed with a ply deck. The hull gains a tremendous strength and resistance against racking and distortion, as viewed from above, when a ply deck is fitted. Old-fashioned decks of planks nailed to the beams used to move at sea. Each plank would slide along its neighbour by a minute amount, but because there were so many planks across the width of the deck the sum of all these tiny movements was significant.

Though plywood is strong for its weight, there are disadvantages. A cubic foot of ply costs a lot more than a cubic foot of plain timber, even timber which has been machined all over. If the builder has a large stock of wood left over from planking, he may find it is cheaper to cold-mould the deck, so the following section deals with that. But generally the saving in hours and labour costs makes ply the usual solution regardless of the size of boat.

Marine ply must be used, and it is almost the most costly version of this fairly expensive material. Every board is stamped with the marine specification number BSS1088, even though it may be manufactured outside the UK. Ply is virtually always sold in sheets 8 × 4ft (2.440 × 1.220m) though there are a few manufacturers who supply 8 × 5ft (2.440 × 1.524m). Thickness is in millimetres. Deck thickness partly depends on the beam spacing, and this is particularly true when planning boats under about 30ft (9m), also for decks less than $\frac{1}{2}$in (12mm) thick. The figures in the graph and the following section on Cold-Moulded Decks are a guide.

In laying a ply deck some builders like to leave off part of the deck, maybe a third or more, to make it easier to run electric cables aboard, fit furniture, clean the boat out, get in engines or tanks, have extra headroom in tight spaces, or for chatting to a girlfriend without having her aboard cluttering the place up.

A typical working procedure is as follows.
1. Draw up a plan showing where each ply panel is to go, unless the designer has prepared one (only a few do so).
2. Fair off the top of the beams, beam shelves, hull top edges, stem, transom top – in fact all the top faces onto which the ply must rest.
3. Lay down the first sheet, holding it in place with two or four clamps. Go underneath and mark with pencil or chalk the edges of all the beams, carlines, planking outside edge, etc.
4. Remove the ply and turn it over so that all the marked lines show.
5. Cut off the surplus wood round the deck edge, leaving about $\frac{1}{8}$in (3mm), or half that width for the skilled shipwright. This will be planed away after the whole deck has been fastened and glued.
6. Drill the holes for the screws and nails.
7. Apply glue on the tops of the beams, deck edges, transom top etc. With *some* two-part glues the hardener goes onto the underside of the ply.
8. Put the ply panel in place on deck and secure it down with weights and fastenings. Now go back to (3) and lay the second panel, and so on.
9. When the whole deck is on go underneath and fit the butt straps that connect the panels.
10. When the glue is fully dry, plane round the sheer to trim off the surplus ply.

Enlarging on these steps:
1. The drawing should be arranged so that joins in the ply are kept away from corners of cabin tops and cockpits, away from hatches and high-stress points like big winches.

For anyone not used to this type of work it is best to cut out of tracing paper pieces which are 8 × 4ft to the same scale as the deck plan. Slide these rectangular pieces of paper, each of which represents a ply panel, over the drawing until the best and least wasteful arrangement is achieved. Offcuts may be used to fill a small corner. An L-

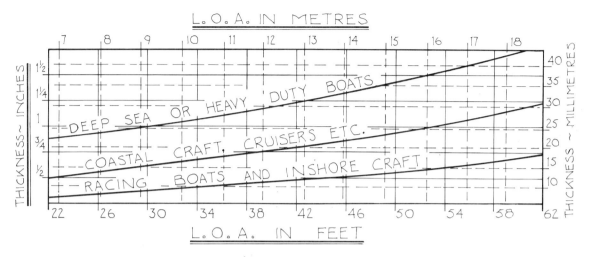

L.O.A. IN METRES

THICKNESS ~ INCHES

THICKNESS ~ MILLIMETRES

DEEP SEA OR HEAVY DUTY BOATS

COASTAL CRAFT, CRUISERS ETC.

RACING BOATS AND INSHORE CRAFT

L.O.A. IN FEET

Deck thickness figures, intended as a preliminary guide. For the type of craft select the appropriate curve. It may be advisable to interpolate between two curves. If the deck is sheathed a reduction of thickness might be considered if the material is a strong and well bonded layer of glassfibre or Dynel. It is hard to justify a reduction for a plywood or cold-moulded deck simply because it has a waterproof, non-strength anti-slip skin such as Treadmaster.

These curves are for a ply or cold-moulded deck; a solid planked, caulked and payed deck based on the upper one should prove satisfactory, or it may be used for a ply or cold-moulded deck. In practice marine ply is seldom available thicker than 1in (25mm) so either two layers have to be used or cold-moulding built up to a suitable thickness, or ply ordered specially.

shaped piece which fits round the forward starboard corner of the coachroof, when cut from a standard panel may leave another L-shaped piece which will fit at the port corner. At the bow a single sheet will cover a good length if the ply is first cut diagonally from opposite corner to corner; the cut is laid outside the sheer and a join is made down the centreline of the boat. Each side of this join is a long side of the original panel.

2. To fair the tops of the beams, carlines etc slide a batten or straightedge over the deck, in time covering the whole area, and make sure that nothing stands high. The batten should lie so that no beam, part of the hull edge or carline pushes it up at all. If a beam sags it may be necessary to put a thin packing piece on top. The aim is to have the whole length of every beam, all the carlines, the full length of the beam shelves, etc in continuous contact with the decking.

3. There is disagreement about where the decking should start, as there is with just about every aspect of boatbuilding. (Shipwrights are such an independent lot, mostly working in small teams isolated from other yards, and it has to be admitted that circumstances vary from boat to boat.) A good case can be made for starting with the stern panel first. When it is on it forms a good

platform for the next one forward. The bow piece is sometimes slightly more awkward than the others so it is sensible to do it last. Staging is almost always needed round the hull to put the deck on, and if the staging happens to be located at the bow it may be best to start there and work aft. It probably does not matter much where a start is made provided the sketch plan of the panel placings is followed, and provided port and starboard decks are worked at about the same rate, to avoid distortion.

Wood should not be marked with pencil where it is later to be varnished. Accidental pencil marks come off best if a hard india rubber is used across the grain. Sandpaper is seldom effective. Once the first coat of varnish goes on over a pencil mark the blemish shows for all time.

4. Handle ply with care. If a panel is dropped on edge the resulting dinge may be the place where a leak starts. Because ply is made up of thin layers of wood, sometimes of relatively vulnerable species, it is easily damaged. Two people at least are needed to handle even a 10mm ($\frac{3}{8}$in) thick standard panel without risk.

5. An electric jigsaw is quick, but in skilled hands a normal panel saw often quicker. The saw must be held at a small angle to the ply to avoid splitting

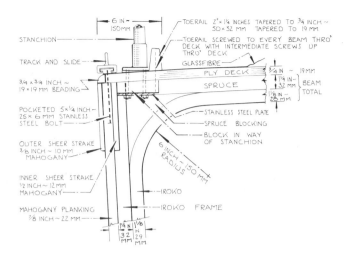

Typical scantlings for a sailing yacht 41.5ft overall and 30ft on the waterline (12.7 × 9.1m), designed by Holman & Pye. She has an elegant rounded deck edge with an inserted beading to cover the vulnerable outer edge of the deck covering.

Because deck edges are potentially weak careful designing is needed. To give the decking ample landing an inner sheer strake has been added, thin enough to bend round easily and deep enough for well staggered fastenings. It also serves to bulk up the top edge of the hull shell to take the vertical bolts which holds the headsail sheet track.

the edge. As the cut will be from the bottom, where the pencil line is, this splitting is on the top surface and serious. If there is any lack of skill, cut $\frac{1}{4}$in (6mm) or more outside the pancil line even though this means more planing later.

6. The holes have to be drilled from the bottom, because this is where the pencil lines are. Use sharp drills to avoid splitting, and a backing block so that the drill goes right on into it, with no gap under the ply to encourage splitting away as the drill emerges. To save time and further limit the chances of splitting, have a depth stop on the drill. Countersinking, where required, is done at this stage because once the ply is down there is a rush to secure it before the glue sets.

For a boat about 20ft long (6m) the fastenings will be about 2in apart (50mm) round the edges and something like 3in apart (75mm) along the beams and beam shelf. These distances will increase to about 3in (75mm) along the edges and 5in (125mm) along beams for a 45-footer (14m). Use countersunk screws or barbed nails, or both (see Cold-Moulded Decks), and between $2\frac{3}{4}$ and $3\frac{1}{2}$ times the ply thickness in length. They should be all ready close to hand because once the glue is

spread there is no time for anything but getting the ply fully fastened.

7. The glue or its hardener, which is put on the underside of the ply, can be spread after the ply panel has been lifted up onto the deck, but not of course onto that part of the deck where it is to be finally fitted. The best glue to use is epoxy. This stage of the operation, and the next, are not work to do singlehanded; at least one other person, and preferably a team of four, are needed.

8. The ply panel will 'locate itself' as its edge has been cut to fit the boat. Cramps, weights or both are put on to hold it down and round the camber while the fastenings are driven in. Work from one corner towards the diagonally opposite corner. To speed up this stage some shipwrights put in every other or every third fastening. Sandbags don't dent the top of the ply and cost little. Weights may not be needed if there is a full team working on the deck: three or four people all kneeling on one ply panel while they secure it provide plenty of weight. The least skilled puts the fastenings into the holes, which have been drilled down into the beams and carlines by the second least skilled. A stop on the drill is essential as this stage of the job is one long rush, especially in warm weather when the glue may be hardening rapidly. The most skilled workers drive the screws in using pump screwdrivers, and the nails with a hammer used carefully so as not to bruise the surface.

9. The butt straps will be bedded or glued, with screws or countersunk bolts (heads on deck top) in a pattern all over the pad. Ply thinner than 12mm ($\frac{1}{2}$in), is hard to screw because there is scarcely enough wood for the thread to grip. Decking offcuts can be used. To make a neat strong job, the butt strap should extend from beam to beam. Some builders butt ply on a beam, but this gives trouble: few beams are wide enough to give a good landing for two pieces of ply, and there is no strong join between the adjacent panels. A well secured butt strap holds two ply panels together so well that they are not much weaker than one continuous piece.

10. As the edge is planed away all round, check that there are no gaps in the glue. It should have been used most copiously, so that it squeezed out at all mating surfaces. Just before it sets the surplus is wiped or cut away with care, to avoid scooping any glue away from recesses. At the same time the minimum excess is left to blunten tools during the cleaning off stage.

To cut down the number of joins that need seam battens or butt blocks, the ply may be scarphed up before being fitted to the deck. A few builders cut the scarphs on the workbench, then glue them up as the panels are fitted on the deck. This seems risky: scarphing is a skilled job and very good case can be made for having it done in the ply factory. Panels can be scarphed up to any length, but the slope of the scarph means that there is a slight loss of length. Two pieces 8ft long and 12mm ($\frac{1}{2}$in) thick end up about 15ft 8in long (a loss from 4.880m to 4.775m). Long pieces are hard to handle and it is seldom advisable to scarph together more than three standard panels, which will require at least four people to handle when in one long strip.

Fore-and-aft seam joins can be over deck stringers recessed into the beams. These stringers are in this instance seam battens. The centreline join may be on a king plank recessed into the beams. If the boat is just too wide to be covered by two (or four) ply panels, a little extra width of decking material is gained by having a rebated solid king plank down the centreline. The ply lodges in the rebates on each side of the king plank, and the width between the rebates is the gain. For instance if the boat's beam at the aft end of the foredeck is 8ft 8in (2.642m) it cannot be covered by two standard panels; but by using a king plank 12in (305mm) wide with a rebate each side of 2in

(50mm), the ply will be wide enough, and still have adequate landings for the fastenings.

Where a deck is heavily cambered it may be difficult to get ply to bend over the curve. In particular a well rounded coachroof is likely to be hard to skin over with 12mm ($\frac{1}{2}$in) ply, which is commonly used. The alternative is to use two or three thinner layers, but they have to be very well glued together with painstaking care to avoid air bubbles or glue starvation. If water gets between the plies rot, delamination and buckling follow swiftly, so the ply panels have to be meticulously pressed and secured together.

Where several layers are used factory scarphs are much safer than handmade joins. If no scarphs are used the butts and seams must be well staggered and glued. Where glue is not used bedding compounds which do not harden are suitable, as described in an earlier section.

If there is camber of the order of 1 in 10 or even steeper, by using several layers of ply it is

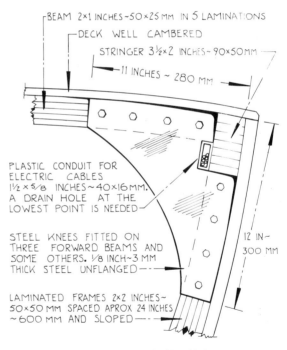

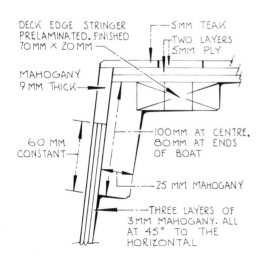

A Norlin designed Three-quarter Tonner deck-edge construction. The beam has been omitted for clarity. The unusual deck-edge stringer has been laminated to the shape of the deck *off* the hull and then fitted.

The deck-edge structure of this 41-footer racer is remarkably light. The designer has gone to considerable lengths to save weight. For long-range offshore work it would be usual to have scantlings perhaps twice this size. Since the steel brackets are thin they twist easily, and so can be bolted tight onto the beam face and frame edge even though these are not in the same plane.

sometimes possible to omit all the beams. This is seen in coachroofs, but beams cannot be omitted under main decks. The ply must be bent in place and then well glued, soft beddings being no use in this type of beamless construction. To get the ply to follow the correct curve, and to support it while the glue is curing, there have to be temporary beams or moulds underneath.

The edges of a ply deck can be painted if the deck is painted, or covered by whatever sheathing is put on the deck. If mouldings or battens are laid over ply edges more than average care is needed with glue or bedding. Any water which creeps between a moulding and the edge of a ply panel makes trouble, especially in frosty conditions. As the water freezes it expands, making room for more water to seep in when the first thaw comes. In time the water soaks the ply edge and drying out never occurs because the moulding keeps away the sun and breeze. This is just the condition to encourage rot, which is why some of the best builders take so much trouble to leave ply deck edges exposed, though they are still sealed.

A trick which may help beginners, provided it is used with caution, is to fit the seam battens and sometimes even the butt straps *on top* of the deck. The work is easier and quicker, with less risk that the filling compound is skimped or fastenings spread too far apart. Fastenings for these components should be spaced as for the ply deck. Seam battens on deck can only be done after careful planning, otherwise the deck will look a mess and have hazards all over to trip the crew on dark nights. A king plank laid on top forms a handy toehold, especially on a sailing foredeck, but the other battens will normally be made cambered on top and given well rounded edges so that they can be walked over effortlessly. On the side-decks of sailing craft battens may also be located under sheet lead tracks, and on any craft they may form part of cockpit coamings.

Cold-moulded Decks

Complex curves in the shape of a deck may be a good argument for using cold-moulding techniques generally similar to those for hulls. Where a coachroof blends into the deck and there are beams with double curvature, it is almost certainly the best approach. Quite a few modern racers have such a deck shape for strength, headroom without the weight and weakness of cabin sides, and to give a large working deck area.

It is possible to build sweeping decks using fairly wide strips of plywood, or a combination of ply and cold-moulding. The width of ply sheet used will depend on the sharpness of the beam curve and if in doubt it is important to keep the strip narrow. Because there are so many variables, a mock-up could be worthwhile.

As with hull planking there can be two or three layers of veneers, or even more, but there will seldom be over four because of the extra labour. Using the same thickness and width of planking for the deck as was used for the topsides simplifies buying, reduces waste and saves money. For the lightest deck one will go for veneers of a wood like spruce or one of the better locally available pines. Because decks are high up it is doubly important to save weight. For economy the lower laminates might be of pine and the top one spruce, which is wonderfully clear wood, free from knots, attractive in colour and though not hard wearing it has in the past been popular on racing craft.

For deep-sea work it is a well established principle that the deck should be as strong as the topsides. Waves breaking aboard fall from a height and come suddenly. So though the weight of water expected on a 30ft (9m) boat will seldom exceed a total of 5 tons, one must allow for 10 tons. And of course the sea does not conveniently spread itself evenly at the same depth all over the deck. It has a despicable habit of piling up deep and frightening, sometimes just at a weak point like between the forehatch and the corner of the coachroof. To make things worse a deck is virtually flat, whereas hulls have curvature in many areas, so the topsides and bottom tend to have 'shape strength' which the deck seldom has. Then again the hull shell may be supported by more internal stiffening than the deck, which often has only the beams and maybe a few bulkheads. To make the deck potentially weaker, it is pierced by hatches and other larger openings such as a coachroof and cockpit, unlike the hull shell. For offshore work it is easy to make out a case for having the deck *thicker* than the hull planking.

For weight-saving, particularly in well sheltered

waters, deck thickness can be cut down considerably. However this has to be done with care and special attention to the placing of the beams. What matters is not the *spacing* of the beams, but the *gap* between the adjacent faces of two neighbouring beams. This gap is the beam spacing minus the beam siding, i.e. the distance each deck panel spans without support. A rough guide is:

Deck thickness		Gap	
$\frac{1}{4}$in	6.5mm	5in	125mm
$\frac{3}{8}$	9.5	7	175
$\frac{1}{2}$	12	9	225
$\frac{5}{8}$	16	11	280

As with all these rough guides, allowances have to be made for factors like the quality of the timber, the builder's skill and the work the boat is to do.

Turning to alternative deck surfaces, nothing surpasses teak for appearance, long life, and it is also more slip-resistant than most timbers. It is a moderately heavy wood (about 45lbs/cu ft) and shakingly expensive, so it is used only for the last layer. It needs degreasing before gluing down otherwise the glue will not adhere. A natural oil permeates teak, and is one reason why rot so seldom gains a foothold, but the oil also rejects glue. A proprietary degreaser such as MEK, or carbon tetrachloride (which is toxic) wiped over removes surface oil.

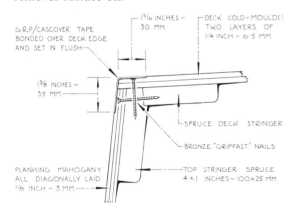

Deck-edge construction on a high-performance sailing yacht 34ft (10.3m) overall. The edge tape is recessed otherwise it is likely to be chafed and forced up off the wood.

The use of barbed nails is typical of modern practice. They give quicker and lighter joins than screws but are not so reliable, and if they have to be taken out for any reason the job is time-consuming and likely to result in chewed wood round the hole.

Whatever deck is laid, there is a choice of fastening techniques. Glue alone is seldom used and fastenings without glue are not ideal; best of all is a combination of glue and metal fastenings. If glue is used without nails or screws, each laminate has to be loaded in turn with weights or sandbags to make sure it is well pressed down while the glue cures. Glue is put on not just the beam and hull top faces, but also on the carlines, beam shelves, quarter knees, deck chocks and so on.

Using metal fastenings alone is throwing away a chance to give the boat a big bonus in extra strength. The strength of a structure (in this context) varies as the square of the depth of the beam plus deck thickness. If the deck is just nailed to the beams there will be a slight movement between the two when load is applied. Gluing bonds the deck to the beams in such a way that they work entirely together. The deflection is typically twice as much when only nails are used.

If the fastenings are put in before the final lamination there will be no visible heads or dowels or stopping. Barbed nails such as Anchorfast and Gripfast have been criticized in the past when used in certain locations, such as for the principal links between frames and planking, but there is general agreement that for fixing down decks this type of fastening is hard to beat. It will not corrode, is quick to use, not heavy or expensive, and it holds well if the correct size of hole has been drilled. Follow the maker's instructions when drilling the holes, but if in doubt first try test holes about two-fifths the diameter of the shank inside the barb. Experiment with a dozen nails in the same wood that is on the boat, and if the nails drive in with just the usual amount of firm determination behind the hammer then the holes are the correct diameter. If the nails go in easily the hole size is too large, though this is unlikely at two-fifths the shank diameter. If the nails bend, the holes are too small.

Galvanized nails might be used instead of barbed nails, but only as a last resort. If they start to rust the whole of the top veneer has to be removed, then all the nails removed . . . a long costly job. However, on cheap boats galvanized nails are used, and if the quality of the galvanizing is good (a very hard thing to discern by eye alone) rusting will not commence for say ten years provided the nails go in without damage to the protective zinc.

The alternative to nails is countersunk screws. Many good builders use screws at important deck locations like beam ends, and barbed nails elsewhere, or a combination of 30 per cent screws and the rest nails. Whatever is used, all fastening heads must be sunk below the timber prior to applying the final laminate.

The procedure for veneering a deck is similar to cold-moulding a hull. Instead of working over frames or stringers or battens, there are beams spaced fairly closely, about 12in (30cm) being a common distance. For thin laminations, say $\frac{3}{16}$in (5mm) or less, the beams may be farther apart with multiple stringers at 8in (20cm). The veneers will seldom be under $\frac{3}{16}$in (5mm), and $\frac{1}{4}$in (6.4mm) is more usual, because there are normally no steep or complex curves to follow. Laminations $\frac{5}{16}$in (8mm) in stiff wood allow the supporting structure, whether it is beams or stringers, to be about 12in (30cm) apart, especially where there is little curvature. On a hump deck, which is a rounded hillock instead of a conventional step-up coachroof, there will be a hollow port and starboard. The veneers must be pushed down into these concavities and held there, so there must be extra support structure. This is where the beams must be spaced at more like 8in (20cm) centres, or better still stringers at about 6in (15cm).

There should be glue between the first layer of veneer and the beams (or deck stringers), but if as sometimes happens to speed up the job none is used, there must be some fastenings at least in the hollows. Where the deck has a normal camber fixing the ends of the pieces will hold the middle down enough under most circumstances until the full set of deck fastenings are put in. Builders occasionally use stainless steel, bronze or nylon staples which are pushed well in below the top surface of the wood and left there when the next layer of veneer is applied.

Normally the second layer is stapled on and the staples left in until the glue has set, as for a hull. As the staples are best put in along the line of each beam, it is essential to know where each one lurks. When the first layer of veneer is put on, the edges of the beams are marked on each plank as it is fitted, and these lines are transferred onto the top of each successive layer. Then, when deck fittings are being put on one still knows exactly where the beams are. This makes it easy to miss a beam when cutting for a vent, or to pick one up when an eyeplate or cleat is being fastened down.

If a mistake is made and the beams are not marked, a long thin drill is driven up from below

through the middle of each end of the first beam. The location of the beam is established on top of the deck, and subsequent beams are measured carefully from the first. Fastenings or wood plugs seal the little holes from the top. Only the most meticulous surveyor ever gets right up under the forward beam, so the holes there are unimportant if thoroughly sealed shut. This trick of drilling the smallest possible hole has uses elsewhere, such as for marking the waterlines through from the inside outwards.

There is a snag to putting the fastenings through the last-but-one veneer: when the deck fittings are put on no-one knows where the fastenings are, so cutting or drilling holes is likely to be frustrating and tool-blunting. Careful shipwrights note before putting in the fastenings just where the deck fittings are to go and avoid screwing or nailing in the vicinity, allowing say a 2in (50mm) margin of error.

The spacing and length of the fastenings will generally be the same as for ply decks, but when trying to cut costs or weight the length of the fastenings might be reduced to $2\frac{1}{2}$ times the thickness of the part of the deck through which the fastening actually goes. That is, if a deck is of four veneers but the fastening only goes through three of them, and each is $\frac{3}{16}$in thick, the minimum fastening length would be $\frac{9}{16} \times 2\frac{1}{2}$ which is $1\frac{1}{2}$in long. The available diameters of barbed nails are strictly limited. Where there is a choice the thicker size is much to be preferred, especially by amateurs, as these nails have a tendency to bend unless carefully driven.

Deck planks are never laid athwartships; on the contrary, to look good the top veneer should follow the sweep of the sheer seen in plan view. This gives long lengths of deck planking, which makes for strength but is expensive. These planks must be kept narrow otherwise they will not bend to follow the curvature of the deck edge, and as wood varies in quality so much, experiments should be made to see how wide a plank can be and still follow round the curve. If in doubt, make the planks no more than $1\frac{1}{2}$in (40mm) wide for boats up to about 40ft (12m), and about 2in (50mm) wide thereafter. For very sharply curved deck edges the planking may have to be kept down to 1in (25mm) wide, or steamed, or cut with some curvature in the planks.

When the top skin is laid with the sweep of the sheer, decking starts with the outside and works inwards. A king plank down the centreline takes the plank ends, which are recessed into it. It is essential to work the port and starboard sides together, great care being taken that each pair of planks is recessed the same amount, otherwise the deck will look dreadful. If the planks are not easy to lay, for instance if there is a lot of beam relative to the length, they may be tapered at each end. This involves a lot of work, and skill too, since the tapering must be even and the planks must all taper the same amount at the same point in the boat's length. Small wonder that this form of traditional deck finish is seldom seen now. The outer plank on each side is made extra wide (often two or three times as wide as the others) and called the covering board. It may be thicker, or from better wood, as it has to take extra wear in places as well as the stanchion bases and other fittings.

Deck top planks laid parallel and running fore and aft are acceptable in quick or cheap building. If they are simply run parallel with the double or triple width king plank they present few problems; laying up starts from the king plank and works outwards. At the deck edge the simplest procedure is to run the planks out over the edge and later cut them off flush with the topsides, putting a toerail on top. This is easy but it looks less than perfect. One way to improve the appearance and add a little strength to the deck edge, also protect the short-grain plank ends, is to fit a covering board on top of the last or second last veneer. It should be of good quality hardwood, ideally teak, but iroko or perhaps makori or one of the harder mahoganies or mahogany substitutes is adequate. It is important to cut waterways or fit drains through the deck, otherwise puddles will lie against the false covering board. The toerail or bulwark is set on top.

A better approach is to fit a proper covering board with the deck plank ends either notched into it or run to it with simple butt ends. Some builders will fit the covering board before the deck, others draw the inboard edge of the covering board on the beam shelf and lay the veneers up to the pencil line.

To save the cost of long deck planks, and to get a quickly laid cheap deck, the top veneer is laid diagonally. It is essential to have the forward end of each plank angled in towards the centreline, so the planks form Vs pointing forwards. The alternative, with the top veneer laid angled outwards at the forward end, is too horrible to contemplate.

To save money there will be no covering board, just a toerail fastened on deck, and for racing this may be a metal extrusion. To improve the appearance a real or false covering board may be fitted as described above for fore-and-aft planking. There should be a king plank: to omit it will seldom cheapen or speed up construction. Rather the reverse, and a king plank has so many subsidiary uses such as to form a centreline toehold (when it is extra thick), to cover the centreline seams of the lower veneers, to form a deck chock for the anchor winch, samson post, inner forestay fitting, etc.

The angle which the top veneer planks makes with the centreline may be 45° if the shortest planks have to be used. I prefer 30° or even 25° as it looks subtly more elegant. The next layer down would traditionally be at right angles to the top layer, but there are strong arguments against this. Wood expands and contracts with changing temperature as well as moisture: even if water never penetrates to the inner veneers the ambient temperature certainly will. This being so, it is logical to have the layers of planking at a small angle to minimize the stress on the glue and fastenings holding them together. Thus, if the top veneer is at 25° to the centreline tapering in towards the bow, the next might be at the same angle but angled outwards towards the bow, making the intersection of the seams 50°. The bottom layer looks better if it is tapered in towards the bow like the top one, and the finer the angle the smarter the appearance.

For diagonally laid decks there has to be some form of landing for the plank ends at the king plank. One way to get a watertight join is to have a rebated king plank. The lower veneer or veneers butt on the outside of the king plank, and the top one or two lie in the rebate. Another technique is to have a row of pads between the beams, so that the tops of the pads and the beams form a landing for the first one or two veneers, the ends of which meet along the centreline. The king plank is next laid, and the final laminations are laid up to it.

There is a totally different approach which is crude, but quick and effective. Here the deck laminations are laid diagonally from port to starboard, right across the centreline. The next layer also goes right across from sheer to sheer. The angle between the layers may be 90° or less. A good case can be made for keeping the angle of the first layer to about 25° to the centreline going leftwards and the next layer the same going rightwards, quite apart from avoiding stresses between the laminations. The strength of a boat longitudinally depends largely on the deck strength. Anyone who has handled an undecked boat will know how floppy it can be, just as a box with no lid is far weaker than one with a tight-fitting lid. If this lid (in this case the deck) has all its strength fore and aft, the boat will tend to be strong longitudinally. So where the need is for lengthways strength the laminations should be run as near fore and aft as possible.

Another approach to the decking centreline join starts with a king plank recessed into all the beam tops: the beams need additional depth to compensate. The first layer ends in a herringbone pattern down one side of the buried king plank and the next down the other side. Each plank length is cut to butt onto the end of the one coming in from the opposite side of the boat, so the join line is a zig-zag and the next layer of decking has another zig-zag but not right over it. This avoids the weakness of a straight join down the centre or near the centre, and minimizes the chances of leaks.

The king plank can also be laid on top, or it can be level with the last one or two veneers. If the king plank is intended to finish flush with the decking it should be made about $\frac{1}{16}$in (1.5mm) too thick and planed down flush when the glue has cured.

Cold-moulded decks are usually laid over the carlines and the coachroof coamings are set on top. This keeps the coaming height to a minimum, always good sense because it is hard to find wide planks of wood and harder still to prevent them splitting in service. Some designers set the coamings inside the carlines, but there are few advantages to this: there must be a line of caulking along the outer face of the coaming at the deck edge and this is not easy to keep tight.

The top surface of a cold-moulded deck can be sheathed over or finished with paint or varnish. Whatever is done, the surface must be perfectly smooth and free from undulations. One way to achieve this is with a large belt sander, such as can be hired from firms which specialize in laying hardwood flooring. It is seldom worth getting one of these for a boat under 40ft (12m) and great care is needed when using it otherwise it will grind down trenches. Because it cannot get into corners and up against all vertical surfaces, the sander should be used before cabin coamings or any other excrescence is put on the deck.

Hull Finishing

Most of the cleaning off, painting, varnishing or sheathing should be done while the hull is still upside-down. Working downhand is far less tiring, quicker and less material is wasted. More important, everything goes on better and stays on more surely. However, turning a boat over seldom goes without some mild hitch. Unless she is really quite small in relation to the equipment available for turning over, it is likely that the hull will be slightly scratched and chafed. The subsequent finishing work is also likely to cause some damage to paintwork. So the final coat or two of varnish or paint is usually left until just before launching. The last veneer layer may be slightly thicker than the others, to allow for smoothing down the surface.

For smoothing off a wooden hull the best tool is a hand plane. Careful and frequent sharpening is the secret. Pause often so that the hull can be examined from different angles to make sure that the precise amount from the right place is being taken off. Because of these reservations, people use belt sanders for smoothing hulls even though they do not make such a good job and tend to give slight ripples or undulations. More serious, a moment's inattention and the belt sander has taken off too much. Because a hand plane requires muscle, it does not breed over-exuberance.

Where a sanding tool is used it is best to suspend it from an overhead rail or beam to carry the weight. Some sort of roller on an overhead rail allows the tool to be moved back and forth and the suspension wire requires a quickly adjustable arrangement (something like a tent toggle) for varying the length. The suspension wire should also have a length of elastic shockcord attached so that the sander is held just above the working surface. The operator then pushes the tool down onto the wood against the tension of the shockcord and this helps to prevent oversanding and dips being ground into the hull. Any suspension system must be variable so that the sander can be used on a horizontal or vertical surface. The bottom will be roughly horizontal, while the topsides will be nearly vertical.

Anyone who has no electric tools except a drill will be tempted to use a disc sander, but even in the most skilled hands these are almost always totally unsatisfactory. Even using a very soft well-cushioned disc, it is impossible to avoid producing at least a few half-moon scours. These can only be eliminated by filling, which means the topsides cannot be varnished, and they have an unpleasant habit of showing up year after year even after careful cosmetics. If mechanical sanding must be done and no belt or orbital sander is available, the type with a cylindrical foam plastic drum with an abrasive belt round it should be used. But even here a good deal of care and skill is needed otherwise scouring and gouge marks will appear.

Paint and varnish should be applied in the same conditions as glue: dryness is essential, the temperature must be right (20°C/68°F is a good all-round average, if in doubt), no drafts and plenty of light. Above all the conscientiousness of a guardian angel is needed. It is worth getting a thermometer, sealing off drafts, spending half a day on the roof sealing up every last leak, vacuuming and sweeping the floor three days in succession well before operations start, and finally damping down the floor with a watering can fitted with a fine rose just before starting so that no dust rises. I have known boatyard painters who will only work when everybody else has gone home so that there is no risk of interference and no-one is likely to come barging in, throwing open the door and raising dust or letting the heat out. These dedicated men add thousands of pounds to the value of the boats they cosset, achieving a gloss that is breathtaking. It is worth being so fanatical.

Paint tins should be turned upside down a fortnight before they are to be used so to reduce the amount of stirring. Varnish tins should be put on a *warm* radiator for a day before using so that the varnish comes out smooth and flowing like the finest warm syrup. It is well worth writing out a complete painter's schedule to ensure that there is the proper time interval between each application. It should state the number of hours to be spent rubbing down because this job is so boring that everyone tends to skip it. As a rough guide half a full day should be allowed for rubbing down a 35ft (11m) boat's topsides. Wet-and-dry sanding between each coat is the best way of getting a really fine finish but takes time, and further time then has

to be set aside to allow the hull to dry properly. After using wet-and-dry the hull will be covered in a white dust once the water has evaporated; this has to be carefully removed with clean cloths and before painting starts tack rags are wiped over to remove any remaining dust.

Varnish looks superb when it is well done over a beautifully finished wooden hull. But defects in the wood can be seen through the varnish so the woodwork must be impeccable. One of the advantages of varnish is that troubles in the hull are often detected almost as soon as they occur. Woods like mahogany which blacken as they start to deteriorate give little warning if painted, but shout aloud about impending troubles when varnish is used. I have personal reservations about varnishing a boat when the outer planking is diagonal, though it is done. To my eye the run of the planks takes a lot away from the perfection of the final appearance if they do not follow the sheer; there is a disharmony between the run of the grain and the line of the deck, boot-top and so on. Admittedly this does not apply when the vessel is seen from a sufficient distance. Varnish does not last as well as paint, especially in hot bright sun, though it is worth remembering that some protection from the effects of ultraviolet light can be obtained in modern varnishes.

Paints which might be described as 'modern' include those with polyurethane or epoxy bases and they do give sensational finishes – sometimes! If conditions are not just right they have a nasty habit of being temperamental and giving not only a bad finish but a coat which is very difficult to remove and replace. So there is much to be said for sticking to the 'old-fashioned' paints which are in fact relatively new. They are the result of a great deal of research, and able to stand up to less-than-perfect conditions while the paint is transferred from pot to boat. After talking to paint salesmen I have no doubt that it is better to use 'traditional' paints if there is any risk that conditions will not be ideally warm and dry when it is being put on.

To choose the right colour scheme the above-water profile plan of the boat should be printed on a heavy quality dyeline paper. Have four or six or even ten prints taken off and, using water colours, paint each print with different colour schemes. Pin these up on an empty white wall, perhaps for a few days. Take down the least acceptable two or three and gradually eliminate those which find least favour. This process of elimination is a remarkably effective way of choosing a good colour scheme. If in doubt, a combination of one colour in different shades can be used.

Light colours last the best and especially on decks and cabin tops should be selected for hot climates because they absorb least heat from the sun. Blue is notorious for fading, and this rule seems to apply regardless of the type of paint or pigment. Dark colours are generally much worse than light ones for fading; they also tend to make a boat look smaller.

Bulkheads and Pillars

Along the taut horizontal centreline wire stretched from bow to stern, the position of each bulkhead is marked. Measure from both the bow and the stern, as a check. From the wire drop a plumb-bob to the inside of the keel or stem and mark both the front and back of each one. This eliminates the chance that a single mark may be for the *forward* side of the bulkhead, but forgotten later when it is put in with its *aft* face against the mark.

Using a large set-square, mark the gunwale port and starboard where the bulkhead is to go, again with double marks. If no large set-square is available lay a straightedge across the gunwales precisely at right angles to the wire and in line with the mark, checking that it's at 90° by measuring diagonally from a point on the wire a few feet from the bulkhead, first to one side then to the other. The diagonals must be equal. Installed bulkheads can be checked for squareness to the centreline and to see if they are parallel by diagonals, which should be equal.

The marks on the top of the keel and at the sheer are joined, using a stiff batten as a guide for the pencil point. This might seem superfluous because the bulkhead should be correctly fitted if it touches all three pairs of marks, but the extra precaution deals with the risk that the bulkhead may be flexible and wobble out of line when being fitted.

FITTING AND SECURING
The bulkhead is cut slightly over-size to the shape taken off either the mould loft floor or the hull. It is lowered in place and the edge marked for final fairing and bevelling. If the bulkhead is to be glassed in place (see below) no bevelling will be done in most commercial yards. During fitting a straight batten should be laid across the bulkhead diagonally, first sloped down to port, then down to starboard. This is to ensure that the bulkhead is going in flat and true. In spite of the marking inside the hull it is possible to put the bulkhead in distorted.

If sawn fillet (fashion) pieces are to be fitted to the hull to take the bulkhead, they may be shaped using the edge of the bulkhead as a template. Normally fillets are put on one side of the bulkhead only. Occasionally they are made by taking straight sections of hardwood and making close-spaced cuts almost through where the fillet needs to bend round a tight curve. The resulting fillet is easy to make and fit, but it needs plenty of

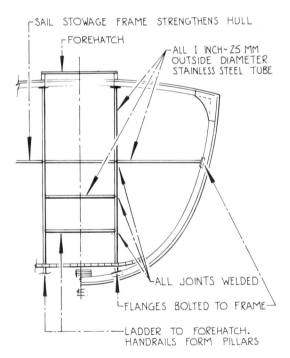

SAIL STOWAGE FRAME STRENGTHENS HULL
FOREHATCH
ALL 1 INCH~25 MM OUTSIDE DIAMETER STAINLESS STEEL TUBE
ALL JOINTS WELDED
FLANGES BOLTED TO FRAME
LADDER TO FOREHATCH. HANDRAILS FORM PILLARS

Light racing boats, like this 41-footer which comes into the Two Ton class need stiffening because the hull shell is made as thin as the designer dares. In this craft he has specified an athwartships web of 1in (25mm) outside diameter stainless steel tubing. To avoid clutter inside and to further save weight, the tubes all have two functions. There is no top rung in the ladder under the forehatch, which is inconvenient for the crew but typical of ruthless racing practice.

fastenings to be effective and is not elegant. However, if it does not show this may not matter.

Fillets can be steamed and bent, but to make a good fit the edges need to be bevelled. Bevelling one edge only is not a good idea because the wood will not bend so well, and if it is put in with the wrong end downwards the bevel will be on the wrong edge. Fillets can also be laminated in, though it is not easy to get the correct bevel and also get the laminates to lie neatly together.

Whatever type of fillet is put in, it must be on the forward side of forward bulkheads and aft of aft bulkheads. This is to allow the bulkhead to slip in place despite the taper towards the ends of the hull sides and bottom.

Screws from the outside in hold the fillets; more screws fix the bulkhead to its fillets. It is never a bad idea to use glue as well as screws, but because of the difficulty of getting an exact fit glue alone is not recommended. Bolts or clenches may be used instead of screws, and as they tend to be stronger they can be spaced farther apart. Fastenings should be spaced at between 5 and 8in (125 and 200mm) centres, according to the strength of the fastenings and the stresses to which the boat is likely to be subject.

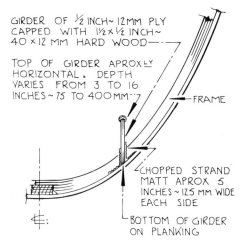

GIRDER OF ½ INCH~ 12MM PLY CAPPED WITH 1½ x ½ INCH~ 40 × 12 MM HARD WOOD

TOP OF GIRDER APROX ½ HORIZONTAL. DEPTH VARIES FROM 3 TO 16 INCHES~ 75 TO 400 MM

FRAME

CHOPPED STRAND MATT APROX 5 INCHES~ 125 MM WIDE EACH SIDE

BOTTOM OF GIRDER ON PLANKING

A lightly built Two Tonner about 41ft overall was fitted with vertical girders port and starboard. The designer had found from past experience that when the backstay was set up with a hydraulic tensioner hulls of this size were liable to bend, sometimes several inches. To stiffen the hull these girders are effective because amidships they are deep, and everywhere bonded strongly to the hull. The girders also double as fronts for settees and the galley bench parts of the ship. This is a good example of how the furniture can be combined with hull structure.

A modern method of securing bulkheads is by glassing-in using the techniques seen in GRP boats. The glassfibre should be on both sides of the bulkhead, and laid in using a minimum of three runs of 1½oz chopped strand mat about 2 per cent of the hull length in width. It is hard to make a truly neat job, but it helps if tape is used rather than CSM or sliced-up woven cloth for the final run of glass. Narrow strips should be used first, not just because each subsequent layer being wider covers the previous edges, but also because each one has its own grip on the wood. So if one layer of glassfibre is poorly applied the bulkhead is not left badly attached.

The glassing-in can be covered by lockers or built-in fittings and lining material or even a stipled paint may be applied to improve the final appearance. It's best to start work on the bulkheads near the ends of the hull, where they are seen less.

The glassfibre strips should be put in over triangular-section filler pieces but this is not always done. Also the timber must be cross-scored with a spike to help the glass adhere. Complete cleanliness is essential. The glassing must be to a high standard and must not be disturbed till it is fully hard and cured, which will be within a week.

BUILDING BULKHEADS

Usually bulkheads are made of plywood but sometimes double or triple or even four skins of diagonal planking are used. If there is a lot of hull timber and glue left over it is only common sense to use up this material. Also, since plywood is relatively expensive a made-up bulkhead, cold-moulded by hand, is cheaper in materials, though it takes more time.

Before cold-moulding bulkheads it is important to decide which way the grain is to run if the bulkhead is to be varnished or polished. Normally the grain in the main saloon will be vertical on the bulkhead and this may mean that grain on the opposite side will either be horizontal or diagonal. Diagonal grain does not look good in the accommodation, so if only two layers are used it will be best to put them at right angles. If three layers are used the outer layers will be vertical (also the strongest arrangement) and the inner one horizontal or diagonal. Occasionally a cabin may seem cramped for width but not for height. For appearance it may be sensible to run the grain horizontally, but it is probably better to paint the bulkhead a light colour instead of varnishing it.

The usual technique, when making up cold-moulded bulkheads, is first to assemble a framework the exact size and shape of the final bulkhead, though sometimes it may be worth making up sheets of 'home made' plywood from the veneers and glue left over from the hull. These cold-moulded sheets should be made as big as needed and then the bulkhead is cut out, as if from a sheet of ply. The offcuts left over can be used for knees, web brackets, deck boxes, furniture, etc. Careful positioning of the framework will get two bulkheads out of one sheet.

Dimensions for the framework can be taken either off the mould loft floor or from the hull. The framework should be a full 'hoop', i.e. not be discontinued in any way. The hoop consists of the sides, a piece across the bottom which will be like a floor, and full beam. In way of the coachroof there will be half-beams each side, then pillar pieces to go up the coaming and a beam across. The framework should be strongly joined at its corners using halved glued joints, or plywood or cold-moulded knees. Door pillars will also be put into the framework and any major apertures may be framed round as well. Any bulkhead stiffeners could be fitted at this stage. The final framework is fitted into the hull with its edges correctly bevelled.

After checking, the framework is lifted out of the boat and laid on a flat floor with newspaper or plastic underneath to catch glue drips. The wood veneers are glued and screwed onto the framework, remembering to get the grain direction correct, with weights to press them together. It will be usual to use relatively few non-ferrous nails to hold the first layer onto the framework. The

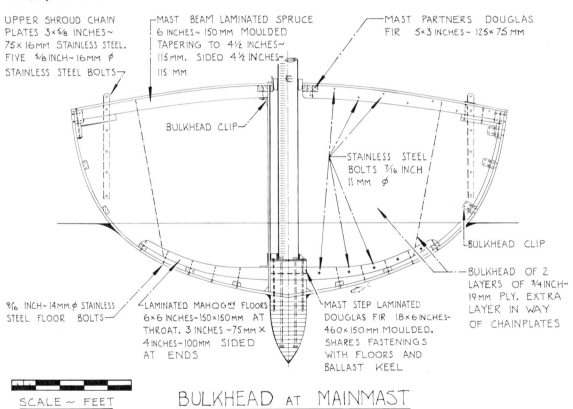

UPPER SHROUD CHAIN PLATES 3×⅝ INCHES~ 75×16MM STAINLESS STEEL. FIVE ⅝ INCH~16MM ∅ STAINLESS STEEL BOLTS

MAST BEAM LAMINATED SPRUCE 6 INCHES~ 150 MM MOULDED TAPERING TO 4½ INCHES~ 115MM. SIDED 4½ INCHES~ 115 MM

MAST PARTNERS DOUGLAS FIR 5×3 INCHES~ 125×75 MM

BULKHEAD CLIP

STAINLESS STEEL BOLTS 7/16 INCH 11 MM ∅

BULKHEAD CLIP

BULKHEAD OF 2 LAYERS OF ¾ INCH~ 19MM PLY. EXTRA LAYER IN WAY OF CHAINPLATES

9/16 INCH~ 14MM ∅ STAINLESS STEEL FLOOR BOLTS

LAMINATED MAHOG NY FLOORS 6×6 INCHES~150×150MM AT THROAT. 3 INCHES ~75MM × 4 INCHES~100MM SIDED AT ENDS

MAST STEP LAMINATED DOUGLAS FIR 18×6 INCHES~ 460×150 MM MOULDED. SHARES FASTENINGS WITH FLOORS AND BALLAST KEEL

SCALE ~ FEET

BULKHEAD AT MAINMAST

Designed by Alan Gurney, this 65ft (20m) LWL ketch has her mainmast stepped down on the keel, as is usual with boats over about 45ft (14m). To stiffen the hull against racking strains there is an athwartships bulkhead bolted to a strong beam and laminated floor, with a fore-and-aft bulkhead ensuring that wracking strains are contained. The number and size of the bolts is instructive, not just through the beam and floor but through the chainplates and bulkhead clips. An unusual feature is the use of Douglas fir for the mast step.

second and any subsequent layers will also have the minimum number of nails at the ends of each plank strip, since they are only to hold the wood in place until the final layer is fitted. Before the last layer of wood is glued on ample nails or screws are driven through all the inner laminates into the framework.

Once the glue has hardened the edges are trimmed off at the correct level. Before putting the bulkhead into the hull both sides are cleaned off and the first, second and possibly the third coats of paint or varnish are applied.

Thickness depends a good deal on how much work the bulkheads have to do. The table below assumes that the function is partly to divide up the interior and partly to help support the hull. It applies for both cold-moulding and plywood.

Approx hull length		Typical bulkhead thickness	
7.5m	23ft	9mm	$\frac{3}{8}$in
9	28	12	$\frac{1}{2}$
12	37	15	$\frac{5}{8}$
15.5	47	18	$\frac{3}{4}$
18.5	56	25	1

These dimensions assume proper stiffening with pillars each side of all doorways and major openings. If a bulkhead is extra wide or high it needs extra pillars or other stiffening. For exposed waters the size would be increased by at least one stage and possibly two. On the other hand when building to a minimum weight, the thickness might be reduced one stage and sometimes even two but strength gained in other ways e.g. pillars.

PLYWOOD BULKHEADS

If the beam in way of a bulkhead happens to be just over 8ft (2.44m) inside of planking, then it would seem necessary to buy three sheets of ply even though the third one will be scarcely used.

There are all sorts of tricks to save buying extra ply. For instance, it is not necessary to carry a bulkhead right down to the top of the keel because a floor can be fitted in way of the bulkhead and will provide extra strength if there is a good join between the two. The bulkhead can even stop above the sole, with the floor carried up to form a strong threshold. Side pieces cut from the lower part where the hull sides taper in can be scarphed on up under the outer deck edges. The joins may be hidden behind lockers or lining so that the bulkhead appears to be all in one piece. The

centreline join can be filled out using either plywood or solid timber with stout doublers which form the beams and the lintel of the doorway.

An entirely different approach is to follow the cold-moulded principle but with thin plywood sheets. The butts and seams are staggered for strength. The sheets are glued and bolted or clenched (not screwed) together and here again ply offcuts can be used since the bulkhead required is boat shaped not rectangular. In passing, it is worth mentioning that clenching using copper nails and rooves looks seamanlike and can be decorative if it is well done. It is also quite easy to do and reasonably quick once the rhythm has been built up. So an amateur who has never tried clenching should consider it because it is convenient and generally speaking cheaper in material costs than bolting.

CUTTING APERTURES AND FINISHING OFF

Regardless of whether a bulkhead is cold-moulded or of plywood, the method of cutting out an aperture or doorway is the same. The hole is marked *very* lightly in pencil and first drawn with the side and top lines meeting at right angles. But of course it is bad engineering to have holes with sharp corners since they make weak points; it also improves the general appearance to have well rounded corners.

To mark a round corner use a paint tin or any round object such as a bowl or cup. It is placed on the two intersecting lines and a firm arc drawn round in pencil. When all the rounded corners have been marked in, the curved lines are joined up with a heavy pencil line. Once all the apertures have been cut out the original faint lines are rubbed out with a coarse india rubber. A hole about 1in across is drilled through the bulkhead well inside the line. This allows the keyhole or sabre saw to be inserted and the aperture is then cut out. The straight lines may be cut with an ordinary handsaw to speed up the work and give a straight cut; sabre and keyhole saws tend to give a wiggly cut. Provided the edge moulding will be sufficiently deep and the wiggles in the saw line are quite modest, this lack of precision is unimportant. Small apertures for vents and electric wiring or piping are sometimes left until the bulkhead is fitted in the boat. This can raise difficulties: it can be extremely hard to work an electric jigsaw in close under a deckhead or down

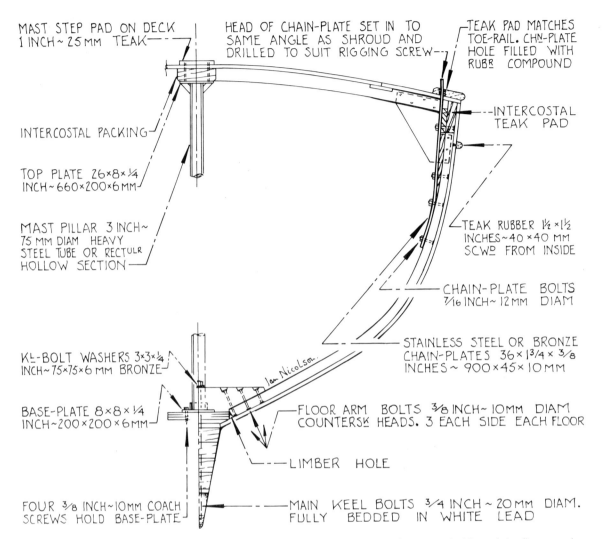

MAST STEP PAD ON DECK 1 INCH ~ 25 MM TEAK

HEAD OF CHAIN-PLATE SET IN TO SAME ANGLE AS SHROUD AND DRILLED TO SUIT RIGGING SCREW

TEAK PAD MATCHES TOE-RAIL. CHN-PLATE HOLE FILLED WITH RUBᴿ COMPOUND

INTERCOSTAL PACKING

TOP PLATE 26 × 8 × ¼ INCH ~ 660 × 200 × 6 MM

MAST PILLAR 3 INCH ~ 75 MM DIAM HEAVY STEEL TUBE OR RECTᵁᴸᴿ HOLLOW SECTION

INTERCOSTAL TEAK PAD

TEAK RUBBER 1½ × 1½ INCHES ~ 40 × 40 MM SCWᴰ FROM INSIDE

CHAIN-PLATE BOLTS ⁷⁄₁₆ INCH ~ 12 MM DIAM

Ian Nicolson

STAINLESS STEEL OR BRONZE CHAIN-PLATES 36 × 1¾ × ⅜ INCHES ~ 900 × 45 × 10 MM

Kᴸ-BOLT WASHERS 3 × 3 × ¼ INCH ~ 75 × 75 × 6 MM BRONZE

BASE-PLATE 8 × 8 × ¼ INCH ~ 200 × 200 × 6 MM

FLOOR ARM BOLTS ⅜ INCH ~ 10 MM DIAM COUNTERSᴷ HEADS. 3 EACH SIDE EACH FLOOR

LIMBER HOLE

FOUR ⅜ INCH ~ 10 MM COACH SCREWS HOLD BASE-PLATE

MAIN KEEL BOLTS ¾ INCH ~ 20 MM DIAM. FULLY BEDDED IN WHITE LEAD

Mast support structure where strength is more important than weight, but weight is not added unnecessarily. On this 38ft cutter from the board of Alfred Mylne of Rosneath, laminating has been used for many of the main construction members. Important details are: ease of construction, the strong bolting of the floors to the frames, the careful packing round the chainplates and the absence of large pieces of solid timber which are likely to warp or split.

in the bilge. So every hole should be cut before the bulkhead goes in.

Also, as much structure as possible should be added beforehand. Berth front and top supports, any framework for lavatory pedestals, doubling pads for bilge pumps and support pieces for shelves are just some of the components which are much easier to fit when the bulkhead is lying down flat, out of the boat.

It is current practice to attach chainplates to bulkheads. Whereas they used to be at the deck edge and bolted through the topsides, now they are often set well inboard. Chainplates carry massive strains so they have to be secured to strong bases; bulkheads can be ideal because they spread the load and are easy to stiffen locally. Doubling pieces are needed in way of each chainplate on at least one side of the bulkhead. If the boat is over about 37ft (12m) it is good practice to put doublers on both sides, using material about half or three-quarters the thickness of the bulkhead. For ocean cruising or racing the

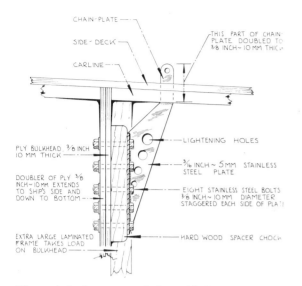

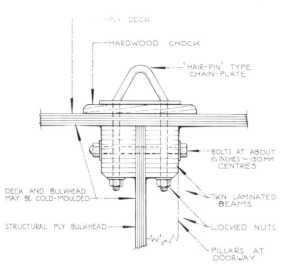

Where chainplates are not in line with the mast support bulkhead, arrangements have to be made to transfer the rigging stresses diagonally downwards. On this 33ft racer the bulkhead is strengthened by a doubler piece made from offcuts of the same plywood. The doubler extends right out to the frame and vertically down to the hull at the turn of the bilge. An additional doubler in the form of a thick chock is glued onto the aft side of the bulkhead. By using a thick doubler the length of the diagonal lower part of the chainplate is reduced, and of course a wood doubler is often lighter than the metal which it replaces.

The loadings on chainplates are very high so the strengthening round them must be reliable, inspectable and yet simple to keep down cost.

doublers may be as thick as the bulkhead. The doublers are no good unless they spread the load and help prevent the bulkhead pulling apart, so if the boat is going to be really driven in shocking conditions the extra thickness should be carried well beyond the fitting in every direction. For normal cruisers a doubler which is 50 per cent longer than the chainplate and six times its width should work well. All this doubling is much easier to do before the bulkheads are fitted into the boat.

On some yachts there is an inner forestay which meets the deck roughly halfway between the mast and the stemhead. Here the deck is weak, so to take the upward pull a wire or rod is lead from the underside of the deck to a strong point lower down which may be a full or partial bulkhead. It will need stiffening and an inside chainplate where the wire or rod meets it. Both the doubling and the inner chainplate can be fitted before the bulkhead

The high local loading on chainplates has to be matched by a structure which spreads the strain. Here the deck is asked to do little work, as the twin beams are bolted and glued to a full bulkhead which extends across and down the hull and is attached to it over a long edge. The beam edges are planed off for appearance and to ensure that the paint or varnish stays on. The nuts must be locked on the chainplate so that rigging vibration does not loosen them. Fore-and-aft bolts through the bulkhead and beams have capping nuts so they can be exposed in the accommodation and still look acceptable.

is put into the boat, but other chainplates have to wait until much later.

Any hole cut in a bulkhead needs a neat moulding round it, to cover and protect the end grain and absorb knocks.

Solid wood mouldings are fine along straight edges, but can be the very devil at rounded corners. A moulding should be rebated, and the complications involved in getting a rebated moulding round bends call for a fairly high standard of woodworking if the result is to look professional. With a rotary spindle or router it is not a long job, without one it takes ages, and without a jigsaw or bandsaw it takes longer yet.

Laminated mouldings make a lot of sense, especially if very thin strips of wood are used. If the apertures have been accurately cut the laminating can be done direct onto the bulkhead, otherwise it has to be done on a jig. Once the glue has set the mouldings are cleaned up before fitting. Such laminations done with just adequate skill look good. Done really well they provoke that quiet

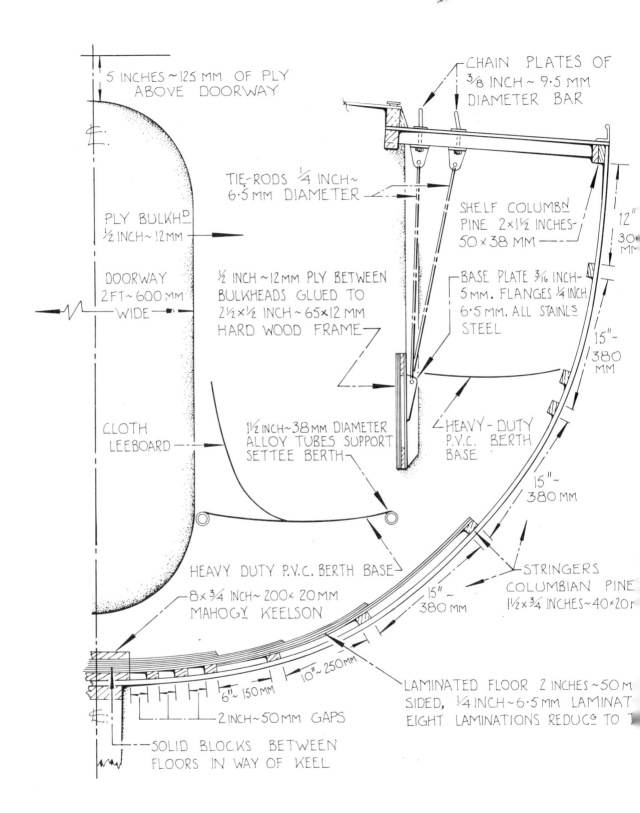

5 INCHES ~ 125 MM OF PLY ABOVE DOORWAY

CHAIN PLATES OF $\frac{3}{8}$ INCH ~ 9·5 MM DIAMETER BAR

TIE-RODS $\frac{1}{4}$ INCH ~ 6·5 MM DIAMETER

PLY BULKH^{D} $\frac{1}{2}$ INCH ~ 12MM

SHELF COLUMB^{N} PINE 2 × 1$\frac{1}{2}$ INCHES ~ 50 × 38 MM

DOORWAY 2 FT ~ 600 MM WIDE

$\frac{1}{2}$ INCH ~ 12MM PLY BETWEEN BULKHEADS GLUED TO 2$\frac{1}{2}$ × $\frac{1}{2}$ INCH ~ 65 × 12 MM HARD WOOD FRAME

BASE PLATE $\frac{3}{16}$ INCH ~ 5 MM. FLANGES $\frac{1}{4}$ INCH 6·5 MM. ALL STAIN$\underline{LS}$ STEEL

12" 30 MM

CLOTH LEEBOARD

1$\frac{1}{2}$ INCH ~ 38MM DIAMETER ALLOY TUBES SUPPORT SETTEE BERTH

HEAVY-DUTY P.V.C. BERTH BASE

15" ~ 380 MM

HEAVY DUTY P.V.C. BERTH BASE

8 × $\frac{3}{4}$ INCH ~ 200 × 20 MM MAHOG$\underline{Y}$ KEELSON

15" ~ 380 MM

STRINGERS COLUMBIAN PINE 1$\frac{1}{2}$ × $\frac{3}{4}$ INCHES ~ 40 × 20

10" ~ 250MM

LAMINATED FLOOR 2 INCHES ~ 50 M SIDED, $\frac{1}{4}$ INCH ~ 6·5 MM LAMINAT EIGHT LAMINATIONS REDUC$\underline{D}$ TO 7

6" ~ 150 MM

2 INCH ~ 50 MM GAPS

SOLID BLOCKS BETWEEN FLOORS IN WAY OF KEEL

To make a fibreglass production boat a female mould is used, for which a male mould, a 'plug' or full-size model, is a prerequisite. Sometimes the plug is cold-moulded in wood. So that the class prototype can be tested afloat it is built as a complete operational boat; modifications can often be made on the cold-moulded hull before it is used as a plug.

Laurent Giles & Partners designed this prototype of the GK29 for Westerly Marine, who built the boat and had Michael Pocock of the design firm campaign her. Problems were ironed out and the boat's racing

nod from the knowledgeable which is worth a hundred words of praise from the ignorant.

These days it is common to see plastic edge moulding. Thick, good quality plastic extrusion may look tidy, but seldom reaches the pinnacle of fine yacht building. Fastenings need to be close-spaced, and the join in the plastic should be put somewhere unobtrusive. There must be no wrinkles in the plastic, and the extrusion must fit the thickness of the bulkhead exactly. A popular section is one like the letter J with the bend at the

potential explored before committing the builders to production.

Of special interest is the way the loading on the chainplates is carried down by a pair of rods to a vertical ply girder 13in (33cm) deep and extending between strength bulkheads. Bolted to it is a plate bracket with a pair of flanges to take the ends of the tension rods. The girder forms the inboard support of the pilot berth, the backrest of the settee berth and also holds the bulkheads rigid. Each end is secured to full-height glued vertical bulkhead stiffeners.

bottom abbreviated. It is called 'hockey stick' section and is available in different widths and colours from big hardware shops, do-it-yourself stores and some timber yards which cater for small firms and amateurs.

Aluminium and brass strip are sometimes used as edging. They are hard-wearing but seldom elegant. The metal must be bent in slowly otherwise kinking occurs and is hard to eradicate. Fastenings should be close, and in aluminium stainless steel screws are needed.

Building up a Fin Keel

A traditional way to make up a fin keel is to use layers of wood. This technique is sometimes called 'bread and butter', the implication being that the wood is the slices of bread and the glue or bedding material the butter. But of course bread and butter is seldom more than two layers thick whereas a fin keel may have ten layers of wood, possibly even more. The method is similar to that for making a half-model of a hull.

It is always good practice to use relatively thin pieces of wood rather than massive chunks, because they warp less and are less likely to conceal defects. An extra bonus is that small thicknesses of wood tend to be cheaper than thick ones because they are more plentiful and come from smaller, cheaper trees.

Normally a fin keel will be made up off the boat, being assembled layer by layer usually upside-down. Done this way the largest piece can be laid down first. However, if the boat is a big one and each piece is too heavy for two or three people to lift easily, it may pay to make up the keel directly on the boat. With the hull the right way up, it is not easy to lift a massive assembly up under the boat. To ease the job there are various tricks which can be used, such as drilling holes right through an

assembled fin so that ropes or lifting bars can be passed through. Alternatively, eyeplates can be screwed or bolted on to help move the finished fin. Once it is in place any unwanted holes are plugged or filled and smoothed off.

Each layer of the fin is made up to a shape which is taken direct from the mould loft floor. The procedure is as follows:
1. Find out which thickness of wood is conveniently available. Let us work on the basis that 6in finished thickness of a good quality, properly kiln or air dried timber is available at a reasonable price.
2. On the mould loft floor horizontal waterlines are drawn through the fin keel at 6in intervals, to suit the 6in thicknesses of timber or 'slices'.
3. The shape in plan view of each of these waterlines is drawn out on the mould loft floor, the shape being taken from the designer's lines plan.
4. The timber for the fin is run through a planing machine so that its thickness is exactly correct, in this case 6in. Both top and bottom surfaces must be fully planed and parallel but the ends and sides can be ignored.
5. Centrelines are marked on each piece and down the ends.

6. Athwartships lines are marked across the centreline at 90° angles. These lines are at the same spacing as those on the mould loft floor, normally at stations and half-stations.

7. The plan view shape is transferred from the mould loft to each piece of timber, by drawing on the waterlines above and below each slice.

8. The timber is cut round exactly on the waterline which makes the *larger* profile.

9. The athwartships lines and centrelines are continued down the sides of each shaped piece, so that the top and bottom profiles are correctly aligned.

10. The pieces of the fin are stacked together without fastening, the lines down the sides being carefully aligned so that the fin is the correct shape seen from the side and ahead.

11. The top of the second piece in the stack must exactly coincide with the waterline on the bottom face of the piece above it.

12. The stack is taken apart and the excess wood trimmed off each slice, so that a fair surface eventually connects the waterlines of each slice.

13. The keel is now reassembled and apart from the final fairing it should be almost the finished shape.

At this stage the fin may either be secured together or put on the boat piece by piece. The ideal way to secure it together is with glue only, since this will leave no fastenings that might subsequently be in the way of the keelbolts or those holding on the ballast. If fastenings are used then ideally they should not be through-bolts since they will be hidden once the keel is on and cannot be inspected during the life of the boat. The hog will be over the top of the bolts and the ballast keel underneath. If by accident one of these bolts comes in way of a keelbolt serious problems could arise. A good compromise is to use a few long screws and glue to hold the fin together. The screws should be carefully marked on the drawings and outside of the fin so that the keelbolts can be kept clear of them later. Also the minimum number of screws should be used; since bronze is the ideal material here and long bronze screws are very pricey there is every encouragement to go easy on the number of fastenings.

When starting to build a wooden fin, remember:
1. Use only good quality, rot resistant hardwood.
2. Select wood free from knots. This means going for one of the 'mahoganies' rather than one of the

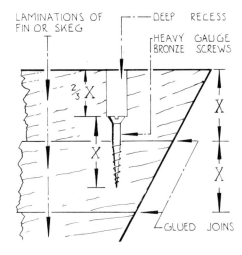

In assembling a fin or skeg the pieces will be bolted together and onto the boat at the same time, but before the bolts are put in they need holding together. This can be done with a few bronze screws and glue (as well as clamps until the glue dries). All the screws are marked on the outside of the assembly so that the bolts are kept clear of them. The recess holes for the screws are made wide enough to take a large screwdriver. To save the expense of very long screws recesses are made about two-thirds into the thickness of the pieces, and screws nearly as long as the laminate thickness are used.

'pines', and if the latter are chosen select a boatbuilding rather than a merchantable grade.
3. If there are knots, try to arrange the pieces of wood so that most knots are cut out, or are located clear of the edge where they will not make the final fairing hard work.
4. Lay the pieces of wood so that the grain of each one viewed from ahead or astern is reversed in direction from its neighbour. The idea here is that if the wood tends to 'cap' then the distortion of one piece is counteracted by the reverse distortion of the next. I have seen fin keels with clearly visible twists.
5. Without a bandsaw it may be worth taking the marked pieces of timber to a mill just to have the waterline profiles cut out, and perhaps for planing the top and bottom.

Wood is easy to cut and work so it is no trouble to have a keel of the best hydrodynamic shape. As so many cold-moulded racing yachts are built, this easy method of fashioning a precise and maybe complicated form is particularly handy. However, there is an offsetting disadvantage. The normal wooden fin is solid right through. As a result there is nowhere for the bilgewater except just below the cabin sole: when the boat heels even a little the water sloshes up under the furniture and unless precautions are taken it wets bedding, clothes and stores. It is often possible to build in a small sump in a wooden boat, so that a few gallons of bilgewater can be collected and held low down, but this may complicate the hull building.

BOX KEELS

For cruising a deep sump is prized. It is a convenient place not only for bilgewater but also water and fuel tanks. Steel box keels are seen on a few cold-moulded boats because they do make life easy in several respects. Ballast can be quickly and easily put inside and sealed down, whereas a laminated fin needs a cast ballast keel. In turn this calls for a pattern and then a mould, the former almost always made by the boatbuilder, the latter now most often made by a keel casting firm.

Steel box fins will normally be subcontracted and so they are made while the rest of the boat is being built. Once the fin is in place about half the ballast may be put in before launching. When the boat is afloat the rest of the ballast is placed so that she trims just right. Since even the best designer has trouble predicting the exact fore-and-aft location as well as the precise amount of ballast to get the right trim, this foolproof method of getting the bow and stern at just the right level is a tremendous asset.

Since cold-moulded boats tend to be perform-ance oriented, it is logical to get the tanks and bilgewater as low as possible. This becomes simpler with a box type fin. Against this, however, a big steel casing is not easy to secure to a relatively light, perhaps flexible, cold-moulded hull. It needs an extra wide hog to take the extra width of a hollow box keel. The hog can be built around an opening made to match that in the top of the keel, to allow access and drainage into it; enough width of hog is built out to either side of the opening to take the bolting-on flange of the keel. A large number of closely spaced small bolts should be used all round. It is hard to lay down rules for bolt sizes because so much will depend on the length of the fin, the thickness of the top flange, the type of bolts being used and so on. As a rough guide, on a 27ft (8m) boat the bolts would be of the order of $\frac{1}{2}$in (12mm) in diameter, and on a 55-footer (17m) about 1in (25mm) would be about right. Spacing would be around six times the bolt diameter, and

the fin flange must be so thick that there is no distortion when the bolts are tightened up strongly (one-half the bolt diameter will be about right in most circumstances).

To stiffen a box keel it is common practice to have vertical floor plates inside, in effect full-depth bulkheads. By extending these up through slots cut in the extra wide but otherwise solid hog, they can be used in addition to an outside flange for attachment to the hull. Fore-and-aft bolts through the plates join the box keel to the wooden floors in the hull; the keel is put on first, then the wooden floors. Though this might seem a good application for laminated 'leaf spring' floors, solid timber with well tapered ends is likely to be better because fore-and-aft bolts may tend to force apart the layers at the glue lines.

STEEL PLATE KEELS

The simplest type of keel, made from flat steel plate, is a little primitive and hydrodynamically less efficient, and it detracts from a boat's resale value and her charms when she is on shore. However, it costs little, can be made in less than half the time for a box fin, and might be replaced later on. A single-thickness plate keel should not be used on a boat over about 35ft (10.5m) long, and even this size is large.

The profile of the fin is cut out of mild steel plate, or if reduced rusting is important one of the more expensive steels like Cor-Ten. Along the top there is a flange to bolt to the hull, on the bottom ballast is secured, the leading edges should be rounded to improve performance, and the aft edge may be tapered for the same reason. The thickness of the keel plate is important. It must not break at the top, so some reinforcing (steel angle-bar welded on each side) is going to be needed for boats over about 22ft overall (6.7m). Allowance has to be made for corrosion over the years, and a keel which sags more than about 5 per cent of its depth when the boat is heeled at 45° would be considered too flimsy by most designers.

Attachment to a cold-moulded hull needs careful planning because this is a typical 'unhappy' join between a slightly flexy structure and a rigid one. If the hull shell has a flat area onto which the keel flange can be bolted this will speed up the job of fitting the keel and should eliminate misfits. More usually the flange has to follow the rocker of the keel, so a template is needed of this shape. During the design stage the bottom of the hull across the keel should be made flat athwartships to avoid curvature in two directions with the need for a shaped curved flange made in two halves along the top of the fin.

To avoid a hard spot at each end the top flange is carried beyond the vertical fin: just how far depends on factors like the hull shape and the length of the fin relative to the boat's overall length. As a rough guide, aim to extend the flange about 5 per cent of the boat's length beyond the vertical part of the fin at its ends. These extensions also make it possible to fit extra keel bolts.

Countersunk bolts are used, made from galvanized mild steel. They will normally be in pairs, up through floors at least six times as wide as the bolt's diameter. A minimum of six bolts each side is needed with a diameter giving a factor of safety of 12. When working out the necessary number and strength the worst possible condition should be taken: when the boat is heeled right down and drops off a wave sideways, or rolls right over. In either case the motion is violent and shock loadings must be considered. For a builder who is more artistic than scientific, a rough guide is: for a $\frac{3}{4}$ ton keel use 12 bolts of $\frac{1}{2}$in (12mm) diameter; for a $1\frac{1}{2}$ ton keel use 16 bolts $\frac{5}{8}$in (16mm) in diameter. Bolts thinner than $\frac{1}{2}$in (12mm) should not be used because the thread has insufficient meat to allow for later corrosion.

The join of the vertical plate to the top flange is potentially the weakest part of this type of keel, so some doubling is needed on keels weighing over about a ton. Angle-bar can be welded to the vertical and horizontal plates, and sometimes instead of a top flange plate a pair of angle-bars are welded on to make the top flange. Full continuous welds are essential throughout.

The usual form of ballast is in slabs bolted on each side of the bottom of the plate fin. The ballast is normally cast steel because lead, though more efficient due to its density, tends to have corrosion problems with the steel and is more expensive. Bolts securing the ballast to the plate fin use the same factors of safety as for the top flange. These bolts and their nuts should be recessed and filled over so that water flows smoothly past them. Before adding the wooden fairings the steelwork is fully painted using five coats of International Paints Metallic Primocon or a similar compound, applied to the freshly ground or wire-brushed bright steel.

One advantage of the plate fin is that it can be fitted onto the hull before its ballast is put on. The procedure would be:
1. Make the fin from templates.
2. Make the ballast lozenges and fit them.
3. Make and fit any fairing round the ballast.
4. For ease of handling and so the hull is not distorted, remove the ballast lozenges.
5. Fit the fin onto the hull. This may be done while the hull is upside down to simplify fitting, drilling holes etc. Or it may be best to fit the fin onto the inverted shell, take it off, turn the hull the right way up, and check the fit again. Leaving the fin on the shell makes turning over the hull heavier and more awkward.
6. The ballast lozenges may be left off until the boat is at the water's edge if there are problems getting suitable lifting gear and transport to the water. As the ballast will be around a quarter of the total weight of the boat, leaving it off makes a substantial difference.

Engine Installation

In many ways installing an engine is the same in a cold-moulded or strip-plank hull as it is for other forms of construction. The shaft line is laid off on the mould loft floor in elevation. Where the shaft line is not on the centreline of the vessel it also has to be laid off in plan view on the floor. The shaft log, which is usually a solid lump of wood to take the stern tube, is drawn in on the loft floor in plan and elevation.

The shaft log has to be secured in the hull with a row of bolts each side of the shaft line. Because it is all too easy to bore out for the tube slightly off the correct line, the bolts should be kept back from the hole at least 1in (25mm). A hardwood free from knots, iroko perhaps or in the best boats teak, is used for the shaft log. Its forward face must be at right angles to the propeller shaft in both plan and elevation, because the flange of the stern tube must lie flat on it. Where an external shaft log is fitted its aft face must be parallel with the forward face of the inside log, since the external flange of the stern tube lies on the aft face of the outer log.

The outer log is usually made as narrow and shallow as possible, with maybe no more than $1\frac{1}{2}$

times the thickness of the securing bolts outside them. The aft end is faired to give the best possible water flow to the propeller and the edges are well rounded for the same reason.

Inside the hull the main shaft log is made with plenty of width and height because it needs a good bearing surface onto the inside of the hull. This is a place where circumstances very much affect individual cases; a rough rule might be that the log should be about four or five times the tube diameter in width and maximum depth.

The log lies flush on the inside of the hull, so frames and stringers which would be in its way are cut back, or during framing-up they are placed short of the log position. Where this causes a noticeable loss of strength, or where there is a lot of horsepower going through the shaft, compensation must be made for the lost frames. This may take the form of wood or metal floors going over the top of the stern log, bolted onto the short frame ends each side. Reinforcing like this is seldom needed if the engine is less than about 10hp or if only one frame is cut.

Even skilled shipwrights have trouble getting the stern log to match exactly, so it is a good policy to use a lot of semi-soft bedding rather than glue on the faying surface. Bedding on fibreglass has been done, but if the boring-out tool is not truly sharp it may be deflected when it meets the hard glass and the hole may not be precisely straight. There is a school of thought which considers the whole idea of a stern log outdated: instead, a stern tube is glassed in just as in a fibreglass hull. It is certainly a quick job; the hull is cut away at the correct slope where the tube is to go and the tube laid in place, sometimes with a plywood floor bolted to its forward flange. Using at least six layers of epoxy resin and woven glass cloth the tube is secured to the wooden hull. Glass cloth in lengths of about 18×5in (450×125mm) is easy to handle. It is laid across the tube, lapping onto the wood, under the tube onto the wood, along the edge of the tube onto the wood, and so on, shorter pieces first and then larger ones. Where this technique has failed it is probably because there has not been enough glassing-in or adequate overlap onto the surrounding hull. The glassing-in should be done strongly because if it fails the resulting leak is likely to be large and hard to cure. The glass should extend on either side about $\frac{1}{2}$in for every foot of length of boat (i.e. 1 in 24), and in the fore-and-aft direction *at least* the same overlap

should be used. The ply floor at the forward end of the tube can be used as a dam, to hold poured-in resin. The glassing round the tube ought to be half the tube diameter in thickness, and as with all reinforcing it should taper away all round.

A wooden shaft log should be secured with *at least* four bolts each side, countersunk with the nuts on top. Because of vibration the best builders put locking nuts on also. These bolts will be about $\frac{3}{8}$in (10mm) thick for boats up to about 30ft (9m), $\frac{1}{2}$in (12mm) up to about 45ft (14m), and $\frac{5}{8}$in (16mm) up to about 65 ft (20m). Fibreglassing *over* the shaft log, in addition to bolting, is an accepted practice and will not complicate boring.

The top of an inside stern log runs parallel with the shaft, and the sides almost always do too. In the same way the underside of an external log is normally parallel to the shaft. So when fitting an inner and an outer log, a single large chunk of wood may be cut diagonally at the correct slope so that one part fits inside and the other outside. Some shaping of the faying surface is likely to be needed, not least because along the length and perhaps width of the log the hull may curve, but this is unlikely to be great so much trimming off is seldom needed. Chalk rubbed on the faying surface will indicate where the wood needs planing off to fit.

When an inner and outer log are fitted boring usually starts from the outside, though if there is only an inner log it is customary to start from inside. Outside boring is usual on boats which have a sternpost, deadwood or similar external near-vertical face. In principle, boring is always done into a flat wooden face which is exactly at right angles to the shaft line.

Occasionally it's impossible to bore out from the inside, perhaps because there is a bulkhead in the way, no room or the hull is still upside down. When external boring is necessary but there is no external log, a temporary log is fitted to give the boring tool a proper start; even when boring from inside with no external log it may pay to fit a chock on the outside of the hull, so that the bit emerges square. Otherwise the tool may deflect slightly as it emerges on a sloping face.

Instead of drilling the log for the stern tube sometimes the log is made in two halves, each with a trench scooped out such that when the two halves are glued and bolted together the tube fits exactly. Then, before fitting the log the hull is cut through for the tube. This technique avoids the

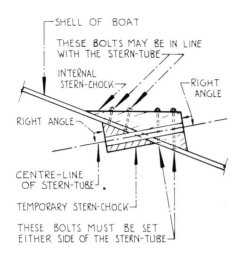

SHELL OF BOAT

THESE BOLTS MAY BE IN LINE WITH THE STERN-TUBE

INTERNAL STERN-CHOCK

RIGHT ANGLE

RIGHT ANGLE

CENTRE-LINE OF STERN-TUBE

TEMPORARY STERN-CHOCK

THESE BOLTS MUST BE SET EITHER SIDE OF THE STERN-TUBE

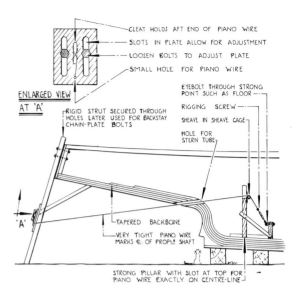

CLEAT HOLDS AFT END OF PIANO WIRE
SLOTS IN PLATE ALLOW FOR ADJUSTMENT
LOOSEN BOLTS TO ADJUST PLATE
SMALL HOLE FOR PIANO WIRE

ENLARGED VIEW AT 'A'

RIGID STRUT SECURED THROUGH HOLES LATER USED FOR BACKSTAY CHAIN-PLATE BOLTS

EYEBOLT THROUGH STRONG POINT SUCH AS FLOOR
RIGGING SCREW
SHEAVE IN SHEAVE CAGE
HOLE FOR STERN TUBE

'A'

TAPERED BACKBONE
VERY TIGHT PIANO WIRE MARKS ₵ OF PROP⊑ SHAFT

STRONG PILLAR WITH SLOT AT TOP FOR PIANO WIRE EXACTLY ON CENTRE-LINE

The face of a stern chock must be at right angles to the tube in plan and elevation, otherwise the flange on the tube will not lie tight. When drilling for the stern tube a temporary chock may be needed if there is no deadwood or sternpost to drill through. Screws or bolts are used to hold the temporary chock on very securely, and after its chock has been removed their holes through the hull must be filled and finished off. Drilling should start and finish through faces at right angles to the shaft line, and where possible the drilling should be from the outside inwards.

need for a special boring tool; and it may save time too if a router is available but no suitable power drilling equipment can be obtained.

Once the hole has been bored out a shaft line or centreline wire is stretched through it, and left in place throughout the fitting of the engine bearers to help align them. The coupling on many engines is centred on a line through the base of the engine feet, so the centreline wire marks the top of the engine bearers – almost. The bearers have to be a little below this line to allow for washers and packing up during engine alignment: an allowance of say $\frac{1}{2}$in (12mm) is about right. The centreline wire is also used to line up external P-brackets, A-brackets and so on.

Engine bearers are made from a pattern taken from the mould loft floor. Since most craft have the engine on the centreline a single pattern will do for both bearers. On a twin-screw boat two patterns (one for the inboard and one for the outboard bearers) will do for the four bearers. Where an engine is offset or not exactly on a fore-and-aft line, a case can be made for taking the bearer dimensions off the hull.

A dense, stable hardwood such as agba, iroko or

For propeller shaft alignment the centreline of the shaft is marked on the plans and transferred to the mould loft floor. It will probably be shown on some of the moulds, and eventually must be transferred to the hull. For fitting the shaft bracket and engine bearers the exact shaft line is shown by a taut wire. Most small marine engines have their feet exactly in line with the centre of the crankshaft, so that provided there is no reduction gearing in the form of a 'drop-down' gearbox the centreline of the shaft is level with the top of the engine bearers. They will be set a little lower to allow for lining up and metal bearer plates under the feet.

The wire being so tight needs ample strength of structure at each end, otherwise tightening it will merely deflect the end supports. To line up the ends of the wire precisely movable plates (top left) may be used.

makore should be used for the engine bearers. However, they are heavy and expensive, so a pine or larch may be used, with a thick piece of hardwood along the top to take the weight and the 'hammer' effect of the engine; this results from vibration and tends to punch the engine feet down into the bearers. For even the lightest engine the top hardwood strip should be at least 2in (50mm) thick. Under engines of 20hp the hardwood should be 3in (75mm) or more thick, and for 50hp 4in (10cm). An engine of about 100hp needs a hardwood piece about 8in (20cm) thick.

Instead of a hardwood top for the bearers steel angle is sometimes used, with the vertical flange down the outside of the bearer and the horizontal flange across the top to take the engine feet. Flat bar should not be used because it tends to dent down under the hammer effect.

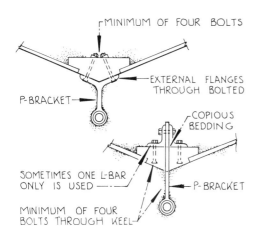

MINIMUM OF FOUR BOLTS

EXTERNAL FLANGES
THROUGH BOLTED

P-BRACKET

COPIOUS
BEDDING

SOMETIMES ONE L-BAR
ONLY IS USED

P-BRACKET

MINIMUM OF FOUR
BOLTS THROUGH KEEL

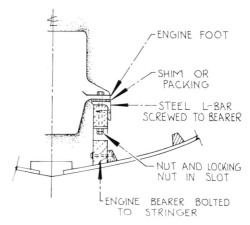

ENGINE FOOT

SHIM OR
PACKING

STEEL L-BAR
SCREWED TO BEARER

NUT AND LOCKING
NUT IN SLOT

ENGINE BEARER BOLTED
TO STRINGER

The older type of P-bracket (top sketch) and the modern type which is in general use. The advantage of the older type is that it can be packed out slightly to one side, if the shaft alignment turns out to be slightly imperfect, and in the event of a sideways bash it is less likely to give serious trouble. But it often has to be packed off the hull to get the correct alignment, and the palms and packing obstruct the smooth flow of water along the hull.

The slot for the modern type should be cut when the backbone is being built. The slot should be made a tight fit, and the plate smeared with bedding when it is driven in. More bedding is needed under the angle-bars, and these should extend well beyond the ends of the vertical plate of the P-bracket. Staggered bolts, at least three in number even on a small boat, are needed through the angle-bar and the P-bracket plate.

Marine plywood is used for engine bearers when it is hard to get sufficiently wide long pieces of solid timber or where weight has to be saved. These bearers are made up like narrow boxes, ply being used for the sides and hardwood on the top and bottom; and as before the bottom length is bolted to the hull. So that one can get inside to put the nuts on the engine bolts and the bolts holding the bearer to the shell, large holes are cut through the ply sides. These holes also act as ventilation slots and give access under the engine.

Engines under about 15hp sometimes have bearers which extend athwartships. This type is easier to fit if the boat is framed athwartships, or if the cabin sole has to be set very low in the hull so that the engine bearers cannot conveniently be put beneath. Athwartships bearers should be extended well up the sides, tapering out gradually to dissipate the engine loads over a big area of the hull. Unless the engine is tiny, say under 7hp, the

A solid wood engine bearer, with slots cut out for the holding-down bolt nuts. These slots should be made slightly too long, as engines often have to be moved fore and aft slightly when finally positioned. It is far better to cut the slots before fitting the bearers. Steel angle-bar makes a good capping for softwood bearers, with screws through the horizontal flange to hold the steel in position. Naturally the steel must be set a little low, in case lining-up the engine makes it necessary to drop it slightly.

bearers ought to reach up to half the hull depth, and extend across under the engine in one piece.

If the engine is small for the size of boat, longitudinal bearers which are only $1\frac{1}{2}$ times its length are just acceptable. 'Small' might be taken as one-third horsepower per foot (30cm) of boat length. As the power increases so the engine bearer length should go up. Bearers *twice* the length of the engine can be taken as a normal *minimum*, and three times the length of the engine should be the aim even if this means sacrificing some comfort or convenience in the accommodation. These are only rough guides, because some engines have their cylinders in two rows so that high power is compressed into short length.

Cold-moulded and strip-plank hulls tend to be light and relatively flexy, and these are just the ones that need extra long and strong engine bearers. Power-driven boats of this type which are even moderately fast will normally have bearers extending a third of the hull length, and truly fast craft often have bearers which run from bow to stern. These long bearers must taper away at each end, or be secured to strong structural parts such as the transom or a strength bulkhead.

All engine bearers have to be well secured to the hull, so through-bolts are best; to save weight and

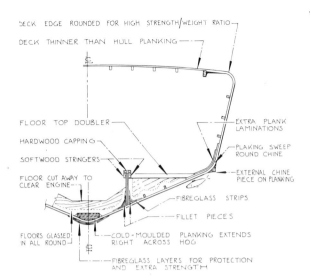

DECK EDGE ROUNDED FOR HIGH STRENGTH/WEIGHT RATIO
DECK THINNER THAN HULL PLANKING
FLOOR TOP DOUBLER
HARDWOOD CAPPING
SOFTWOOD STRINGERS
FLOOR CUT AWAY TO CLEAR ENGINE
FLOORS GLASSED IN ALL ROUND
EXTRA PLANK LAMINATIONS
PLANKING SWEEP ROUND CHINE
EXTERNAL CHINE PIECE ON PLANKING
FIBREGLASS STRIPS
FILLET PIECES
COLD-MOULDED PLANKING EXTENDS RIGHT ACROSS HOG
FIBREGLASS LAYERS FOR PROTECTION AND EXTRA STRENGTH

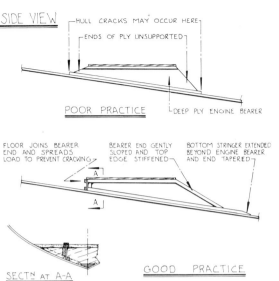

SIDE VIEW — HULL CRACKS MAY OCCUR HERE
ENDS OF PLY UNSUPPORTED
POOR PRACTICE — DEEP PLY ENGINE BEARER

FLOOR JOINS BEARER END AND SPREADS LOAD TO PREVENT CRACKING
BEARER END GENTLY SLOPED AND TOP EDGE STIFFENED
BOTTOM STRINGER EXTENDED BEYOND ENGINE BEARER AND END TAPERED

SECTN AT A-A   GOOD PRACTICE

A hard-chine hull, such as on this fast powerboat, may be moulded with rounded bilges and under side of keel, so that the hull strength extends round from one side to the other uninterrupted. Even at the deck edge there need be no sudden sharp turn and no plank endings, so that strength can be maintained. To further stiffen the highly stressed turn of the bilge some extra laminations may be glued in. They are shown extending down as far as the glassed-in engine bed brackets. The glassing is carried all round, leaving limber holes. More glassing is used on the underside of the keel. Just in case one run of glassfibre is not perfectly applied and does not adhere fully, each successive layer is wider than the previous one.

The engine beds are made as light as possible by using ply and softwood stringers. But the engine feet would bite into softwood so a hardwood capping must be run along the top of the bearers, at least in way of the feet. Even when larger metal washers are put under the feet hardwood underneath is necessary otherwise the washers will sink down. The bottoms of the bearers are fillets to avoid glassing-in over an acute angle.

money alternate heavy screws and bolts may be used. Vertical bolts through the shell are put in with their countersunk heads on the bottom. The nuts on top should be locked, either by using self-locking nuts or by peening the bolt end over the nut, or by adding locking washers or nuts. Bolts will be the same size as for the stern log and spaced at roughly 8in (20cm) centres.

The bottom of each bearer is shaped to fit the hull and cut away to straddle any frames it crosses. The amount of wood cut away should be enough so that the bearer is not a tight fit on any of the frames, and there must be large limber holes at each intersection of frame and bearer.

Any strong component, but particularly the engine bearers, must be designed to blend in with the rest of the hull. If bearers stop short they are likely to cause local cracking, especially with a heavy engine.

The top sketch shows a typical bearer, at first sight apparently drawn with forethought; each end tapers down which is much better than a vertical termination. However, for seriously stressed conditions the tapering away of the engine bearers must be carefully worked out so that the ends can actually flex. Alternatively, the ends can be tied to another structural member such as an athwartships strength component, in this case a floor. A bulkhead is an even better location for the ends of the bearers, as it spreads the loads farther.

If the hull is only stringered rather than framed, the designer might with advantage site stringers so that the engine bearers are beside them. This will give a strength member to secure the bearers onto and also help to run the strength of the bearers on forward and aft. Lightweight hulls with thin planking are often built with stringers, and this is where the engine bearers may be blended into stringers with particular advantage. A thin shell cannot be expected to give bolts a good hold, so it is logical to link the bearers to stringers and to use a large number of small bolts through the shell. In addition the bearers may be glassed in, with at least four runs of $1\frac{1}{2}$oz chopped strand mat worked in tightly along both sides of each bearer and round the ends. The angle between the bearer and the hull shell will be acute, particularly on the outboard side. Glassfibre does not easily bend into such a sharp recess, so it is good practice to fit wooden fillets an inch or two (25–50mm) wide, to make a better job, and as usual to put on narrow strips first.

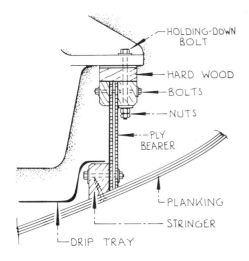

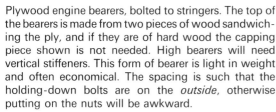

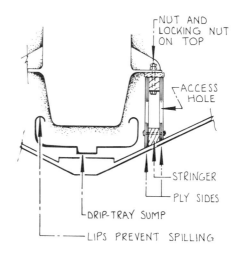

Plywood engine bearers, bolted to stringers. The top of the bearers is made from two pieces of wood sandwiching the ply, and if they are of hard wood the capping piece shown is not needed. High bearers will need vertical stiffeners. This form of bearer is light in weight and often economical. The spacing is such that the holding-down bolts are on the *outside*, otherwise putting on the nuts will be awkward.

Though it is usual to align the bearers fore and aft, this may not suit the construction or the interior layout. To save weight they can be run fore and aft in way of the machinery, then angled out or in to double as furniture supports and continue as longitudinal stiffening.

Athwartships strength is given to engine bearers by floors, which are likely to be similar to those used to link the frames to the backbone. The size and spacing will be the same as in the rest of the boat.

Drip trays under an engine are advisable in all wooden hulls, because oil soaks easily into timber and in time goes right through strip-planking. It is less likely to go through cold-moulded planking because the glue acts as a barrier, but glue lines are not in every case totally impermeable. Signs of oil on the outside of the planking take the form of irregular dark stains in the area of the engine, and sometimes under the fuel tank if it weeps at its pipe joins and similar weak points. Such oil stains result in a smell which is hard to remove, and antifouling peels off in the tainted areas. As the oil tends to creep along the grain of the wood, the affected areas get slowly larger. In theory the wood cannot become rotten if oil-soaked, but oil in the planking seems to put off potential buyers of secondhand boats. Furthermore, without a drip tray the

Engine bearers made of two pieces of ply, in the form of a hollow box, are light and strong. Access holes are needed to get the holding-down bolts in. If these bolts are put in with their heads at the bottom it is often easier to tighten the nut and locking nut. Should the engine vibration loosen the nuts this defect is more quickly noticed when the nuts are above the engine feet.

Curled-over lips on a drip-tray give strength and prevent the mucky contents from slopping into the bilge. The drip-tray sump makes it possible to suck out almost every last drop.

bilgewater becomes oily so that greasy dirty muck is spread through the boat and eventually pumped out – which in some areas has lead to regulations concerning bilge pumping.

If the engine bearers are glassed in the glassing may be extended between them and turned up at each end, to form a fixed fibreglass drip tray. The glass is worked over frames and stringers, but since at the aft end a cut-away will be needed to clear the propeller shaft the idea may not work.

ENGINE BEARER THICKNESS RELATED TO HORSEPOWER

The lighter thickness is for high performance craft, inshore boats etc. For rugged offshore craft use a figure halfway between the higher and lower figure. For extremely heavy boats and/or exceptionally heavy engines select the higher figure.

Horsepower	Bearer thickness		
4hp	between $\frac{3}{4}$ and $1\frac{1}{2}$in		(20–40mm)
8	1	2	(25–50mm)
16	$1\frac{1}{4}$	$2\frac{1}{2}$	(32–60mm)
30	$1\frac{1}{2}$	$3\frac{1}{2}$	(40–90mm)
60	2	$4\frac{1}{2}$	(50–115mm)
120	3	$4\frac{1}{2}$	(75–115mm)

Coachroof and Cockpit Coamings

The majority of coamings are made from solid wood or plywood to save time. Ply is used for high coamings because it is hard to get solid wood of great width except by paying a big price, and often suitable timber is only found after a long search. Even carefully selected solid timber is liable to crack if used in widths over about 12in (30cm), especially if subject to high temperatures; wood varnished and exposed to prolonged sunshine gets very hot and cracks. However, plywood has several disadvantages. The edge is unsightly and may soak up water unless covered with a moulding, which is not quickly and easily fitted around windows; irregular and sharp curves are hard to make; and also there is still some prejudice against ply, even the finest marine ply which has hardwood inside as well as on the faces.

So apart from the time it takes, there is little against laminating coamings. The extra glue needed involves some additional cost, and the designer will have to do more work, such as showing the lay of the veneers, where any extra stiffening goes, and the precise run of the curves in plan view, indicated by offsets at regular intervals.

The outer layers can be of a superb wood carefully finished and varnished and the inner layers of a lighter less expensive wood, to save weight high up and money. That great attribute of laminating, the ease with which extra strength can be worked in precisely where it is needed, applies here especially. Cutting out a window in a coachroof coaming results in a local weakness, which can be compensated for by extra layers around the window, these forming a frame to take the glazing. If the same coaming rises aft to form a doghouse, extra laminates can be added to give additional thickness and strength. Deep-sea experience has shown that waves breaking aboard heavily over-stress doghouse (and also coachroof) sides. The usual place for a crack to appear is along the bottom, just above deck level. A coaming 6in (150mm) high might be about ¾in (19mm) thick even for an ocean cruiser. If the height is increased to 12in (300mm) the thickness need not be double, even though the loading may be more than double when a wave breaks aboard. The *strength* must certainly be double, and an allowance must be made for fastenings and windows, so the thickness will probably be 1¼in

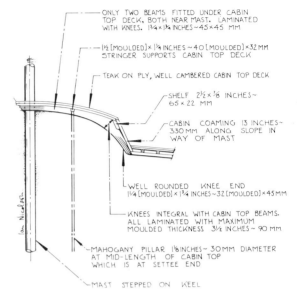

ONLY TWO BEAMS FITTED UNDER CABIN TOP DECK, BOTH NEAR MAST. LAMINATED WITH KNEES. 1¾×1¾ INCHES ~ 45×45 MM

1½ [MOULDED]×1¼ INCHES ~ 40 [MOULDED]×32 MM STRINGER SUPPORTS CABIN TOP DECK

TEAK ON PLY, WELL CAMBERED CABIN TOP DECK

SHELF 2½×⅞ INCHES ~ 65×22 MM

CABIN COAMING 13 INCHES ~ 330 MM ALONG SLOPE IN WAY OF MAST

WELL ROUNDED KNEE END 1¼ [MOULDED]×1¾ INCHES ~ 32 [MOULDED]×45 MM

KNEES INTEGRAL WITH CABIN TOP BEAMS. ALL LAMINATED WITH MAXIMUM MOULDED THICKNESS 3½ INCHES ~ 90 MM

MAHOGANY PILLAR 1⅛ INCHES ~ 30 MM DIAMETER AT MID-LENGTH OF CABIN TOP WHICH IS AT SETTEE END

MAST STEPPED ON KEEL

For a very light racing yacht 32ft (10m) long, McGruers produced this almost beamless structure to support the cabin top (coachroof). The deck gains strength from its bold camber and from the single stringer each side. Each stringer has a single slender pillar at the aft end of the settee where it is out of the way and forms a handy grabrail.

To brace the keel-stepped mast there are a pair of beams which are delightfully blended into knees at each end and support the cabin top. Being laminated they look terrific and have no hidden defects.

The steep slope of the coachroof coaming helps to feed a smooth airflow to the sails and ensures a strong join with the top deck. Loss of interior space is acceptable in a racing boat, and is made less obvious by the pleasing appearance of the moulded wood structure.

(32mm) for deep-sea work. This is because strength goes up roughly in proportion to the square of the thickness. Farther aft, in way of a doghouse with a big window the coaming height may be 2ft (600mm) and here the thickness might be of the order of 2in (50mm) round the glazing and along the bottom and 1½in (38mm) elsewhere.

For racing much depends on how far offshore the boat is to go, how much the coachroof coamings have to help support the mast, and the coaming length. If the coaming is steeply angled inboard it may form part of the deck and should be as strong. But a small coaming on an out-and-out racing machine can be made very thin, perhaps $\frac{3}{8}$in (9.5mm) on a 30ft (9m) boat. This is an area where fanatical weight-saving should not go too far, because coamings form part of the 'lid' of the hull and as such contribute to the stiffness and strength of the whole structure. Do not follow the lead of a bright young designer who made one of his creations so light that when modifications were required the owner set to using a bread-knife!

Laminated coamings, whether for coachroof or the cockpit, can be made very simple. In effect the builder makes his own plywood. He may build up a big sheet of laminated wood the length of the required coaming and twice the width, saw it down the middle lengthways and there are the two coamings. If the cabin coaming is 12in deep at the fore end and 18in deep at the aft end, the piece can be about 33in wide and cut diagonally to give the necessary shape. It is advisable not to make the laminated plank up to the neat size because there will possibly be edge blemishes, bevels have to be put on and the edge may get chipped in handling. Also allowance has to be made for 'set' if the coaming is curved and tilted inward.

Both outer laminates should show the grain running longitudinally, but the inner concealed layers may be at an angle to use up short lengths of timber. The stresses sometime placed on such coamings mean that vertical or angled grain are desirable for strengthening and to counter any tendency of the outer skins to split along their grain. Short horizontal lengths can also be used on the visible surfaces with careful butts, provided trouble is taken to match the tone and grain if the wood is to be varnished. Where the grain is hard to match an inside butt can be located at a bulkhead so that the change is not obvious.

A more elaborate type of coaming is built up not as a simple slab of wood but a structure of variable thickness. The top edge is increased to take the coachroof top and maybe its beam ends. The bottom is thickened to form a carline or deck edge facia or both, and perhaps a handrail is worked in too. These extra laminates may be added to the 'basic slab' described above, or built on as part of a single operation, best if there is curvature in the coaming.

When making up cockpit coamings the same considerations apply. Long light coamings can be made up using relatively short lengths of wood. The top edge can be thickened to form a flange on

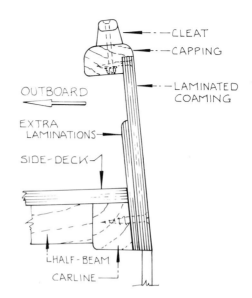

Because the bottom of the cockpit coaming has to take greater stresses than the top, extra laminations have been put in. The top edge is sealed with a capping which is well rounded at the upper corners so that it looks smart, holds the paint or varnish well, and is comfortable for sitting on. The bottom outer edge is kept to a fairly small radius to help keep water on deck from tumbling over into the cockpit.

the outside for strength, keeping out water and for sitting on, or for attaching cleats that are not heavily stressed. The practice of putting cleats on the outside of a coaming has disadvantages: the cleats are not easy to see especially at night and it is easier to fix or free a sheet on a cleat which is secured to the upper edge of a coaming.

Laminated coamings can be made curved on the sort of jig needed for other components. The procedure is the same as making up frames or beams except that some layers may be set diagonally, and extra clamps are needed because of the extra width. Pairs of hardwood bars tightened down by bolts threaded up to their heads are handy clamps. For quick tightening use either butterfly nuts or common nuts with handles of round rod welded on.

Metal fastenings are not used in coamings like this because they make cutting out windows, edge bevelling and similar work more difficult. Any windows are marked and cut out with a jigsaw after the piece has been cleaned off on both sides. Partly because this tool is awkward to train round tight bends, partly because it is bad engineering, the corners of windows should not have radii less than about 1½in (40mm). To speed up work it is best to have a radius of 3in (75mm) because the saw can be eased round quicker and there is generally less fairing off to do inside the smooth curve. Window manufacturers and designers tend to believe that small windows must have small-radii corners, whereas it is better to have the window ends a continuous curve. On ply or laminated coamings the exposed grain edge by windows changes direction round the opening so it is desirable to keep the smoothing off as simple as possible. This is done by masking the end grain either with the window frame or with an edge moulding.

Portable routers can be used to make the rebate for the glazing, but often it will be quicker to add laminations on the inside to form a lip. On all boats, even for sheltered conditions, the rebate must be on the *outside* so that the glazing is braced against waves, which tend to force it inwards. So the extra laminations will be on the inside of the coaming, and it is logical and simplest to have all the other additional laminations, for the beam shelf, carline, etc also on that side.

Coachroof coamings may curve round the forward end, and the cockpit coamings bend

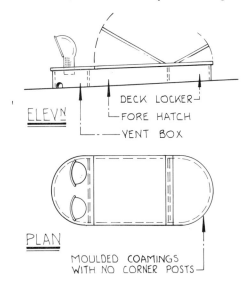

ELEVⁿ
DECK LOCKER
FORE HATCH
VENT BOX

PLAN
MOULDED COAMINGS
WITH NO CORNER POSTS

By laminating coamings quite sharp curves can be worked in. This foredeck unit has no corner posts: it looks smart, heavy seas find nowhere to pile up against, sheets are less likely to catch since there are no corners, and those drying-out gaps besides the posts are avoided even in hot sun conditions.

round aft. In this way there are no corner posts. Coamings shrink little in the longitudinal direction, but corner posts, having their grain vertical, dry and open the seam along the coaming. Curved coamings are also strong, and easy to keep painted or varnished because there are no sharp edges. Admittedly the work involved in laminating is substantial because the corner bends are sharp, except on very large boats.

Almost always, when laminating up a curved shape the first layer is the one on the inside of the curve. If a coaming is to have integral internal stiffening such as a beam shelf, the laminating procedure will be as follows.

1. Set up the jig to the correct curve, which is taken off the mould loft floor, or (less often) off the plans or the boat.
2. Laminate up the main thickness of the coaming working from the inside of the bend outwards.
3. When the glue has fully cured remove the coaming from the jig and clean up both sides.
4. The curve may spring back when taking off the jig but this does not matter. The coaming is replaced in a jig so that the inside is accessible and the extra laminates for beam shelf, etc are added. Some builders make up laminated beam shelves separately and glue them to the coaming after separate finishing.
5. Top and bottom bevels are cut or planed on the completed coaming, but the top one may not be finalized until the coaming has been fitted in place. This is to allow one to fair in the beams and coaming together and to get the exact final angle 'off the ship'. It shouldn't vary from the angle lifted off the mould loft, but as there may be a change of angle fore and aft and athwartships every few feet along the coaming, it is better not to plane off too much in the early shaping stages.

Extra laminations are theoretically needed on cockpit coamings in way of winch bases and perhaps cleats. In practice wooden coamings on cruising boats are not usually pared down, so there is ample strength all along. Racing yachts tend to have their sheet winches mounted separately on deck, but if the coaming forms part of the winch support some extra thickening, even if only to compensate for loss of strength in way of the bolt holes, is desirable.

Just how much extra strength to add is not the sort of figure which can be precisely calculated. We have to remember that one of the most famous yacht designers of all time suffered the awful embarrassment of loosing a yacht to his design amid a world-wide blaze of publicity. The owner was even more celebrated than the designer and loss of life was involved. The boat appeared to split open in what seems to have been no more than a severe gale, not an out-an-out hurricane. Yet this designer is well known for the number and complexity of the calculations which he does for boats from his board. It boils down to what every boatbuilder knows: there's as much art as science in designing and building small craft.

To give a crude example of the simplest scientific approach, which is convenient even if not absolutely precise: take a cockpit coaming $\frac{3}{4}$in thick, 6in high, pierced with a row of $\frac{1}{2}$in thick bolts in line. The hole of one bolt removes $\frac{1}{2} \times \frac{3}{4}$sq in. Allowing a factor of safety of 3, we ought to put on additional timber having a cross-section of $3 \times \frac{1}{2} \times \frac{3}{4}$sq in. The extra laminate will normally extend the full depth of the coaming, i.e. 6in. So only *one* extra layer is needed if the coaming is made up of six or fewer laminates.

The number of layers to use for coamings depends on the wood available, the amount of curvature, the time which can be spent on the job and so on. Since coamings are small compared to the hull, they should be made from timber available for other parts, unless there is a very tight bend in which case the laminates will have to be made up with the thickest layers that will go round the bend comfortably. Sometimes components such as small coach roof coamings are made up of only two thicker laminates, but three is the more usual minimum.

Four layers can be economical, with the inner layers of thick cheaper wood in short lengths and the outer thin layers of teak (always the best wood for coamings) running fore and aft. Mahogany is one of the most popular woods for coamings but once water gets to it it tends to blacken under the varnish, especially at corners and joins. The blackening is the first sign of softening, and is usually 'cured' by layering paint on where previously there was varnish. If teak cannot be used (and I would go for it even if I had to do without something else), one of the hardwoods which has taken over so much from the mahoganies should

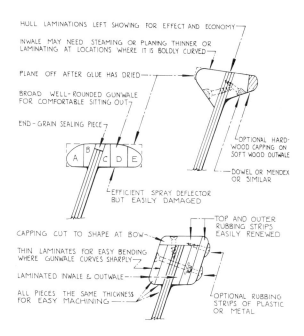

Top right: a simple type of gunwale made from an inwale, outwale, and outwale capping of hardwood and suitable for open boats or cockpits. Rounding the edges is usually best done after the strips have been fitted and their glued edges are dry. Leaving the faces square until after gluing helps clamping; it is hard to get a clamp to stay on a rounded edge without forcing it into the wood. The top of the hull laminates are left showing and give an attractive appearance provided the whole of the top edge is planed smooth.

If the gunwale or coaming (centre) will be sat on a wide, well rounded capping is needed. The two strips B and C are cut from a single length, using a saw blade set at the correct angle to give a diagonal cut. For economy pieces A, D and E are all the same width as the combined B and C so that they all go through the planer at the same setting. The sealing piece is made oversize and glued in, then planed off at the same time as the rounded edges.

Bottom: a more elaborate capping made from strips of equal thickness. The top and outer pieces are easily renewed for repair without disturbing the glued and bolted main strength structure.

be used. Iroko is a typical example, and afrormosia is used, but I do not like it because it has a 'sooty' appearance after weathering. Merante and agba are also possibilities.

Deck Fittings and Furniture

It is logical to use cold-moulding for minor parts of a boat built by the same method. Offcuts can be used up, and it is always a good idea, before starting the main hull, to get a little practice by making perhaps a forehatch or a steering wheel. These can be glued up in a small workshop or even at home. This is a version of the oldest ploy in boatbuilding, which is to make a small boat first to try out ideas and skills before going on to something bigger.

Where possible several fittings should be combined into one, not just to cut down the amount of work though it should do that: it saves weight and windage, gives a neater more unified appearance and cuts down maintenance. There is more deck space, and less chance of damage as each part reinforces its neighbour and there are fewer vulnerable corners or edges.

Some forms of deck strengthening can be worked in with deck components too. For instance the important reinforcing needed round mooring bitts or cleats can be combined with the forward part of a forehatch. Or the deck doubling needed

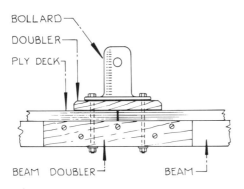

BOLLARD
DOUBLER
PLY DECK

BEAM DOUBLER   BEAM

Deck fittings such as mooring strong-points have to take heavy forces, especially when a boat is being battered by waves. They cannot be simply bolted down without additional local stiffening. This bollard has been bolted through a king plank which also serves to seal the centreline join of the plywood deck. If the king plank was put under the deck it would be in short lengths between the beams, or it would be necessary to recess the beams which would weaken them substantially. Running the king plank continuously not only ensures that it and the associated structure are strong, but also the forces on the bollard are extended well fore and aft and taken by several beams. Here it also forms a useful toehold to prevent slipping around the foredeck.

around a mast might incorporate that for turning blocks or winches for halyards, and continue into halyard and ventilator boxes or a gas bottle or liferaft locker.

Other items which can be cold-moulded are curved cockpit seats, winch bases, dinghy and liferaft chocks, and boom gallows. The fashion for using alternate light and dark coloured wood has died out and parts made like this may look contrived. But using two shades of a similar wood can look attractive. Alternatively, items like liferaft chocks can be made up of hardwood top and bottom laminates, with some softwood layers grouped together to form spacers. The hardwood takes the fastenings and resists damage, the softwood provides bulk.

Inside a hull there are opportunities to use cold-moulding, partly to achieve strong light furniture, but just as much to get an attractive, solid appearance. Also it is pleasant to extend the concept of cold-moulding right through the craft, giving an effect of uniformity and craftsmanship. A berth front which curves round to form the berth end, all in cold-moulded hardwood, is not just extremely pleasing to see; the absence of a sharp corner reduces annoyance and the chances of the crew being injured in severe conditions. Sail locker fronts and tops, cabin steps, fiddles, binocular or instrument brackets and many other parts look terrific if well made in cold-moulded wood with every corner well rounded.

On deck a bulwark or toerail always looks better if it sweeps round a corner and has no join. On power boats with bold flares and decks which sweep sharply in to the stem, the only way to get the toerail or bulwark to look good and retain ample strength with no short grain is by laminating. At the transom edge a laminated corner is stronger and will not open in dry weather. The whole length of a toerail or bulwark can be made up with staggered butts for the laminates so that there is no apparent join at any point.

Under the deck, where there is a high local stress such as around winches, there must be a doubler pad. In way of an anchor winch, stem fitting or mooring point the pad will be as thick as the adjacent beams are deep, with a king plank extending under three or five beams to spread the load well fore and aft. There will be bolts through

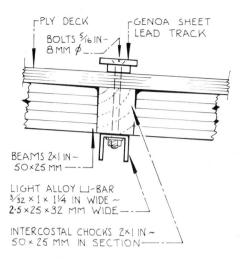

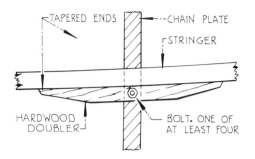

Any fitting which has to carry a severe load needs careful fastening through not just planking but also some additional structure. A bolt hole through a stringer weakens it so a doubler is fitted. Since the pull on the chainplate is upwards it is logical to fit the doubler on the underside. The ends are tapered away so that there is not a hard spot there.

On a 41 ft Two Tonner this method of strengthening the deck also provided a base for the heavily loaded sheet lead tracks. The beams were laminated because they had a lot of curvature, but as the chocks between them were almost straight they were made from solid timber. The alloy inverted channel bar runs continuously fore and aft below the beams and being strongly bolted helps to make up a substantial girder. But for the size of boat the scantlings here are light, meant for weight-saving even at some risk of failure in severe conditions.

the deck and bottom king plank, in addition to those through the mooring fitting. For economy all the bolts may be the same thickness, but on the finest boats the fastenings clear of the bollard will be about three-quarters the diameter of those through it.

Beneath each stanchion doublers are also needed, typically about half the deck thickness on a racing boat and the same thickness as the deck on heavier craft. To make this sort of doubler look tidy it should extend from beam to beam, out to the shelf and in to the carline. When done none of the doubler edges show and the load is well spread. But the majority of builders only make doublers about $1\frac{1}{2}$ times as big as the stanchion base flange.

All doublers should be of hardwood. Ply is often used, but where it shows its edge looks unattractive. In practice the best builders use offcuts from the better timber used in the boat, and splash on some Cuprinol anti-rot fluid because leaks round deck fitting bolts are common. They bevel the edges at 45°, and use glue or if not a waterproof non-hardening bedding.

Tillers

If a boat is cold-moulded it is logical to laminate the tiller. On yachts with wheel steering it is attractive to have a varnished laminated emergency tiller stowed on special chocks, at once a practical ornament and conveniently to hand if the steering gear fails. Carefully designed wooden tillers (especially laminated ones) can be lighter than steel, perhaps half the weight.

A tiller that is straight from rudderhead to handle will not be stronger if laminated instead of solid, but the more curvature there is the more important it is to use laminating. If a solid tiller curves through 90° and the grain runs along it at the handle, right aft it will be completely cross-

grained. The reduction in strength from handle to rudderhead will be the difference between the timber's longitudinal strength and across the short grain, which may be 75 per cent, or more in some woods. Cutting a curved tiller from solid timber which has a swept grain, like a solid sawn frame, is an out-dated idea. Few are the timber yards and boatbuilders who can between them produce wood to match a particular curve. With solid sawn frames some latitude is allowable, but with tillers the grain must run along the curve of the tiller.

Tillers seldom do have to turn through as much as 90° but they are most unlikely to be perfectly straight. Plenty of mass-produced boats have tillers which are roughly horizontal at the handle, whereas the most comfortable angle for the hand is about 45°. This is easy to produce by laminating even if it means a double curve over the length of the tiller.

It is usual to laminate tillers with the layers horizontal, following the sweep of the curve. This also ensures that the glue lines are horizontal, and it has been suggested that this minimizes water penetration. There is little in this argument, because if the glue line is not perfect moisture will seep in anyway by capillary action.

A tiller will be laminated up on a baseboard or jig just like a frame or beam. It is usual to taper it by about 50 per cent of its depth, from the rudderhead to the handle. Some are made to taper in width too, but this seems an unnecessary complication, and as the main strains are athwartships it seems doubtful engineering. As the taper is across the layers it has to be made after the gluing is completed. The excess wood should be taken off the bottom side, to ensure that the top laminate continues for the full length. On the underside the tapered-out laminates will not be very tidy but they are not obvious. The handle is pared down to a circular section about $1\frac{1}{4}$in (32mm) across, or 1in (25mm) if the boat is to be sailed by children.

One way to taper a tiller so as not to slice across the laminations is to have a tapered inner chock at the aft end, with laminations added above and below.

A popular way to make the tiller decorative is to use alternating woods. Mahogany and spruce are commonly used because the reddish hardwood and the creamy softer wood contrast. It might be thought that two woods which have such different weights, hardness, expension when wet and so on might 'fight', but no trouble is experienced in practice provided the gluing is well done.

For anyone who finds a striped tiller too common, three different woods or vertical laminations might be worth trying. Another variation is to combine thick and thin layers.

When designing a tiller it is worth remembering that sometimes two people have to heave on it together. Each can exert say 200lbs when sufficiently worried, so the siding and moulding are easily calculated, depending on the tiller length. For boats over about 35ft (10m) the greatest strain will not be when the tiller is being yanked over by the helmsman, but when it is lashed and a sea breaks against the rudder, or the boat is hove-to and driven backwards by a wave so that she has a tendency to 'sit' on her rudder. Boats which venture far offshore therefore need exceptionally strong tillers, perhaps 75 per cent stronger than those used inshore. For deep-sea work there should be at least three vertical through-fastenings to hold the laminates together at the aft end, where there are horizontal fastenings through the rudderhead fitting and the tiller. The ideal rudderhead fitting is in the form of a metal socket which totally surrounds the tiller end, holding it together and bearing on its entire lateral surface. But an undrained socket anywhere on a boat is a risk: if water lies in it undiscovered rot may start and creep up the wood. So a tiller socket should have an open bottom at the aft end to let water out, and the metal must fit tightly round the wood.

PART 7

REINFORCEMENT AND REPAIRS

Carbon Fibre

Reinforcing with steel is easy, but it adds too much weight and bolting it to the wood requires holes through structural parts resulting in local weaknesses. Aluminium can be used, but it puts up the cost and still adds weight and just as many bolt holes.

Ideally a material is needed that can be glued in; it should be light, easily handled, unobtrusive when installed, versatile, easy to store, unaffected by water when in use – indeed something of a paragon. The material exists and is 'carbon fibre'. An advertisement describes its advantages as: high 'specific strength' and 'specific stiffness' (i.e. good strength and stiffness for its weight), low wastage, simple to use and allowing selective stiffening. It goes on to say that structures reinforced with CF gain in terms of increased stiffness, weight-saving, robustness, localization of damage, minimized vibration, and improved fatigue resistance.

It is hard to quarrel with this, except to say that the care and labour involved in both design and building, plus the materials costs, all make CF reinforced hulls more costly than simple unstiffened ones. For racing and other high-performance boats the increase is almost certainly less than 5 per cent of the total cost for hulls over 25ft (7.5m), however, and for craft double this size, it could be below 2 per cent extra. These figures are necessarily vague because CF can be used liberally or sparingly, as desired. Never was a material so easy to tailor according to the available cash or time, or the required strength, or almost any other criterion.

Carbon fibre is a relatively new material so that innovation through experience is quick. Before contemplating its use it is sensible to go to one of the manufacturers for up-to-date information (see Appendix). The material is normally used in consultation with the suppliers to get the best stiffness for a limited quantity. As a rough guide, weight-saving of about 25 per cent is not hard to achieve, with no loss of stiffness and without going to extremes in design and fabrication. This saving is in the hull and deck shell; the rest of the craft remains unchanged. As the weight of ballast, engine, rig and equipment is likely to be around three-quarters of the total, in both powered and sailing high-performance craft, a saving of 25 per cent of the hull weight alone is of the order of 6 per cent of the total displacement. This is worth having and probably hard to achieve any other way, but it does explain why carbon fibre has not swept the board up to now.

Two similar cold-moulded hulls had these characteristics:

	Normal unstiffened hull	Hull with carbon fibre
Hull thickness	24.6mm	16mm
Cold-moulded lay-up	Inner and outer skins mahogany, four inner skins obeche. Six in all.	Inner and outer skins mahogany, three inner skins obeche. Five in all, plus CF.
Stiffness, approx.	4.5lbf/mm	4.6lbf/mm
Weight per sq ft of topsides	2.5lbs	1.9lbs

The savings in time and material in applying five instead of six timber laminations partly offset the CF cost. The use of obeche for the middle laminations is to save weight and cost. Experience has shown that when using CF one should be wary of reducing the amount of wood too much, however.

Data on the effect of reinforcement in timber panels is hard to get, because though CF is a consistent material wood is not. It is therefore relevant and helpful to see how CF works in fibreglass (GRP). Tests on thin strips of fibreglass show that with two CF tows (made up into ribbons) the panel is almost three times as stiff as without CF, even though the amount of glass included in the stiffer panel is half that in the panel with no CF. Increase the number of tows in the ribbon to three and again reduce the glass content, and the stiffness is over six times. These sensational improvements should not be expected in cold-moulded wood hulls, however, not least because broad panels show less benefit than thin strips. In practice even thick strips show up less well than thin ones when stiffened.

Tests on fibreglass panels 12in (30cm) square (which is fairly typical of the size of hull panels stiffened by frames or stringers, or both) show that deflection measured at the middle of a panel is halved when reinforced by CF, taking the sort of additions which are in regular use.

It is noteworthy that Courtaulds give data for using carbon fibre and then add: 'The basic choice in design of ribbon-stiffened panels is between weight-saving and an increase in stiffness. Using graphs, the laminate construction can be selected to achieve the required performance. *A test piece should then be made to confirm that the chosen lay-up is satisfactory.*' (Author's italics.)

Few people will have the technical knowledge to specify the type of carbon fibre they require, and even when they feel they are qualified it still makes sense to tell the suppliers exactly what the material has to do and get them to decide on the specification. This is doubly true because of the wide choice of CF types and because this is an advancing field. For instance, in Grafil, which is Courtauld's trade name, there is a choice of: Type A which is for high strains, to resist elongation, Type HT for high tensile strength, Type HM for high modulus (stiffness). The suffix S is usually added to denote that the material has been surface treated so that resin bonding is more effective.

It is usual to hold CF in place and secure it immovably to the timber with an epoxy resin, the specification of which varies according to the type being used. For this reason the CF must be ordered first, then the resin to bind it.

Though it is virtually unaffected by water, it is not a good idea to expose CF to physical damage, so it is not ideal laid inside a hull where boots can tread on it and gear fall against the lines of strengthening. The good impact strength and the ability to limit damage only come into effect when the CF is built in, and it depends on the continuous bond to the wood remaining intact.

The logical way to apply it is therefore between the layers of timber. Typically the builder will lay up two or three laminations, then take a hand-held routing tool or portable spindle moulder and make grooves in the outer surface. They must be just deep enough for the CF ribbon, plus an allowance of say 20 per cent extra to ensure that there is room for the resin under and on top.

A thixotropic resin is applied, otherwise it will flow away and not bind the full length of the CF. Before gluing the ribbons must be pulled tight and secured at each end. This tensioning is important and explains why CF is less easy to apply on the inside of a hull. If it is put on the inside of a curve, say in a cold-moulded hull which has been set the right way up after being taken off the mould, with the idea of putting an inner layer of timber veneer over the CF, there will be trouble holding it into its groove. Any tension on the ribbon will cause it to pull up out of the groove. It cannot be stapled or nailed down.

Carbon fibre is very handy for *selective* stiffening. Most boats need fore-and-aft strengthening, with special emphasis on the lower forward areas, so the runs will normally be most numerous there. But wherever it is applied it must be laid so that the runs do not terminate along a straight line. Arranging the stagger of the ends of the CF is probably best done on site, or on a model rather than on a drawing. The aim must be to have no two runs of the ribbon ending on the same athwartships line, and adjacent ribbons should have their endings as far apart as practical, to avoid hard spots. Probably the best way to arrange the runs is to plan them on a print of the lines plan, carry out the strength calculations, then make minor modifications on the actual boat. It will be usual to order the carbon fibre in the exact quantity required plus about 5 per cent extra for contingencies. There is little point in keeping this surplus, since the resin has a limited shelf life (variable, but in some cases as little as two weeks) and some versions of CF have a short shelf life. So whatever is left over might as well be used.

For powerboats the CF will normally be arranged fore and aft, perhaps tapering towards the bow. In sailing boats the high stresses round the keel or centreboard case and chainplates call for additional stiffness, with diagonal runs.

On frames, the easiest technique is to use CF between the timber laminates. The CF should cover nearly the full width (siding) of the frame and there can be one layer of it or more, say between the second and third timber laminates, and again between the sixth and seventh. If only one run is to be used place it nearer the outside of the curve of the frames. It is not good practice to apply the CF without making a groove to fit. If possible select a ribbon slightly narrower than the frame. As it is important not to leave any of the CF exposed, either side doubling or fibreglass sheathing can be applied to the finished frame if any CF extends on the outside: avoid trimming down the CF, however, as this can damage and weaken it.

Rudders, skegs, spreaders, strong beams, bulkheads and indeed all load-bearing members can gain from the inclusion of CF. The following conversion factors will be useful.

$1 \text{ GN/m}^2 = 10^3 \text{ MN/m}^2 = 10^6 \text{kN/m}^2 = 102 \text{ kgf/mm}^2 = 1.02 \times 10^4 \text{ kgf/cm}^2 = 100 \text{ hbar} = 145 \times 10^3 \text{lbf/in}^2$.

Repairs to Cold-moulding

It is important to make repairs really strong, a full belt-and-braces job. Damage caused by normal operations as opposed to an accident is clear evidence that the boat is not stout enough and the repair should be appreciably stronger than the original condition. If a defect occurs on the port side through normal use not only should that side be repaired but logically the starboard side must also be strengthened. Following the same line of thought, if a forestay fitting starts to come loose it must be resecured; at the same time the backstay fitting needs attention because it is almost certainly fastened down in the same general way, by the same person, using the same type of fastenings.

If there is no time or if conditions are wrong for a good repair, it is best to restore watertightness and strength with a temporary repair and do a good job later.

It almost always pays to make the last layer thicker than the surrounding woodwork. Once the glue has set this layer is planed flush to give a neat invisible patch. Also, timber ordered from a mill seldom arrives with exactly the right thickness, which confirms the need for an extra thick final laminate because nothing looks so suspicious as a subtle hollow in the topsides, deck or moulded coachroof.

It is worth taking a great deal of trouble to match the timber if it is to be varnished. The match should be made with it varnished, that is to say a sample of the patching timber should be cleaned up and finished. Once the varnish is *dry* this sample is compared with the intact area round the damage. Two pieces of bare wood from different trees may appear identical but may not have the same tone and texture after varnishing. If a repair is to be painted the area treated should extend far beyond the damaged region. Normally the whole topsides will be repainted after a plank repair, unless a temporary job is being done or repainting is planned for the near future.

MINOR DAMAGE

If topsides or the bottom have been scraped or chafed so that a little wood has been damaged but the main trouble is just ruined paint or varnish, it may be possible to sand off the damage. Planing lightly is acceptable for damage only about $\frac{1}{16}$in (1.5mm) deep, but beyond this something more elaborate is going to be needed unless the boat is over about 40ft (12m) when perhaps up to $\frac{1}{8}$in (3mm) might be planed away. It is not satisfactory to plane away more than half the thickness of any outer laminate. The work must be done precisely, tapering the amount of wood removed in every direction so that there is no suspicion of a flat spot or hollow.

Minor gouges can be filled, but if the boat is varnished the material has to match. Experimenting may take hours rather than minutes. The problem is that the finished job must have no visible blemish after the final varnishing; the filler and the wood around it both change colour and shade when varnish is applied but they seldom change the same way. If the filler tends to darken more when varnished it has to be made lighter than the wood prior to varnishing. Such matching up can only be done by trial and error. A filler which has been used successfully is Mendex. Two parts are mixed together and setting starts immediately, but there is plenty of time to work the putty-like mixture into cracks and hollows. Once set it can be worked like wood.

If varnished topsides are damaged quite extensively but in a lengthwise direction it may be possible to disguise a repair by blending art and cunning. For instance repairs very near the waterline could be covered up by raising the boot-top. Damage higher up might be disguised by a broad painted band, perhaps interrupted by the boat's name or number painted boldly. But there is a limit to ingenuity, and really badly damaged varnished topsides generally have to be painted unless there is a great deal of skill, patience and money available. An owner who rightly values his varnished topsides might salvage something in his sorrow by leaving a broad varnished band from bow to stern high up on the topsides, like a decorative cove line.

Gouges such as are made by bolts protruding from a quay wall can often be repaired with filler, but if several layers of wood have been penetrated a covering piece is needed. The first job is to cut away all the damaged wood so that no cracks or splintered ends are left. If the damage does not go right through, the ruptured laminates are chiselled away and it is easy to see how deep to go since there is a glue line between each layer. A new piece of wood is cut to fit the gap which has been chiselled out, but the replacement block should be made a good fit and about $\frac{1}{8}$in (3mm) too thick. It is glued in with a few well countersunk fastenings. When the glue has set the excess wood is planed

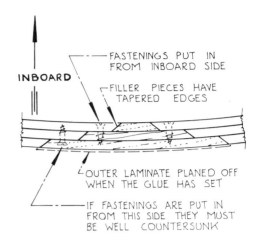

The most sophisticated repair method for cold-moulding involves wedge-shaped filler pieces. Cutting out the laminates needs careful chisel work, but this gives a strong join when the filler pieces fit exactly. In theory no fastenings are needed, each new part being held in by a shore and wedge or similar force from outboard, but in practice a few screws to pull it tightly in place are worth having.

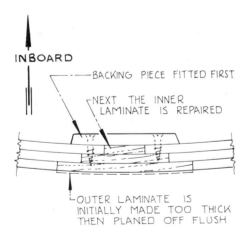

Repairing a cold-moulded hull can be done this way quite quickly. A backing piece not only strengthens the repair, it also holds in the first filler piece. Each one is rectangular and fits closely into the slot cut in the laminate. Ample glue must be used, but it should be wiped away where it squeezes out before it has time to harden.

off, the final plane strokes being carried over the surrounding topsides very lightly.

If a hole is right through the planking, the procedure is much as described above. The damage is removed by cutting a rectangular hole right through. The top of the rectangle will normally follow the sheer; just occasionally this hole is made in the form of a diamond with the long axis extending fore and aft, sometimes called a 'Dutchman'. A backing piece about 30 per cent larger all round is fitted inside the hull, well fastened and bedded with glue or a filling compound to make it totally watertight. A filler piece is now put in, made an exact fit but over-thick, glued and fastened. This type of repair is not likely to be used unless the hole is quite small, perhaps no bigger than 6in (15cm) in any direction and only half that on boats under 22ft (6m).

MAJOR DAMAGE

For larger holes the laminates are cut back successively in steps, to get to solid wood and sound glue lines. The area of damage can 'travel' beyond obvious crushing, etc of the wood fibres, and glue lines should be examined closely. Cutting back calls for sharp chisels and patience, but is not all that difficult. The glue lines act as guides, and the steps are used to stagger each join in the built-up patch. The largest replacement layer will be on the outside, although a case *might* be made for having it on the inside surface. In theory the timber for each layer of the laminated patch should be exactly the same thickness as before, but in practice new layers might be just slightly undersize. (They may be too thin, but never too thick except in the final layer.) The usual finishing off is done, and fastenings should be put in even though the boat has none in her original hull planking. They may be bolts, clenches or screws as seems appropriate to hold the repair together while the glue is curing and pull the wood tight so that glue is squeezed into every tiny gap.

Naturally every piece of wood put in must fit perfectly, but in practice repairs are made by human beings and gaps of up to $\frac{1}{16}$in (1.5mm) are acceptable in a few places around the edges of the *inner* (middle) laminates. The outermost laminates must fit perfectly, however, particularly if the area is varnished.

Big holes cannot be repaired without some sort of internal support such as frames. These may be temporary but they must follow the lines of the hull and be fair. If there is any doubt about the need for supports then they should be put in. A light racing hull with damage in excess of 18in (50cm) in any one direction will almost certainly need some supporting. Bent timbers are sometimes used but they must not be so thin that they protrude slightly at the hole or lie too flat. This will result in a subtle ugliness and unfairness in the finished job. It is better to make up a sawn or laminated frame, taking the shape from the mould loft floor if available, or from the opposite side of the hull provided this has not been distorted when the damage occurred. A bump on the port side sometimes causes slight shape changes on the starboard side. (This subject is covered more fully in the author's book *Surveying Small Craft*.)

If a hole is so big that it needs bridging by frames before the first lamination is put in, then very likely the support structure should be secured in place before the damage is cut away and cleaned up into a neat rectangle. It is logical to leave the frames in after a repair of this size, as even an immaculate repair is likely to leave the boat slightly weakened. Such extra structure should be put in both port and starboard, to keep up the value of the boat, bamboozle future buyers and surveyors, and because it is illogical to have more strength on one side than on the other, especially in a lightly built hull.

In a hull built with longitudinal stringers, instead of putting in extra frames add fore-and-aft stringers. If they are short taper them away at each end, if long secure them to a bulkhead or the stem or some other strong point with knees or brackets. Like frames they should be hidden if possible, perhaps close up under berth bases or the sole, just as additional frames should be disguised as locker end supports or fillets for partial bulkheads or cleating for holding furniture.

Where the damage comes in way of a bulkhead check first that there is no movement or distortion in the bulkhead. Lay a straightedge all over the bulkhead and make sure that it is in contact with the bulkhead along its length. Push or tap the bulkhead back in position. If force is needed try laying a piece of wood on the bulkhead and tapping it. The bulkhead itself is never hammered because this would damage the surface.

Damage at a bulkhead edge is repaired by cutting out the jagged piece. A filler piece is put in secured by a butt strap or doubling. It may be good policy to put a doubler on each side of the bulkhead and fasten right through. The wider repair will help support new laminates being put in to repair the hull shell.

When damage includes an area of deck edge as well as the topsides, it is logical (but not common practice) to mend the deck first. As usual the rough edges are cleaned up by sawing out the ruptured timber and a new piece is fitted with an under-deck doubler. No doubler is needed if a piece can be scarphed in with sloping joins between the old wood and the new. The repair, which will normally be rectangular with one edge parallel with the centreline, is left with the outboard edge extending very slightly beyond the topsides. The planking is now repaired in the usual way, and when a plane is used to clean off the outer hull laminates it takes off the slight excess of deck planking at the same time to give a flush finish.

Broken frames and beams are mended in the conventional way if they are of solid timber. Laminated members should, as far as possible, be mended so that they look as new. A chunk out of a laminated frame or beam is repaired by putting in new layers with well staggered scarphs or butts. This can be difficult, sometimes impossible. When a solid timber filler piece is used, cut it with a scarph at each end having a slope of 1:10 or longer.

Glue and plenty of fastenings are used to hold the new piece in place but even so the repair is likely to leave the boat with less strength than she originally had. To compensate for this a doubler is needed and ideally a pair should be put on, one each side. If a beam is to look good the doublers should be carried the full width of the boat or at least as far as a locker or bulkhead so that the repair is not obvious.

As with all boatbuilding, doublers are only as effective as their fastenings. If the gap between the fastenings is more than 8in (20cm) they should be viewed with suspicion, and 6in (15cm) is seldom too close. Repairs by professionals seldom reach this standard, usually because they are trying to save money.

Where partial relaminating is needed (in frames, beams and stringers) it should be done as described below for backbones. Partial relaminating is well worth avoiding, partly because it tends to lack strength and partly because it is so hard to mask. Often the best way to make a repair is to take out the damaged piece entirely, make up a replacement and fit this. The replacement may be made clear of the boat or *in situ*, but either way needs some ingenuity. For instance a beam which extends from sheer to sheer can only be removed by cutting it through at some point, and the replacement can only be fitted by cutting out an unacceptably large piece of the beam shelf or stringer unless the deck can be taken off. So in this case it is no use chopping out a damaged beam and making a new one to the full length since it cannot

be fitted. Sometimes the same problem arises with a broken frame, though here is it often only a matter of removing enough furniture.

A badly damaged beam or frame can be totally renewed by laminating up the new part *in situ*, using the hull or deck to give the correct shape. The laminates must be thin enough to bend easily round the hull curves. Each one is put in with the minimum number of fastenings to hold it in place until the next one is fitted. Glue is put on one face and hardener on the touching face of the next layer. Some simple form of U-shaped guide or jig is needed to line up the laminates as they go on and through-fastenings are recommended to hold everything together, not just while the glue is setting but for all time.

A broken main backbone is mercifully rare. Repairing it will take a lot of time and calls for some skill. The principles are the same as for a beam or frame: the strength must be restored and this means putting in more wood than there was originally. Joins should be tapered away, and if new laminates are put in successive ones are cut back beyond the damage and built up in well spaced steps. Glue should be used as well as fastenings, the glue being applied to the butt ends as well as the faces of the pieces. Because the job is almost bound to take quite a lot of time, plenty of screws or perhaps barbed nails should be put onto each part to hold it in tight. In theory the next piece should be on before the glue of the previous one has set, but in a job of this magnitude there can be no guarantee of this.

PART 8

STRIP-PLANKING

Technique and Materials

Strip-planking is a form of carvel planking suited to people who do not have the skill and experience to build in the normal carvel way. Only one layer of planking is used in normal strip-planking, though there are hybrid versions which combine strip-planking and cold-moulded (dealt with earlier in this book).

Narrow planks are used so that no 'bellying' is needed. Bellying is the shaping of each plank as seen in section, usually by hollowing the inside and rounding the outside. The curved inside is needed to fit round frames at the turn of the bilge, and on the outside it is to avoid having a hull made up of a series of longitudinal flat planes. Where the hull curves outwards, at garboards or the flare of the bow for instance, the bellying is reversed, being concave on the inside.

At its simplest, strip-planking involves building with no plank shaping at all, so concessions have to be made. The design must be prepared so that the hull shape has as nearly as possible the same girth at the bow, amidships and at the stern. The run of the planks will not everywhere suit the sweep of the sheer, and it is almost inevitable that the final appearance of the boat will show that concessions have been made in the interests of super-simple construction. At the top end of the quality scale, strip-planking can cope with virtually any hull shape, and can look as good as the best cold-moulded or conventional carvel work.

Because strip-planking has various levels of simplicity it suits amateurs and also professional yards where there are semi-skilled men, or a blend of skilled and barely skilled. With no more than average competence at wood-working there is no reason why a careful amateur's first attempt at strip-planking should not be entirely successful.

Large or small teams can work on the job. Singlehanded, a man should be able to build a 50-footer yet two or even four teams can work on one hull. When two full teams work together, one on each side, they have to take care that one does not

race too far ahead or hull distortion may occur, but a degree of competition speeds up work. If the planking is being worked up from the keel and down from the sheer at the same time, in theory two teams of plankers can work on each side at once. They would have to be tolerant, and careful to avoid dripping glue onto each other and when manoeuvring strips into position, but where hurry is the order of the day four planking teams is the way to get things done.

Even using one team requires organization. One person will be preparing the planks, another gluing them, two or three will be fitting them, with a less skilled helper handing out nails, working the drill or punching down nail heads. One person inside the hull is useful for pulling in the planks, cleaning off the glue that runs down from the seams, and letting the other know if a plank is not tight on the inner edge. Strip-planking with just one team tends to be slower than ordinary carvel because the plank widths are so narrow. Fit one strip and an inch of the hull has been covered; one carvel plank may be 4, 6 or sometimes 8 inches wide. But the equation is not as simple as this. Because strip-planking needs far fewer frames and frame fastenings, and no stringers, time is saved once planking is complete. More important, a strip plank sometimes needs no shaping, and seldom very much, so each one goes on soon after its predecessor. With carvel planking there may be hours of fitting and shaping between plank no. 5 and no. 6, while the garboard or a plank with 'sny' (reverse turns) can take a very long time to make and fit, and this work demands shipwrighting skill.

Costs should be moderately low because cheaper narrow pieces of timber can be used. There are higher sawing costs since each plank has to be a narrow strip, but relatively little planing of the flat surfaces. However, the upper and lower edges are bevelled (rounded or cupped) where adjacent strips fit together (see diagram), and this requires machining. The inboard face should normally be planed, but the outboard face need not be because it will be faired off with a plane later, when planking is finished. If a planer circular saw blade is used the top, bottom and outer faces will be smooth enough. A planer saw gives a finish which is good for gluing and is smooth enough for painting. So if the hull is to be painted or lined inside the planks do not need any further machine planing, provided the planer saw blade has been correctly set and kept sharp.

There is little wasted timber, nothing like as much as with conventional carvel, clinker (lap-strake) or cold-moulded. The quality of the timber must be good, with no knots which extend more than one-third the width of any plank. However an amateur who doesn't count his time can use wood which has a lot of knots, by cutting out the bad ones and scarphing up plank lengths. Some scarphing will almost certainly be needed even if the boat is only 25ft (7.5m) long, so it is a question of balancing the quality and cost of the timber against the time taken to make scarphs. Professionals and amateurs not tied to the tightest budget will select wood with the minimum of knots; the best of the 'pine' and 'mahogany' families can be bought in long lengths virtually free from knots. The only way is to visit the timberyard, discuss with the manager the best available timber, then personally turn over the stock and select the best pieces.

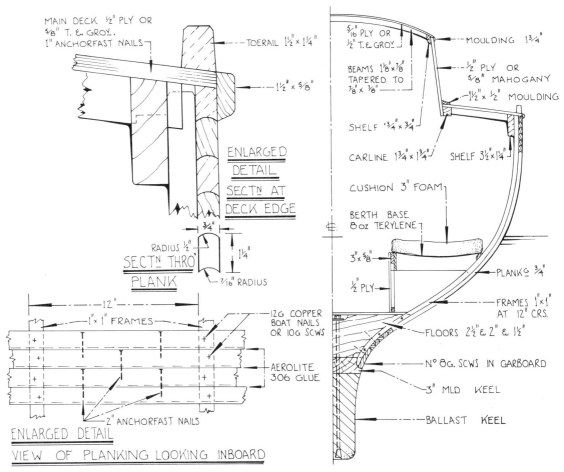

Right: the midsection of a strip-planked auxiliary sloop designed by Alan Buchanan. She is 23ft 8in (7.2m) overall and strong enough for extended cruising. The section through the deck edge and bottom (left) shows the way the designer recommends the nails are driven through the strip-planking. This is a good example of the radiused edge technique and shows the precise shape of the plank section.

Where weight has to be saved, a high-density wood may be used below the waterline and a lighter one above. This is also a good plan if there is a shortage of excellent wood. The lower part of the hull is the area where stresses are highest, so this is where the strongest wood, normally the densest, should be used. If the topsides are to be varnished this method will need modifying, because a 'hard' wood is essential for a varnish finish. Though coniferous woods are occasionally used the results tend to be disappointing and seldom long-lasting.

For the lightest hulls cold-moulding rather than strip-planking is used. The many nails in strip-planking add to the weight, though this is partly offset by the fewer frames and absence of stringers. The planking cannot be very thin because the glued joins are the seams, so there must be enough width to allow for errors and to give a strong bond. Gluing has to be done with enthusiasm so that plenty of surplus oozes out on both sides. To save later work it is wiped off before it can harden but there is no getting away from the fact that a quarter of the expensive glue is likely to be wasted.

WHICH TYPE OF STRIP PLANKS?

Strip planks are usually thought of as being square in section. One advantage of having the same width and depth is that the plank can be laid to best advantage. If it has to curve in tightly, then the grain will be set on edge and this will help the wood to bend. But generally the grain will be set athwartship so that the plank outer edge appears rift sawn (the grain edge shows on the outside faces). This gives long life, the maximum resistance to wear and tear, and reduces the chances of splitting or 'leafing' especially when finishing off.

Because square-section planks each extend only a rather small distance around the girth of the hull, a great many have to be fitted between sheer and keel. The obvious way to speed up the planking is to use a section which is wider than it is thick. In theory, if the plank is twice as wide as it is thick then the working time is cut in half, compared with square-section planks. But of course it does not work out quite like this. Rectangular planks need more bevelling, more skill to fit and more care when edge-nailing. Nevertheless a very good case can be made for using planks about 30 per cent wider than they are thick.

Rectangular or square-section planks are cheaper than the machined type described below, but more work is needed to fit each one because quite a lot of bevelling is required. If the yacht has a lot of hull curvature the bevelling takes time. One way round this is to have square-section planks round the sharpest turn of the bilge and wider planks above and below.

Specially machined planks (either rectangular or square) with one edge concave and the other convex (see diagram) are the easiest to fit. However, the machining of the concavity and the convexity has to be done in a bench-mounted spindle moulder and this is more expensive than straight cutting and planing. These machined strips are probably best for a first attempt, or for someone who is not fully confident of this skill. In remote areas one may not be able to get concave/convex planks machined up. Anyone who is going to use this type of timber should visit the yard where the machining is to be done, to make quite sure the mill operators know exactly what is required. If there is the slightest doubt, then buy a few sample lengths for trial gluing-up into a curved shape. This need not be a waste of time; if the work is well done the resulting piece can be used for a transom, hatch top or some such.

The radius of the convex edge is usually between 110 and 120 per cent of that of the concave edge. The concave section can be worked facing upwards or downwards. If it is upwards each edge forms a trough which the glue lies while the next plank is being prepared, and tends to hold it in the seam once the plank is fitted to it. This is clearly an advantage, but the corresponding disadvantage arises when nails are being driven in; each nail head has to be punched down with a nail punch otherwise the hammer face will damage the plank edges. This is not such a disadvantage since the nails should in any case be punched down even on a convex edge. Because strip-planking simply must involve using excess glue at every seam and it is better to encourage it to stay there, it is logical to have the concave edge upwards, but care is needed to prevent the plank edges from being damaged.

Whatever section is used, more strip planks should be bought than is known to be needed from calculations. A minimum of 3 per cent extra should be on hand; it is unlikely to be wasted as there are plenty of other jobs where leftover strips can be absorbed. In practice 5 per cent over is better, and for beginners or a yard where there is series production 8 per cent extra is reasonable.

NAILS FOR EDGE-FASTENING

Because the nails are totally recessed in the planks they should not get wet, but anybody knows that everything on small boats gets wet sooner or later, so ungalvanized steel nails are just not acceptable. There is a school of thought that advocates galvanized nails on the grounds that they will not rust during the normal lifetime of the boat. This is not necessarily true, partly because some nails are almost certain to become chipped when being hammered in and partly because modern galvanizing cannot be totally trusted. Once the zinc coating is damaged rust must start, and it will quite soon bleed outwards and inwards through the planking seams. The owner is then faced with red weeps, and what is he to do about them? There is no known cure for this disease. Painting may cover the trouble for a short time but it will break out again, generally all over the boat, and she will be unsightly and possibly unsaleable. There are concessions which may be made during construction, but it seems to me unjustified to risk ending up after a few years with a useless hull all for the sake of a relatively small sum of money. Anybody who still remains unconvinced might try a few simple experiments with galvanized nails before deciding to use them for hull planking: for instance, a sample area of topsides might be made up and left exposed to the weather for a few weeks or months. This experiment should include oc-

casional saturation and the nails should be hammered in with the same sort of energetic enthusiasm which will be used during the actual hull construction.

For those who simply have to economize at every turn, there are two types of galvanized nails, boat nails which have a square section, and the conventional wire nail which is an ordinary steel round section. The latter tend to be a bit flimsy and grip less well, so if galvanized nails are used boat nails are much to be preferred even though they are hard to find.

Much better are silicon bronze, barbed nails, which are supplied by many chandlers. They are sold under the trade name of Gripfast and they neither rust nor corrode under normal conditions. In theory barbed nails cannot be pulled out; actually they can be got out if wrongly driven though not without a struggle. In North America Anchorfast nails are used, similar but of Monel metal, so they too strongly resist corrosion.

Barbed nails need pilot holes. In softwood these should be about half the diameter of the nail, and in hardwoods about two-thirds the diameter. But here again it is worth prior experiment to be sure the nails go in only with a well wielded hammer, yet do not bend when hit. In edge-nailing the length should be $1\frac{3}{4}$ times the plank *depth* at least. Some builders go for $2\frac{1}{4}$ times the plank depth, which certainly gives an extra measure of strength, but it makes repairs more difficult because each nail is right through two planks and into a third.

Spacing should be of the order of four times the plank *thickness* where there is a lot of curvature; on straight lengths it can be increased to around seven or even nine times. Staggering them is important, and if the spacing is varied it is necessary to mark on the outside of the planking where the nails are, so that subsequent rows do not interfere with those hidden by the last strip laid.

There are builders who claim that the edge-nails' only job is to hold the strips while the glue is setting. Certainly modern epoxy glues are wonderfully strong, but if the glue is imperfectly mixed, or applied leaving dry gaps and bubbles, the nails give the planking strength. Boats live rugged lives, bumping on each other and harbour walls, so there are severe side loads on plank seams. Nails help to contain these stresses. They give a boat strength in two other ways: (1) strip-planked boats tend to have few frames, so the nails give the shell some additional strength; (2) the glue may adhere

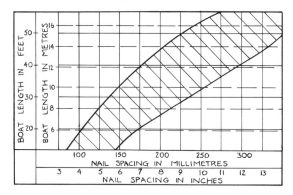

When fitting strip-planking each plank is secured with vertical nails to the previous plank. Nailing should be close in way of tight curves (in plan or section) but where the planks lie straight and clear of the sharp turn of bilge or at the bow wider spacing is acceptable.

This graph shows typical upper and lower limits of nail spacing, but in practice there may be special areas where very close nailing is needed. Too many nails are rarely found; too few will result in leaks.

to the thin film of wood on the edge surfaces of the plank, but when struck sideways this surface layer of wood fibres may tear off even though the glue holds. Nails penetrate right through the plank's depth binding the layers of wood fibres together.

It is theoretically possible to build a strip-plank boat using modern epoxy glues and with no nails. This would save money and final hull weight, but it would be a slow job, because each glued seam would have to have set hard before the next plank could be safely fitted. If glues such as the rescorcinals and ureas are used the nails cannot be skimped, whereas with the epoxies nailing is less critical.

Simplifying the Work

Virtually all cold-moulded hulls are built upside down, but quite a few strip-plank boats are put together the right way up. This is at first baffling, as the many advantages of building upside down apply as much to strip as to cold-moulded. Probably the explanation is that strip-planking has in the past been used by lone builders and people very short of equipment. They may have felt that it was too difficult to turn a hull over so they have got round that particular crisis by building right way up.

My own view is that upside-down building is so much better that it needs very strong arguments to coax me to work in any other way. Strip-planks ought to lie exactly flush, so there should be no difference in level between adjacent planks and therefore little planing off when the glue has set. In real boatbuilding the wood does not co-operate to that extent. Planks will often lie smoothly together, but just as often there will be a difference in the way two neighbouring ones lie. This difference has to be planed away, then the whole hull needs rubbing down just like a cold-moulded shell; there is the same painting or varnishing. All these are easy working downwards. Even with plenty of power tools like belt sanders for cleaning off the hull, it is still quicker and easier to have it upside-down. There are tricks, like arranging overhead support wires to take some of the fatigue out of holding a power tool for hours on end, but they work far better when the hull is upside down.

Clamps for holding each plank in place while it is fastened speed up and simplify the job. They can be in the form of flat-bar metal hooks with just the same jaw width as the plank thickness, the jaws long enough to embrace the plank being fitted *and* the one it lies on. That way each new plank is held flush and precisely positioned relative to the last one. With a hook every 2–4ft (60–120cm) planks will be quickly and positively positioned even by unskilled labour. To hold the hooks down tight there is a choice of strong elastic shockcord with adjustment toggles (like the short lengths of hardwood with a hole at each end, used for tightening tent guys), or tackles, or ropes with weights.

These hooks or clamps may be used when planking upwards or downwards, since the tensioning line has just to extend back over the planks already fitted. A comparable arrangement is a set of Mole-Grips with flat plate 'paws' welded onto the jaws, so that the enlarged jaws grip both the new plank being fitted and the previous one. But this tool is in one respect not as good as hook clamps, since it doesn't force the new plank hard against its neighbour; it only ensures the alignment and that there is a firm grasp on the new and next plank.

Another arrangement is to have ropes or shock-cord secured inside the hull and leading out over each new plank and back to a securing point. As the new plank is put on the ropes are pulled tight and they keep it in place until the nails are driven home. But again ropes only pull the planks together, not help with the alignment, so some form of guide is still needed. A narrow U-shaped piece of ply at least $\frac{1}{2}$in (12mm) thick (similar to the guides for laminating frames) can slide over the new plank and the previous two. A row of these guides makes sure that the new plank is level with its neighbour.

For strip-planking there is nothing so valuable as a very long woodworking bench. Ideally, planks will be put on the hull in one length from bow to stern. This is only possible when the team is big enough to handle long pieces, as few people alone can properly control more than about 12ft ($3\frac{1}{2}$m). Where the team is large enough and has the skill, planking-up is quicker and neater if each strip is laid on in a single length. When the timber is not long enough pieces are scarphed together, for which the long bench, with plenty of stops or chocks to hold the pieces every few feet, is a great help.

Even when the planking is put on in more than one piece for each length, a scarph-cutting box is essential. It is nothing more than a channel of wood open at each end, like a mitre box, with a pair of diagonal cuts in the sides at the correct scarph angle. A plank end is laid in the box and sawn through diagonally using the cuts in the box sides as guides. The piece is joined to another prepared in the same way. Since both have been cut in the same guide they have the same angle of cut and match perfectly. Anyone with a universal woodworking tool, or a power saw set on a guide which can have its travel angle varied, will set up the tool permanently while planking. The angle of set will be correct for the scarphs (about 1 in 8) and will be locked until the last scarph has been cut.

Where the planking has to bend sharply in a fore-and-aft direction it may be necessary to steam it. It is easy to recommend that a design is selected which does not call for this sort of work; it is just as easy to suggest that where there is curvature which the planks are going to fight (and ten minutes experimenting with the proposed type and thickness of timber will quickly show what is easy to

bend) it is better to go for cold-moulding. But when someone has selected strip-planking for other reasons, and then finds he cannot get planks to bend without breaking or at least creaking and sometimes splitting, the steam box is the answer. (Details are found in the earlier section on steamed frame timbers.) Only that part of the timber which has to be bent need be in the hot chamber. However, it is inconvenient, and sometimes plain madness, to have a very long piece in the cooker. So here is a situation where planking-up with a single piece extending from bow to stern is seldom sensible. Remember that any steamed wood is too damp for epoxy gluing, so one of the glues which are mixed up with water will be necessary.

One gadget which is always needed, not just to speed up strip-planking but to ensure accurate nailing, is a stop on the drill used for pre-drilling the holes in the plank edges. The stop may be a solid metal or wood cylinder put on the drill so that only a precise pre-determined length of bit can enter the wood. Or the bit can be shortened so that just the right amount sticks out of the chuck, then the chuck end acts as a stop. Beware of the chuck teeth or the stop damaging the plank edges.

Procedure for Strip-planking

For the initial stages of building, before the actual hull planking-up, this method follows the same steps as cold-moulding or ordinary carvel, so study the earlier sections of this book in conjunction with the following.

After lofting, when making up the moulds, it is vital to remember that the mould size is the same as the finished hull size minus only the finished plank (shell) thickness. Moulds are fixed down, braced and protected against contact with the glue in the usual way, but spaced at about one-fifteenth of the waterline length. Experienced builders may space them at one-twelfth or even one-tenth, but at the bow and stern where there is most curvature they then put in half-station moulds. Though there is a school of thought that says the mould supports need not be as tough as for cold-moulding, I disagree.

The backbone is fitted on the moulds following cold-moulding practice. It is common not to rebate the stem, so that the plank ends run on beyond it. When all the planks are fitted and the

glue cured the ends are sawn off and planed smooth. Then one, two or more laminates are laid over the stem and plank ends, with ample glue and fastenings according to the degree of strength required and inversely according to how much weight and money is being saved. In theory no metal fastenings are needed for these outer laminates but for deep-sea work it would be good practice to put in a bolt or screw every 18in (50cm) or so.

The keel/hog will normally be rebated to take the lower planks, but the transom edge will be left unrebated and the planks run on aft. When they have all been fitted round the transom the outstanding lengths are sawn off and planed. For tugs and working boats that lead rough lives metal or wooden protection may be added.

After the usual fairing, planking-up is started. Some people start at the keel and work towards the sheer, some do the reverse. Others start in the middle and work upwards and then downwards. There are almost as many methods as there are

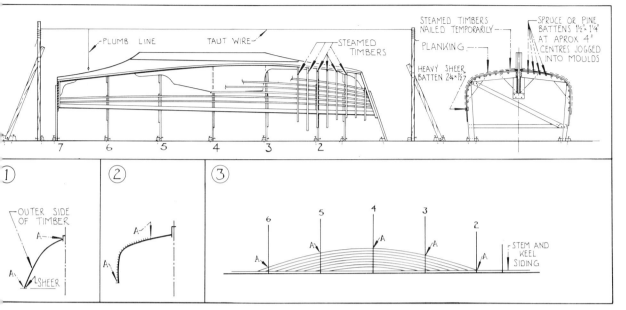

It is usual to build this boat upside down, as shown in the top sketch. She is the 18ft 6in Weevil class camping cruiser designed by Alan Buchanan. The keel is set up exactly under the taut wire which remains over the centreline of the hull throughout building as a constantly available check for accuracy and alignment.

After the backbone has been put up, and the building moulds, softwood battens at about 4in centres are notched into the moulds. In the elevation drawing (top) the battens have been omitted aft, for clarity. Next the steamed timbers (frames) are put on over the battens, the first few starting from the bow being shown.

In (1) the bow section is being measured and then divided by the width of planking. In (2) the same girth as in (1) is laid off around the midships girth and again the girth is divided into widths equal to the plank widths. The lower part of the bottom (3) is planked up to fill the bottom area of the hull up to the point where the fixed girths A-A commence. At the lower A marks the normal planking commences and extends to the sheer.

builders! Starting at the sheer has the advantage that the early planks are easy to fit, and this is a help for beginners. However, the job gets harder towards the keel and it is almost always essential to fit 'stealers', short planks which taper towards both their ends. They compensate for the differences in girth between the bow section, amidships and stern. The more girth difference there is the more stealers are needed. Some builders mark in all the planks, as closely as they can, before laying them in place, to arrange the number and location of the stealers to best advantage. Even if (as is likely) the marking does not work out precisely, it is a great help.

Planking from the keel towards the sheer is virtually bound to end with some planks 'running off' at the sheer near the bow and stern. That is, the upper planks will not run precisely parallel to the sweep of the sheer. This may be acceptable for commercial craft, but it seldom looks good. If the topsides are painted and provided the seams are

perfect, it should not matter that the seam lines conflict visually with the sheer. In practice even the finest paint finish seldom lasts that well through a single year: sooner rather than later the seams become visible and the boat looks less than perfect.

When planking from the keel towards the sheer, with a lot of care and by introducing enough stealers at just the right levels at least the final five planks can be parallel to the sheer. However, planning stealers is just the sort of job that needs experience and skill; these are learned over the years, especially from doing carvel planking, whereas a main reason for strip-planking is to avoid the need for this sort of craftsmanship. Probably the best method is to fit a bilge stringer and work up to that, level off, then continue to the sheer. The procedure is as follows.

1. Recess a bilge stringer into the moulds and bulkheads, locating it below the waterline. It is essential that the top is exactly parallel with the

sheer. A line is drawn along the middle of the stringer on its outer face. Any taper needed to fit this stringer must be cut off at the bottom or inboard face; it must not be on the top edge.

2. The strip-planking is started along the keel and worked as far as the stringer, each plank end being carried beyond the pencil line. When all the planks have been fitted their ends are cut back and planed level with the line.

3. The rest of the planking is completed, all planks now running parallel with the sheer. The first strip in the second stage lies with its lower edge along the pencil line on the bilge stringer.

A major snag is that this technique does not fit in well with having the hull upside down. A variation which does work better with the hull upside down is similar, but the topsides planks are fitted first, starting with the sheer and ending at the line on the bilge stringer. Then the boat's bottom planks are fitted, working from keel down towards the same line. The first batch planks involve nailing downwards, the second nailing upwards – an awkward job.

These general hints will help in planking.

1. At a sharp turn of the bilge or similar awkward place, reduce the width of the planks. Even 5 per cent less thickness eases the job, but for a sharp bend it may pay to slice off a third of the width.

2. Do not be tempted to fit wide, tapered planks to fill the triangular gap often found on sailing yachts where the sternpost meets the keel. Extra wide planks give trouble after a few years, due to the way they expand and contract at a different rate to the others.

3. Pre-drill each plank for the edge-nails, before fitting it onto the shell.

4. After each plank has been nailed remove the surplus glue inside and out using a sharp scraper, palette knife or similar tool or wet rag. Some builders claim that if the glue is removed before it has set there will be glue starvation at the edges of the seams. There is no defect in strip-planking more serious than glue starvation, so these claims have to be taken seriously, but with care it should be possible to get the excess off without pulling or gouging the important glue from the seams, either while still wet or by cutting it off at the 'green' partly-set stage.

Though the main lengths of the planks are nailed, the ends should be screwed. Below the waterline screws should be silicon bronze, not

brass; above it brass is acceptable though bronze is fitted on the best boats. These screws should be twice the plank thickness, and $2\frac{1}{4}$ times is much to be preferred. Dowels are put over these counter-sunk screwheads except in commercial craft where stopping is used.

If rectangular section planks are used, some bevelling will be needed at the turn of bilge or garboards. The amount to be planed off the bottom of one plank so that it fits tightly onto the previous one and against the moulds is easily measured. The new plank is laid in place and there will be a gap at the seam; this is measured in way of each mould and noted down. On the workbench the distance between the moulds is marked on the wall, and each mark is given the appropriate mould number. The plank is laid on the bench and marked with a sharp pencil to show how much has to be planed away at each station. It is important to remember which side of the new plank is planed away, to fit the edge of the previous one. Except for the last plank, only *one* face of each plank is bevelled for this purpose.

It is a waste ot time putting each new plank in place to measure the amount to be planed off for a tight fit. Instead, just carry a 12in (30cm) length of standard planking from mould to mould. Fit this short length along the last plank so that the inboard edge lies tight against the mould and measure the 'want'. When working round the turn of bilge the gap in the seam will be on the outside, so the inside of the new plank is planed away. The reverse is true when working inside the tuck of the garboard, or in a hollow.

THE FINAL PLANK

When planking from both sheer and keel, eventually there is space for only one more plank on each side which will usually need to be shaped to fit the gap. Before distinguishing two simple methods of shaping this piece, sometimes called a 'shutter plank', it is worth noting that some professionals leave it out for quite a long time and also leave out two or three adjacent ones. The gap is used to ease some of the work inside the hull: it is very handy for passing tools and fastenings through, ventilation or cleaning out shavings. If steamed timbers are to be clenched or frames are being bolted, someone will be working outside the hull and his mate inside; even the most skilled pair need to communicate occasionally and this is far easier if there is a long slot. I have known builders to leave out these final few planks while furniture is made, wiring and plumbing put in, and so on.

Getting back to the shaping of the final plank: a strip of stiff paper or cardboard, or maybe a strip of hardboard or veneer, is secured tightly on the outside of the planking and a pencil line is drawn round the gap from the inside so that the exact shape of the final plank is obtained. It may be possible to secure the timber for the final piece over the gap and draw on it. (Securing can be by three or four temporary screws provided the holes can be plugged; if they are going to be on topsides which have to be varnished then screwholes are unacceptable.) The paper pattern is laid on the wood from which the final plank is to be cut and the shape is pricked through; or the shape can be cut out and then laid on the wood as a template and drawn round. The latter method is preferred if the builder is running out of wood and down to a few pieces which are less than perfect: the template can be tried in various positions so that the grain is used to best advantage.

Whichever method is used, the final plank should be made slightly oversize and then planed so that in section it is very slightly wedge-shaped. It is tapped in place and where it is too tight pencil marks are made. These are planed away and the plank is then glued in. It is unlikely that the port and starboard gaps will be identical and so two templates will be needed.

Repairing Strip-planking

One of the main drawbacks of this method of hull construction is its relative difficulty of repair, especially where major damage is concerned. The seams are all-important, and receive very little support from underlying structure: consequently they are more liable to be broken by say a collision, crushing or pounding on the bottom, and when this happens not only is watertightness lost but the hull strength is affected. Seam bonding may be broken for some distance beyond the apparent area of damage, and also one must check the opposite side of the hull. Where rusting edge-fastenings result or are the trouble, there may be no remedy possible.

Minor repairs such as shallow gouges or scratches are made in the same way as on a cold-moulded hull, and it is worth reading the earlier section on the subject. A small hole through the planking can be closed with a filling piece and backing block, a method that is fairly quick and economical but will only be suitable if the damage is not more than 10in (25cm) across. First cut out the damaged timber and make the hole neat and rectangular, following the seam lines at top and bottom. The ends of the hole will probably, but not necessarily, be at right angles. A backing block inside the boat is fastened with screws, bolts or clenches and overlaps the hole by at least 2in (50mm) all round. Glue is used copiously under the backing to ensure a strong and watertight bond, and to reinforce the seams. A filling piece is then put in from the outside, and should be a very good fit with glue and fastenings into the backing block. The filling piece is slightly over-thick and later planed off flush after the glue has cured.

Trimming up any hole in strip-planking can be very awkward. The hidden edge-nails ruin the edges of wood-working tools so metal cutting drills and saws are needed. It is often necessary to work in confined spaces and the inside of the hull may be inaccessible for extensive examination. A metal-cutting blade in a keyhole saw handle or a Stanley knife saw is useful. The blade of a power hacksaw may be the best tool to use. These blades are $22 \times 1\frac{1}{2} \times \frac{1}{16}$in ($560 \times 38 \times 1.5$mm) long and a great deal stronger than an ordinary hacksaw blade; also the teeth are larger so that cutting tends to be appreciably quicker. More important, one person can hold the outside end while another on the inside holds the other end. With two people, like a big cross-cut wood saw, the work is speeded up remarkably. Such hacksaw blades can also be used singlehanded without fear of breaking.

A seriously damaged area has to be built up in approximately the same way as an ordinary planked boat is repaired. The damage has first to be cut out, but this time the hole must *not* be rectangular. There must be staggered butts, or scarphs, so that the hole is made into a neat series of steps, as in cold-moulding.

It is very important to make sure that the new planks fit in such a way that they follow the smooth curve of the hull, so some framework is almost certain to be needed unless the damage is

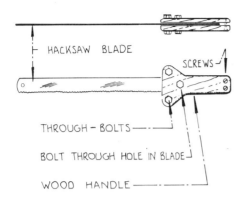

HACKSAW BLADE

SCREWS

THROUGH – BOLTS

BOLT THROUGH HOLE IN BLADE

WOOD HANDLE

For cutting through a strip-planked hull, to make a repair, a good tool is a machine hacksaw blade as it will cope with the edge-nails. It is impossible to buy standard handles for these blades, but not difficult to make up hardwood grips.

very local. The backing can be temporary or permanent: if the frames are going to be taken out once the planking repairs are completed it is only necessary to use some simple bent timbers, screwed on the inside of the planking. Their spacing depends on the amount of curvature but it is far better to put in a lot too many temporary frames than to risk having an unfair repair. Permanent frames should all match the existing ones as closely as possible, and to do a really good job they should be put into both sides of the hull even though the damage is only on one side. Not only surveyors but prospective buyers, seeing that the port side has more frames in one area than the starboard side, will quickly appreciate that the boat has been damaged.

New strip planks are put in using timber that is slightly too thick and the excess planed off later. This is the best way to ensure an absolutely smooth finish to the topsides. No-one wants to spend hours planing away masses of surplus wood, so the repair should only be about $\frac{1}{8}$in (3mm) above the original planking.

The new strips will be edge-nailed vertically so far as possible, but as the hole is gradually filled in the time will come when a hammer can no longer be used. Nails used in the repair should be non-ferrous regardless of the type used elsewhere. By drilling the last few strips and putting the nails almost through them it will be possible to go on nailing in the planks until only one or two remain to be fitted. As the gap above the last few narrows one can use various tricks: the nails may be driven in diagonally, with their heads near the outer edge of the plank, or a flat bar of thick steel, the heavier the better, can be used instead of a conventional hammer. Alternatively, screws can be used instead of nails; a dumpy short-bladed screwdriver with a small handle fits into a small gap and the screws are put almost through the plank being fitted, so that about a third or half their length shows above the wood when it is lodged in place. There are special screwdrivers with blades turned at right angles at the end which can be used (laboriously) in slots about 1–2in high, so this deals with all but the last one or two planks. The very last strips may be glued in with no fastenings and after the glue has cured some form of backing block may be fitted, particularly if the builder is a little uncertain of his skill or lacks experience. For a long replacement plank a backing block at each end, covering the scarph or butt with about 4in (10cm) clear all round should suffice, with perhaps short frame pieces or backing blocks at 18in (50cm) intervals, if there are few or no frames to support the planking.

Backing blocks will normally be about the same or possibly three-quarters of the plank thickness. They need shaping on the outside face if the boat has curvature, and the top face is well sloped down inboard to prevent water lodging there. The edges are rounded and if there are close-spaced frames the block will fit tightly from frame to frame. If the block is low down in the boat so that the top face cannot be sloped enough to ensure that water runs off, it is sloped slightly fore and aft and a gap left beside the adjacent frames to allow water to run away.

In the case of serious damage, where frames as well as planking are damaged, the frames are mended first and extras are put in, then the planking will follow the correct curve as it is renewed. For very bad damage, e.g. stem fractures, ordinary boatbuilding practice is followed.

Temporary moulds erected on a building base here support bulkheads, floors and ring frames that have been fabricated separately. The stem and hog are also in position and the way the floors and frames meet the hog is worth studying. The boat is a Carter 45 and was cold-moulded using West System epoxy resins at Whisstock's Boatyard in Woodbridge.

Another set of moulds, which are notched for the hog and have some laminated frames set up among them. The main part of each frame is made up a continuous piece to run over the hog and additional layers forming a chock to fill the gap and reach the hull shell are added. Strip-planking is proceeding from the sheer upwards, and run out past the transom. So far all the strips are continuous without any 'stealers'. (*Courtesy Whisstock's Boatyard*)

OPPOSITE PAGE Later stages of both boats. The cold-moulded Carter 45 is being planked up, with the planks put on successively and pinned to the moulds. The squares of scrap wood protect the surface while the pins are driven and later removed.

The strip-planked hull has been turned over and is being completed. The frames are very few in number. Provided it is not marked by glue, the inner surface of strip-planking can be interesting and pleasing to look at, though in this boat it will be largely covered by linings and furniture. (*Courtesy Whisstock's Boatyard*)

Here the order of construction relates to that for carvel hulls, starting with the centreline structure and including all the frames and stringers, which are notched into the hog. The rebate for the planking and the widening around the rudder shaft position can be seen. Over this iroko framing was laid a mahogany shell, one layer of 7mm and four of 5mm giving a final thickness of 28mm. The deck was teak. The boat is *Tyfoon VI*, an ocean racer 13.40m overall and 2.45m beam, built by Gustaaf Versluys Jachtwerf in Oostende, Belgium.

OPPOSITE ABOVE The gentle curvature of the lines of this traditional type of boat means a minimum of moulds for strip-planking. She was built using SP Systems epoxy adhesives by Capt. Frank McNulty.

OPPOSITE LEFT By contrast, the highly curved form of this mould would make strip-planking impossible, and thin pliable veneers are necessary. The supporting battens have to be well faired with only slight gaps between them on the curved areas, both to support the veneer and allow it to be close-stapled and to prevent an uneven surface. (*Courtesy Austin Farrar*)

166

FACING AND OPPOSITE PAGE The first cold-moulded Dragon, *Wyner* ex *Ganymede II,* built by Peter Wilson of Aldeburgh Boatyard after the class rules were amended to allow this form of construction. Others have been built in Australia and the USA. The centreline structure of stem, keel and deadwood, horn timber and transom were all incorporated into the mould with temporary fastenings. The hull shell was laid up over battens using six layers of 3mm khaya veneer and resorcinol glue. After lifting off the frames were laminated in at 24in centres over mahogany floors. These were removed for cleaning up and then screwed and glued into position. The entire deck structure was conventional. The resilience of the finished boat was demonstrated when she was knocked off her trailer while being towed: the rudder and cockpit coamings were damaged but the hull itself suffered only abrasion.

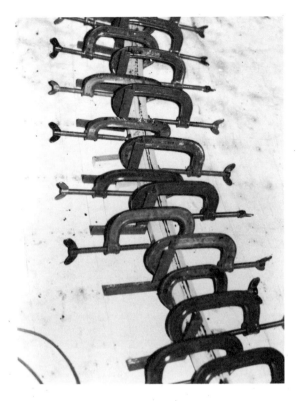

ABOVE The second layer of planking on this dinghy is being laid in alternate strips and nearly at right angles to the diagonal first skin of wider timber, which was also put on alternately over close-spaced battens. Staples were removed from all the layers as work proceeded. The third and final skin ran parallel to the sheer. (*Courtesy Austin Farrar*)

ABOVE LEFT Angle-bar brackets fastened down in a fair curve and used with clamps as a laminating jig.

BELOW LEFT The International 5.5 Metre class rules were originally intended to keep costs and maintenance within reason for these elegant boats, and to encourage new building. When they were amended to allow cold-moulded construction the weight distribution and hull weight were kept the same so that older planked boats would not be outclassed. The hulls are allowed to vary in design, and most new boats are now cold-moulded. They are stronger and could easily be built lighter than the older ones, but are restricted to a max. weight of 2050kg, of which the bare hull is about 300kg and the lead keel 1640kg.

An initial series of five boats was built to the new scantlings. Fitting the stringers and web frames proved time-consuming and Lloyds later gave permission to omit them. To ensure the same weight, subsequent boats have a hull thickness of 17.5mm (instead of 13mm), two conventional frames in way of the mast and one behind the cockpit, and extra floors forward and aft. The veneers are pressed together under vacuum and no staples are used.

PAGES 169–172 INCLUSIVE Stages in the construction of *Santa Evita*, a very successful racer built by C. H. Fox & Son of Ipswich. No framing has been set up prior to moulding the hull shell in this case, and light frames as seen in the photo of the engine beds and shaft log were put into the finished shell. (*Courtesy Richard Riggs*)

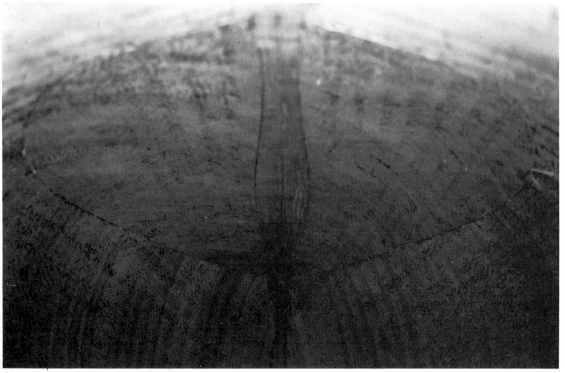

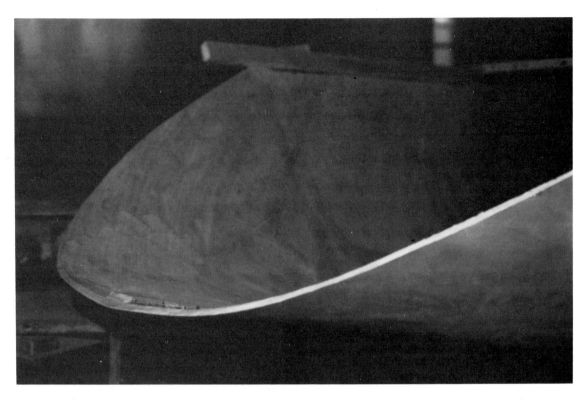

Initial stage of *Santa Evita*'s deck construction (ABOVE), and the finished engine beds with shaft in place (LEFT). (*Courtesy Richard Riggs*)

OPPOSITE PAGE Interior of *Alice's Mirror*, showing the structural function of every visible element of the furniture as well as her laminated frames and beams, the reinforcement at the bottom of the main bulkhead and the lower corners of half-bulkheads, and the substantial floors in the foreground over the keel. The white box-like structures with round holes on top are tanks for water ballast. The view of the bow section shows the three metal tubes of the space-frame (see page 75), the continuous frames running over the hog and the strong shape of the blister deck. All this is enclosed in a hull shell with a panel weight of about 1.31 lbs/sq ft including stringers and coating, cold-moulded using SP106/SP201 adhesives and coated with SP301.

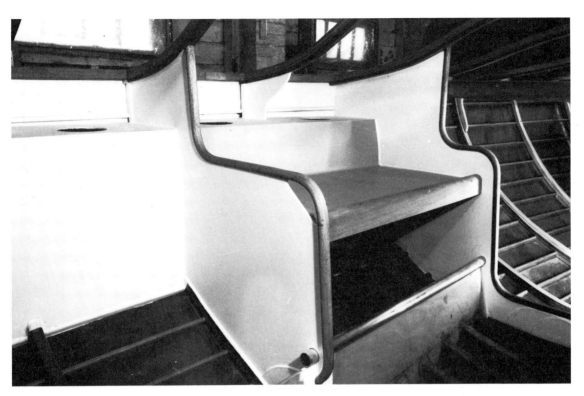

LEFT Vacuum-bagging one side of the hull of *Alice's Mirror*. Both the plastic sheeting and the cord net are polythene, which will not stick to resin squeezed out between the veneers. The edges of the cover have to be well sealed down with tape. The net leaves a slight gap between the timber and the sheet when the air is pumped out, as a path for the air to reach the bleed point and escape, making for a uniform vacuum and even pressure. When planking is thicker and thus too springy the technique is not effective, but here the veneers only needed stapling at top and bottom as the vacuum held them down during curing. (*Courtesy SP Systems*)

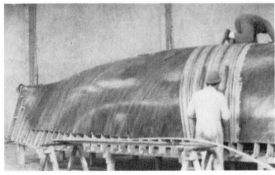

LEFT AND THIS PAGE Three-quarter Tonner designed by Tony Castro and built in Portugal in strip-planking with two cold-moulded layers on the outside. The numerous moulds are quite closely spaced, and set up with the frames and centreline structure over them as usual. The extra framing in the mid-section of the hull, and widened hog in way of the keel, are also visible.

The strip-planking runs parallel to the sheer and was put on working upwards towards the keel. Strips are edge-nailed and glued together with SP106 epoxy and individually pinned to the moulds with extra nails at the ends. The hollow near the stern (second photo) is the most complex curvature on this hull. The two 'double diagonal' veneer layers over the strips are pre-coated with SP106/SP209 and microballoons. The veneers are held down by staples put over plastic banding strips pulled lengthwise along the timber, with pins where curvature is difficult. This combination method is fairly quick to build and suited to one-off designs. Frames are small, as seen in the fourth photo showing a part of the space-frame. The stern was left open, and after the hull shell was turned over the transom was fitted, as well as bulkheads etc. (*Courtesy Tony Castro Design*)

FACING AND FOLLOWING TWO PAGES The Windermere class originated in the early 1900s and its design parameters are similar to the 12 Metre rules. (Though called 17-footers, actual length is 25ft 6in.) *Freedom* was designed by Ian Howlett and built by Franklin-Eldridge Wooden Boats in Windermere. The owner specified that the boat should last at least forty years, but it must be emphasized that the construction used would not be suitable for seagoing though for Lakes racing it is ideal.

Caption continues on opposite page

The procedure was quite different from that for the other boats illustrated here. The first stage, in which a plywood deck panel is fitted with its beams and clamp and set up provided a solid building base over the uneven floor, and was a method used for the aluminium 12 Metre *Victory '83*. On this were erected temporary moulds, also used as templates for laminating the frames and ring frames (Japanese oak on makore webs). The framing was joined to the clamp or shelf after precoating with SP epoxy, and when joined by the backbone structure was rigid enough for the moulds to be removed.

Everything was covered with polythene sheet and western red cedar strips $1\frac{1}{8} \times \frac{7}{8}$in were precoated, edge-nailed with bronze barbed nails, and glued with SP epoxy with microfibres. (As the bond area is smaller in strip-planking the filler used has to contribute to bond strength, whereas in cold-moulding the bond area is much larger and microspheres can be used.) The strips are all at an angle to the centreline so the resin can penetrate the end-grain for good bonding. Each half-shell was planked separately, removed and cleaned off, and smoothed down to $\frac{5}{8}$in thickness while the other was being planked up. When finished they were precoated with SP301 and screwed temporarily onto the structure; the screws were later removed, the holes drilled out, and wood dowels glued in to attach the shell without any metal fastenings.

The centreline join was made by cutting a $\frac{1}{4}$in gap down to the hog and gluing in a wood fillet. Then a wide shallow groove $1\frac{1}{2}$in wide $\times \frac{1}{4}$in deep was cut in the surface and fitted with a glued-in oak strip, in 2ft lengths with the grain crosswise. This provided a much greater bonding area to prevent splitting apart, and protects the planking ends against damage.

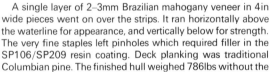

A single layer of 2–3mm Brazilian mahogany veneer in 4in wide pieces went on over the strips. It ran horizontally above the waterline for appearance, and vertically below for strength. The very fine staples left pinholes which required filler in the SP106/SP209 resin coating. Deck planking was traditional Columbian pine. The finished hull weighed 786lbs without the

$18\frac{1}{2}$cwt lead keel, and floated to within $\frac{1}{8}$in of her marks on launching. As the use of cedar makes a much lighter hull than the traditional planking, the class rules had been altered to specify a minimum of 2.4lbs/sq ft to avoid an unfair advantage over older boats. (*Courtesy R. Franklin Pierce*)

PART 9

REFERENCE SECTION

Boatbuilding Woods

AFRORMOSIA (*Afrormosia* spp.)
45lbs/cu ft

When first cut this wood is yellow-brown but it darkens with exposure and in time sometimes becomes almost black, occasionally with a sort of sooty sheen. To call it African Teak is deliberately misleading, since the woods are far apart in quality. To be sure, it does not easily rot even when exposed to conditions which encourage infestation. It is strong, stable and like teak fairly hard, but not nearly as proof against wear and tear as the salesmen of cheap mass-produced boats pretend. Because it is much cheaper than teak it has been used for deck trim, e.g. toerails and handrails. A better location is for keels and the backbone.

A tendency to split is one of the reasons why this is not the ideal wood for trim. Also it stains when in contact with steel, though the dark colour may for a time disguise this. It is a stable wood and might be used for parts like floors, especially as the interlocking grain does not matter in such a location.

AGBA (*Gossweilerodendron balsamiferum*)
30lbs/cu ft

There are so many purposes for which agba can be used that it is a natural choice when available in good quality. It is used for planking, and what is left over will be suitable for components above and below deck. The yellow-brown colour is not to everyone's taste, but where furniture or bulkheads are painted (and agba takes paint well) the colour does not matter.

Agba resists rot well, glues well and does not check or split as much as many other timbers when subject to changing temperature and moisture. Some logs are gummy and they should be rejected, not least because sticky sap is death to good gluing.

This is one of those rare woods which has in the past been used for decking as well as planking, for coamings and trim, for deadwoods and backbone components. It is not the hardest of woods, but entirely adequate for all boatbuilding jobs.

BLUE GUM or EURRABBIE
(*Eucalyptus globulus*)   56lbs/cu ft

Found in Australasia, this hard tough wood is suitable for sawn frames. It is light brown with growth rings which are not easily discerned. Though the grain may be straight, in some logs it is interlocking. This is probably one reason why blue gum is considered hard to work (to saw or nail) and also to season.

The wood is classified as 'very durable' and it seems to stand up against shipworm better than the general run of woods, though this does not mean that normal precautions like sheathing and antifouling can be overlooked. Its properties make it suitable for deadwoods and backbone parts where bending is not needed. It is rarely found in Europe, not least because it is getting scarce even in its native regions.

WESTERN RED CEDAR (*Thuja plicata*)
23lbs/cu ft

Considering how light this wood is for its strength, and that it shrinks only a little, works easily and is durable, it is surprising that more use has not been made of it. Probably the reason is that the trees grow in the Pacific Northwest, in Oregon and British Columbia, so that for European buyers it is likely to be fairly costly.

When freely available, a good case could be made for using it, perhaps not in the most important scantlings but certainly for second-line components. Because of its light weight it is suitable for racing boats and for use high up in the hull.

Though not a wood which gives a good varnished finish, it holds paint well enough. If steel touches it and there is moisture about, staining follows. All the 'pine' characteristics are found in this wood, such as a straight grain which is easy to split with an axe, relative softness and general good temper in that it allows an experienced worker to achieve the shape and finish he wants without its resisting.

In colour it is reddish brown and it is not to be confused with White Cedar (*Thuja occidentalis*) which is lighter in weight at about 21lbs/cu ft. This wood is also found in North America and was popular for small-boat planking. One of its disadvantages is that it blots up water remarkably, and to a serious extent.

GABOON or OKOUME (*Aucoumea klaineana*) 25lbs/cu ft

Gaboon is yellow-brown in colour, and of the mahogany type in many respects though it is in a different family of wood. It is often cheap, and is favoured in low-price yards turning out production craft because it is easily worked and finishes well. It is not a fine timber, nor even a moderately good one, being too susceptible to rot and not particularly strong. However, for its weight it is reasonably strong which may explain why it is used for inner laminates in cold-moulding, and it is found in many varieties of plywood.

Paint and glue adhere well, but varnished and used inside any boat it looks disappointing and suggests building down to a price but without any ingenuity being used to disguise the fact. It is occasionally found externally, but this is a mistake since its resistance to rot is too low.

GUM-TOP STRINGY-BARK, or TASMANIAN OAK, or AUSTRALIAN OAK, or WHITE-TOP STRINGY-BARK (*Eucalyptus gigantea*) 48lbs/cu ft

As the name suggests, this is an Australasian wood, seldom found in Europe. It has a straight grain and easily seen growth rings spaced between 3 and 10 to the inch. The wood texture is open and rather coarse, pale straw, almost like cream in colour. This wood has been used for planking because it is reasonably tough, bends well, planes off without undue effort, is moderately hard and generally good tempered. However it is no more than 'fairly durable'.

SWAMP GUM or STRINGY GUM (*Eucalyptus regnans*) 44lbs/cu ft

It is most unusual to find this wood outside its native Australasia. It suits boatbuilding in being easy to work and bend, however, it is graded as only 'fairly durable'. It has been used for planking because it is moderately tough and hard without being too difficult to saw, plane or fit.

Though the grain is coarse it is straight and even, the growth rings being 3–10 to the inch and clearly seen. Like others in the Eucalyptus family the wood is the colour of slightly bleached straw. Their similarity in texture and shade makes these woods difficult to identify positively.

IROKO (*Chlorophora excelsa*) 41lbs/cu ft

There are all sorts of local African names for this wood including Bang, Tule, Odum and so on. These names are acceptable, if rather confusing, but what is totally outrageous is the way it is sometimes called Nigerian or African Teak. The difference between this wood and teak is greater than the difference between good bronze and the shoddiest brass. There is nothing like teak, and it is low-level salesmanship to imply that lesser woods come anywhere near it.

Iroko has many virtues and there has been a tendency to use it when mahogany is considered to be lacking in strength, hardness or some other quality or is not available. It is much more rot-resistant than mahogany and seasons well without serious warping. it has become fairly widely used, at least in part because it is available in good lengths and widths, clean and free from knots or blemishes. It also holds fastenings well, but it only works moderately, and sometimes it is plain awkward due to the excessive interlocking grain which among other things makes hand planing so grim. Ingrown limestone-like deposits are sometimes found and they play hell with tool edges. It is this harsh presence that may have caused some people to liken this wood to teak.

JARRAH (*Eucalyptus marginata*) 54lbs/cu ft

It is unusual to find this wood outside Australia, where it is concentrated in the southwest. Pale brown with a red tinge, it is available in lengths up to about 24ft. It does not work particularly well, and blunts tools. Like other woods which seem to fight against the boatbuilder, jarrah in fact co-operates with him in the long run, because it is unusually good at resisting rot and the other malaises which attack wood.

Admittedly jarrah warps a fair bit, and needs care when gluing for the best results. But by all accounts it stands up well to weathering.

EUROPEAN LARCH *(Larix decidua)*
35lbs/cu ft

A good wood when bought correctly, and some-times known as 'the Scots boatbuilders' timber'. It comes in a variety of grades, partly depending on the number and size of knots. The quality to specify is 'boat skin' as this is relatively free from blemishes.

Larch is like a pine, being straight grained, moderately hard and a red-brown striped colour with overtones of orange. It resists rot well and might be likened to a poor man's pitch pine. It is used for beams, stringers and frames, also less often for planking and decking. This is not a very stable wood but it takes paint, varnish and glue well except when that usual curse of the 'pines' is present, namely resin. Bolts, nails and screws are all easy to put in. Larch would be more popular if it did not so often grow with so many knots, and because of these it needs careful selection.

AFRICAN MAHOGANY *(Khaya ivorensis)*
35lbs/cu ft

Because it is plentiful African mahogany is widely used in boatbuilding. It is relatively cheap, normally comes free from knots and defects and in ample lengths and widths, and has a good appearance. Colour varies from a dark red to a sort of pinky-brown, with much lighter sapwood at the edges. This sap timber is a fawn colour and often streaked, and it should not be used even though it is frequently included in boards.

This is not a particularly strong wood and it sometimes comes with compression shakes, zig-zag cracks across the grain which are not easy to detect and sometimes are quite small. However, any fracture across the grain means there is total severing of the fibres and the strength is virtually all lost, so these shakes can be very dangerous. Fortunately they do not often occur in large numbers.

Mahogany is reported to be resistant to decay but this seems to me to be only half true. If this wood is left unprotected in the weather it soon blackens and goes soft, especially where water can lodge in a thin opening, like a gap where glue starvation has occurred or under the edge of varnish. In a way this blackening is akin to rust, being a clear and early indication that trouble is brewing. One of the problems about mahogany is that it does not absorb rot-proofing chemicals easily.

Mahogany has only a moderate tendency to warping, and it does take glue properly. It also holds fastenings quite well and is not usually difficult to work. I have seen it damned in publications for having interlocking grain; my own experience is that mahogany is a lot less frustrating in this respect than a great many other tropical hardwoods.

It is probably true to say that between 1945 and 1965 no wood was used half as much as mahogany for general boatbuilding. It was also used in Royal Navy minesweepers built after 1950, but there are people who will say vehemently that the British Admiralty's skill in drawing up small boat specifi-cations is lousy. So perhaps the fact that maho-gany is found in naval craft may not be so much of a recommendation; and possibly it was used in many boats simply because it was cheap and convenient, and lent itself to cutting into veneers. Certainly there has been a swing away from it over the last ten years.

HONDURAS, or CENTRAL AMERICAN MAHOGANY *(Swietenia macrophylla)*
34lbs/cu ft

This wood is of a higher quality than African mahogany, being more resistant to rot, easier to work and good so far as fastenings and glues are concerned. It takes paint well and is certainly worth varnishing. In some ways it is the universal boatbuilding wood, being suitable for virtually everything from planking and backbone to fine trim. However it is not so tough, hard and rot resistant that it is really ideal for backbone structures, and in many ways it is better below decks than on deck.

The colour is a lighter red than African mahogany, and may be a pale pink with an impression of creaminess; it is also seen as a pale brown with plenty of yellow. It does submit to cleaning off wonderfully well, and like many woods is not easy to grade without first planing.

Because of its fine qualities Honduras has been much prized and it is now much harder to find than formerly. It is also more expensive.

RED MERANTI or RED SERAYA *(Shorea)*
35lbs/cu ft, but varies more widely than most woods being found as light as 28 and up to 42lbs/cu ft.

This wood has features in common with African mahogany, in that it comes in different reds, is free from knots, fairly resistant to rot, works easily, has a wide variety of uses afloat and finishes well. It needs selecting to avoid compression shakes, which are particularly found near the centre of the log. On the whole it is more clear-grained than mahogany. Long lengths are not always available; though 30ft logs are reasonably common if sought with enough determination, they are sufficiently rare and prized to be more costly than the average boatbuilding timber price.

The medium red variety is probably the best, though the darker red is likely to be harder. Beware the yellow grade, as seen when first cut, but all grades of the wood tend to bleach on exposure and become a dark brownish-yellow. Meranti takes glue well, and fastens well without undue splitting.

EUROPEAN OAK *(Quercus* spp.*)*
46lbs/cu ft

Oak has always been the boatbuilding timber, particularly in Europe, and is also in demand for furniture. As a result the oak forests have been depleted for centuries, especially during wars. For years there has been a growing shortage of good wood and the scarcity is now acute; there have been reports in some areas that the longest available clear lengths of this fine timber are 6ft (2m). Oak is a wonderfully strong timber, but this strength is achieved, as with so many other woods, by slow growth. So the supply cannot improve for generations, and only then provided there have been years of intelligent forestry (which is possible) coupled with sensible taxation and government (which is unlikely).

Oak resists decay, and when it is going bad it usually turns black, which is fair warning that trouble has started. Rot seems to spread slower through oak than many other woods, even after it has got a good hold. Small wonder that oak has been popular for backbones and frames. It works well but is tough, so plenty of effort is needed with

hand tools. Careful drilling is essential for fastenings: it is all too easy to break screws in oak. Wherever iron (or steel) touches it staining occurs and the acid in the wood attacks metals. In practice this acid attack does not seem to be all that serious, but fastenings should be good sized and at least heavily greased when put in.

For steamed timbers oak is the usual wood to use. Its only rival is American Rock Elm which in the past has cost more, worked less well, rotted sooner and faster, and generally behaved as a poor second in quality.

AMERICAN WHITE OAK *(Quercus alba)*
48lbs/cu ft

There are many species of oak found in North America and they are sometimes classified simply as White and Red Oak. White Oak has been used in the USA quite often for glued laminated components as well as frames. It has many of the features of European Oak and has been used for centuries for building ships. Red oak soaks up water more readily and is softer and more prone to rotting.

HUON PINE or MACQUARIE PINE
(Dacrydium franklinii) 31lbs/cu ft

This Tasmanian wood comes with a very high recommendation for boats. When first cut it has the colour of pale straw, which darkens with prolonged exposure to a matt yellow. The grain is even, straight and sometimes marked with an attractive birds-eye figuring. The texture is close and regular with growth rings spaced at 20 to 30 per inch.

In two respects Huon pine finds special favour with boatbuilders: it seems to be exceptionally rot-proof and it works wonderfully well. Not surprisingly, such an ideal wood is not easily available in large pieces, and it is scarcely found outside Australasia. Among its other virtues Huon pine bends well and finishes with a high polish. The timber can be used inside and out, for planking and for furniture which reduces waste. It can be recognized when cut by the smell of methyl eugenol.

KAURI PINE or NEW ZEALAND PINE
(Agathis australis) 36lbs/cu ft

Not found except in the southern hemisphere, this wood is a useful all-rounder. It is straight grained and has been likened to Pitch Pine, but it is not right to take the comparison too far because kauri takes glue and paint well without problems. Though it works well, it blunts the edges of tools which means frequent resharpening. Perhaps its main weakness is a tendency to split when being drilled. To prevent outward splintering a backing block is held securely to the wood during drilling and the drill is put through the pine into the backing block.

The colour is light grey-brown but where the resin is ample it is darker and red or yellowish brown. The texture is regular, and the finish smooth after seasoning which proceeds well but slowly.

QUEENSLAND KAURI (Agathis robusta, Agatha palmerstonii, and Agatha microstachya)

The poor cousin of Kauri Pine (q.v.). It is lighter, less reliable and therefore not as generally useful but is otherwise similar.

PARANA PINE (Araucaria auguatifolia)
34lbs/cu ft

This wood enjoyed a brief period of popularity in boatbuilding because it was available in large quantities and as wide, thick, long boards and it was cheap. Otherwise it has few virtues except a general absence of knots and ease of working. It rots without trying to put up a fight, and blots up water, then discolours. The basic colour is a pale grey-yellow with red and brown streaks which are random in direction and width and not particularly attractive.

Though this wood has been used for many parts of boats, its lack of virtues, softness and inability to resist abrasion make it a poor selection. To experienced eyes its use throws suspicion on a boat because it has been used so often in a desperate attempt to save pennies. And so often it has cost the owner ten times the money saved.

PITCH PINE (Pinus spp)
40lbs/cu ft

Because it contains a lot of resin pitch pine is highly resistant to rot. This, with its toughness and strength, makes it desirable in many ways, though it can be awkward to work because of the stickiness and bleeding of the resin. The colour is striped red summerwood and fawn spring growth; the differences are marked and the wood is

something like a multiple sandwich with hard-soft-hard-soft layers. It is not usually varnished though the topsides of some fishing boats planked with it, and sometimes beams in yachts, have been kept bright. It is a wood for hard work, and by tradition is used for beams, beam shelves and sometimes decks. It has also been in demand for spars, for ships and yachts, though no longer except by traditionalists.

A few years ago there was a long period when pitch pine was virtually unobtainable in Britain so that it became uncommon, and it has not come back into wide use. This may be in part because it is not easy to fasten, and it does need treating to get rid of the resin before gluing or painting.

SCOTS FIR or SCOTS PINE or REDWOOD or RED DEAL (Pinus sylvestris)
32lbs/cu ft average

Because this wood is easily available in useful lengths and widths it is often used in glued structures which form part of buildings ashore, but is is not so common in boats. And when it is found in small marine craft, they generally tend to be less than best quality.

One of its disadvantages is that when wetted it stains, spoiling the appearance. Of course the glued-up structures can be planed and then protected with varnish or paint before staining can occur. In well run boatyards staining is not allowed because the timber is kept dry. Another trouble with this wood is that it is not particularly strong. However, it glues quite well although even here it does not behave perfectly: the resin which exudes in places stops the glue from getting into the pores and making a perfect bond. But where the glue does reach the wood there is a tendency for it to be blotted up so plenty must be applied.

Careful selection and laminating are necessary because of the numerous knots. These are 'hard spots' and also mean that the wood is not all that easy to work, though clear of the knots tools flow easily through and over it. Like so many species a lot depends on how and where it grows, and careful hand selection is as always well worth the extra trouble for any boat.

Because this wood is not durable it should only be used inside, in protected areas which are well ventilated. Like most softwoods it crushes too easily if heavily loaded so where eyeplates, chainplates or similar stressed fittings are applied there should be hardwood or Tufnol pads between the metal and the timber, and extra large plate washers behind. And as in other softwoods, fastenings do not hold wonderfully well.

SITKA SPRUCE *(Picea sitchensis)*
27lbs/cu ft average

For many years this beautiful wood has been a favourite with boatbuilders. It has an unusually good strength/weight ratio and in the past was known as 'airplane spruce'. But two world wars have decimated forests on every continent and now good Sitka spruce is hard to find. During the mid-'seventies in Britain it was so rare that yards spent days searching the country for quite small parcels. One of the reasons why aluminium masts became universal was the shortage of this wood. Because of its quality and rarity, Sitka commands a higher price than other softwoods and tends to be found in better quality, more expensive craft.

Making allowances for its light weight and low density, the wood has many assets. It holds fastenings well, is generally free from defects and works very easily. The colour is almost white with a silvery overtone and no noticeable grain markings; sometimes there is a slight pinkish tinge. As well as for spars, spruce has always been popular for beams, especially to save top weight, and is used for stringers, framing, beam shelves, etc in fast, lightweight boats.

TEAK *(Tectona grandis)*
45lbs/cu ft

There is nothing like teak: it stands above other timbers and has so few disadvantages apart from its price and the way it blunts tools that anyone building a boat for himself should be tempted to use teak here there and everywhere. Perhaps the only reason why this wood is not used universally on all expensive boats is its weight. Examination of the figures shows that this is not really such a strong argument. Teak weighs something like 20 per cent more than common softwoods; in practice this means that the weight of the finished boat is often increased by no more than 2–4 per cent because so many components are of metal. If weight-saving is the aim, the most effective action is to reduce metal components or substitute wood, plastic or other materials, drill multiple lightening holes and so on.

Teak is a gold-brown colour when cut but darkens when exposed to light; if not kept varnished it weathers to a silver grey. It can be left untreated and unfinished, which partly explains its popularity. It should be given a coating of tung oil every six months, but it can stand up to prolonged exposure without any treatment at all. It is this durability which makes it so ideal for exterior use such as on decks and trim, as well as for underwater areas. The oil in the wood acts as a preservative and prevents rot. However oil on the surface is bad when it comes to gluing, so degreasing has to be done first; also it seems to help if the wood is warmed to around 65°–70° F (18°–21°C). But then all gluing should be done in a warm atmosphere so teak is not particularly difficult in this respect. Apart from its tendency to blunt tools, teak works reasonably well and holds fastenings well, and is relatively free from knots and blemishes. It is getting difficult to buy in long lengths and in the past I have bought to advantage by selecting decking flitches. These come up to about 15ft long in various widths and thicknesses, seldom over 5in (125mm) thick and 12in (300mm) wide.

CIRCULAR SAW BLADES FOR CUTTING WOOD

Type of Wood	No. of Teeth	Pitch in	Pitch mm	Hook Green	Hook Seasoned	Clearance	Top Bevel	Depth of Gullet in	Depth of Gullet mm	Notes
Abrasive hardwoods e.g. teak	32	0.0982 × Diam	2.49 × Diam	20°/25°	15°/20°	15°	10°	0.35 × Pitch	8.89 × Pitch	Tooth pitch not much over 3in (75mm) if a fast feed is required. Therefore number of teeth depends on saw diameter
	40	0.0785 × Diam	1.99 × Diam							
Fibrous hardwoods and fast sawing of less dense hardwoods	40	0.0785 × Diam	1.99 × Diam	20°	15°	20°	25°	0.4 × Pitch	10.16 × Pitch	As above
	46	0.0683 × Diam	1.73 × Diam							
Light softwoods and for fast sawing, e.g. spruce	46	0.0683 × Diam	1.73 × Diam	25°/30°	25°	20°	15°	0.45 × Pitch	11.43 × Pitch	
Heavy softwoods and for finer finish, e.g. pitch pine, larch, etc	54	0.0582 × Diam	1.48 × Diam	25°	25°	20°	15°	0.45 × Pitch	11.43 × Pitch	
Low to medium density hardwoods, e.g. mahogany	54	0.0582 × Diam	1.48 × Diam	25°	20°	15°	15°	0.4 × Pitch	0.16 × Pitch	
Medium to high density hardwood, e.g. dense oak	60	0.0523 × Diam	1.33 × Diam	20°	15°	15°	10°	0.4 × Pitch	10.16 × Pitch	For high density wood use a saw with 66 teeth
	66	0.0477 × Diam	1.21 × Diam							

This table gives specifications for saw blades to suit different types of wood, and is based on a rim speed of about 9500ft/min. It is reproduced by kind permission of the Forest Products Research Laboratory.

Bibliography

Boatbuilding by Peter Cook
Boat Data Book by Ian Nicolson
The Gougeon Brothers on Boat Construction:
Wood and WEST System Materials
Glulam by W. A. Chugg
Metal Corrosion in Boats by Nigel Warren
Corrosion of Fastenings in Timber by Pinion
An Introduction to the Design of Timber
Structures by Phillip O. Reece
Timber Construction Manual by the American
Institute of Timber Construction
Timber Designer's Manual by E. C. Ozelton and
J. A. Baird
Wood Handbook, Forest Products Laboratory,
U.S. Dept of Agriculture
Handbook of Hardwoods, HMSO
Wood Specimens: 100 Reproductions in colour
by H. A. Cox
Wood Bending Handbook by W. C. Stevens and
N. Turner, HMSO
Carbon Fibres in Composite Materials by
R. M. Gill
Carbon Fibres in Engineering by Marcus Langley

A Method of Improving the Bending Properties
of Wood, Technical Note 16, HMSO 1967
Textbook of Laying Off by Attwood and
Cooper
Lofting by Allan Vaitses
Structural Adhesives, Aero Research (Ciba)
Various publications of the Timber Research
and Development Association (TRADA)
Structural Design of Planing Craft by S. R.
Heller and N. H. Jasper, in Trans. RINA 1960
Exploration of bottom pressures and associated
accelerations experienced while running in a
seaway in a high speed launch, by R. B. Page
and H. P. Rader for Ministry of Defence and
Vosper Ltd 1958
Dynamic loading of motor-torpedo boat YP110
during high speed operation in rough waters by
N. H. Jasper. Report C-175, 1949 Dept. of
Navy, David Taylor Yacht Basin, Washington
D.C.
High Speed Small Craft by Peter de Cane
Dhows to Deltas by Renato Levi

Suppliers and Sources of Technical Information

Suppliers of inflatable buildings in the UK include:
Airborne Industries Ltd, Arterial Rd, Leigh-on-Sea, Essex
Clyde Canvas Goods and Structures Ltd, 92 Bay St, Glasgow

Adhesives and sealants for wood:
Wessex Resins and Adhesives Ltd, 189–193 Spring Rd, Sholing, Southampton SO2 7NY
Structural Polymer Systems Ltd, Love Lane, Cowes, Isle of Wight PO31 7EU
Plastics Division of Ciba-Geigy Ltd, Duxford, Cambridge CB2 4QA, UK

Staplers, power and hand:
Forpak Ltd, Romsey Industrial Estate, Greatbridge Rd, Romsey, Hants, UK
Senco Products of Cincinatti, Ohio, USA and Turner Rd, Sandyford Estate, Paisley PA3, Scotland
Dup-Fast Corp., 3702 River Rd, Franklin Park, Illinois 60131 and through distributors.
British Industrial Fastenings Ltd, Gatehouse Rd, Aylesbury, Bucks HP19 3DS
Signode Ltd, Queensway, Forest Fach, Swansea SA5 4ED, Wales
Spotnails Ltd, Bessamer Rd, Basingstoke, Hants RG21 3NT
The Stapling Centre Ltd, Goodwood Rd, London SE14 6BL

'Rapid' model made by Isebergs Verkstabs AB of Haestra, Sweden
Bostitch Div., Textron Ltd, Edenbridge, Kent
J. & H. Rosenheim Ltd, Quay Rd, Glasgow G73 1RN

Wholesalers of barbed nails in UK: Simpson Lawrence, Edmiston Drive, Glasgow G51, Scotland (trade suppliers only)

Sealants and bedding compounds:
Sealastic made by Expandite Ltd, Downmill Rd, Bracknell, Berks
Sylglas Co., Denso House, Chapel Rd, London SE27
DRG Inseal Products, Theobald St, Borehamwood, Herts
Mendex and Liquid Marine Glue are made by Alfred Jeffery & Co., Marshgate Lane, London E15
Farocaulk and Farocure are made by Faro Sealants Ltd, Edgworth Rd, Sudbury, Suffolk

Carbon fibre products and applications:
Courtalds Ltd, Carbon Fibres Unit, PO Box 16, Coventry CV6 5AB, UK
Fothergill & Harvey Ltd, Summit Littleborough, Lancs OL15 9QP, UK
Hyfill Ltd, Avonmouth Rd, Bristol BS11 9DU.

Forest Products Research Laboratory, Princes Risborough, Aylesbury, Bucks, UK